Praise for Dr. Dincalci's forgiveness work:

Being able to work through an issue from childhood so quickly (after years of various other tools) was a thrill. - Trice Bonney

Excellent! Very complete. It helped me. - Howard Deforte

This is very important work! I wish everyone could have on-going forgiveness training. - Christen Connors

The process is much faster than I had thought possible. The surprising thing for me was that everything leads to and proceeds from self-forgiveness. - Cate Griffiths

It gave me specific tools for guiding my own process of forgiveness—excellent accommodation of content to meet any situation.
- Deborah Klass, RN, PhD

I didn't know what questions to ask to analyze my situations. Now I have a roadmap. I not only learned a process for forgiving, I forgave.
- Evan Lloyd

Thank you for helping us all become hero's of our own lives. This work helped me see things in other ways, and gave me tools to use in my relationships. - Debbi Berto

Added new perspectives on what forgiveness is and more importantly for myself, what it isn't, allowing me to move through it easier.
- James Bourke

This work...has felt cathartic and freeing. - VB

Very practical. - Debra Peterson

It really put the processes of how to forgive in "layman's terms" so that I can explain and discuss forgiveness easily with others. Most significant was realizing that I held some myths of forgiveness. - Laura Lutz

It gave me a "how to" process to breakdown an overwhelming issue with many angles to a manageable level. - M. Rolewei

This work feels like the missing piece of the puzzle for deeper love, joy and peace. My overall response was excitement, empowering—New tools. - Ren Nelson

This needs to be shared in our community, schools, etc.
- Olga Senyk RN

Meaningful, and helpful. Intense and Enlightening! - Elizabeth Bakewell

A tremendous help, this set a foundation—the rest is up to me. Defined what forgiveness was and perhaps more importantly what it wasn't. Showed me how to go about the process.   - Danette Ellsworth

Forgiveness is a missing link in social evolution, via the individual heart. The part about self-forgiveness was valuable, especially in a culture that values selfishness, yet not self-forgiveness.   - Kit Lofroos

The explanation of brain function was new and helpful info for me. I am going away with new tools to help me on my path toward continued personal growth.   - Jacqueline Williams

I can see how anytime I get into a forgiveness jam or hold onto a grudge the opportunity is now placed before me to work out the problem and let forgiveness happen.   - Ann Marie Tomczak

Successes From People Who Work With Clients

On a professional level, I am now equipped to teach my clients about forgiveness and to guide them through the process.   - Sally Lobb

I now have the information to help my clients who may be struggling with forgiveness.   - C. Slovonik

This work exceeded my expectations. . . . The personal learning was intense and profound.   - Harriette Linn

I highly recommend this. The Principles of Forgiveness are a blueprint for self-acceptance and compassion, and are wonderful intervention tools for clinicians.   - Suzette Dotson

It gave me the information and the process to resolve issues I was hanging onto that needed forgiveness. — It will also be useful in my work with families.   - Carol Newman

I learned tools to use in my own personal life and also to share with clients. I'm excited about new possibilities in my clinical life.
                                        - J Bennett Jordan

I gained insights and competency in working with clients.
                                        - Jacqueline Doyle

Extremely helpful information framed in a useful way. Every process gave me insight.   - Tawny Martin, MFT

HOW TO
Forgive
WHEN YOU
CAN'T

by DR. JIM DINCALCI

How to
Forgive
When You
Can't

The Breakthrough Guide to
Free Your Heart & Mind

Healing Upsets Without Condoning
or Being Hurt Again

Dr. Jim Dincalci
Founder of The Forgiveness Foundation

Publisher: The Forgiveness Foundation, a 501c3 non-profit charity 11312 US 15-501 N, Suite 107-4, Chapel Hill, NC 27517

www.ForgivenessFoundation.org

Profit from this book go toward building caring families and communities worldwide by people helping each other heal blame, resentment and grudges.

Owing to the limitations of space, acknowledgement of permission to quote from previously published materials will be found at the end of the bibliography.

The Forgiveness Foundation books and products are available through most bookstores. To contact us directly call within the U S - 919-799-2113 or fax 262-244-3823. We also publish in a variety of electronic formats.

Library of Congress Catalogue Number: 2009937128

Publisher's Cataloging-in-Publication Data
Dincalci, Jim.
How to forgive when you can't : the breakthrough guide to free your heart and mind : healing upsets without condoning or being hurt again / Jim Dincalci.
p. cm.
Includes bibliographical references.
ISBN: 978-0-9824307-0-5
1. Forgiveness. 2. Self-acceptance. 3. Mind and body. I. Title.
BF637.F67 D54 2010
158.2—dc22   2009937128

DEDICATION

To my daughter, Erica,
and the young people of the world.
May this book bring you the means to a better future.

To my parents, Grace and Tony,
I guess I will always miss you.

To my wife Rita who enriched my mother's life,
And to all those who take care of people.
May this book lighten your heart.

To those who have been to hell from terrible trauma.
May this book help bring you peace.

There are raised letters and numbers at the end of some sentences. These are either references to publications where I found the information or notes giving more data on what was said. See the "Notes" section at the end of the book for the references in each chapter.

Readers should be aware that Internet Web sites offered as citations and/or sources for further information may have changed or disappeared between the time this was written *and* when it is read.

CONTENTS

FOREWORD

I am the Director of the Stanford Forgiveness Projects and have written two bestselling books on forgiveness, Forgive for Good and Forgive for Love. My work is used all over the world to help people to forgive. I consider Jim Dincalci to be my peer in this work. He is one of those teachers the New York Times has not yet featured. My work has been featured in the New York Times and all other major media. That is in part because I developed my forgiveness work while working at Stanford University. Jim developed his forgiveness program through his life experience, desire to be of help and his multidimensional education. The bottom line is we are both saying the same thing. We are preaching from the same pulpit.

This is a really good forgiveness book. It is clear, helpful and wise and anyone who brings a hurt or grievance to this work will be helped. I recommend *How to Forgive When You Can't* both because of the book and because of Jim. I have known Jim for 7 years. Since our first meeting, I have known him to be sincere and determined to help people forgive. The first time we met was before I was to give a book talk at a bookstore near Jim's home. Before the book talk, he contacted me to meet and we talked forgiveness for a long dinner and walk.

When Jim and I first met in Sonoma, California, we talked about the projective defense mechanism where we picture our wounds. He said to me that we make forgiveness permanent by this simple process, which I found creative and strong:

    A. To pull back the projection (forgiving the other because we have done the same thing in similar manner). Then

    B. To do self-forgiveness so that there is no need to project the personal guilt onto anyone else through blame.

Jim is the only person that I know of who worked full time on forgiveness work outside of those employed in a University setting. The last time I saw Jim was on the other coast and again we talked of forgiveness and of life over a long dinner. Again, I found that mostly we were on the same page and that Jim was sincerely committed to helping people through forgiveness.

Not only does this book have a strong psychological basis but Jim has added a spiritual but non-religious dimension. Thus, his book can be used by pastors, ministers and chaplains to help their parishioners forgive, in addition to therapists, lawyers and counselors in general. As Jim says in the first chapter, he set about to create a manual to help people learn how to help others forgive and of course to do their own forgiving. It took him 9 years and he has used all of what he found in his classes to create this book. Jim is clear that his vision of forgiveness has been a driving force in his life, and this book attests that it has been fruitful.

This is not a Morons Guide to Forgiveness or a Forgive for Dummies book. It is thoughtful and complete and is the product of a lot of hard work and effort. It is for the person who wants to truly leave their wounds behind and who is willing to work at it. And, as importantly it is for the professional who wants to help his/her clients forgive and live a more peaceful and fulfilling life.

Frederic Luskin, Ph.D.

ACKNOWLEDGEMENTS

No one writes a book alone. Everyone who helped me on this book is dear to me. The trite term "I couldn't have done it without you." is true. The changes I went through while writing this book were due to their support. I am blessed to have such first-rate friends, who have all been enthusiastic and encouraging about the book.

Thank you to Angeles Arrien, PhD, whose support through my psychotherapy training and far beyond has been invaluable. The influence of her trainings in cross-cultural healing carried me through my own forgiveness transformation in 1993.

Thank you to Dr. Fred Luskin, a forgiveness pioneer, who acknowledged the validity of my original premises of the *Power Forgiveness Process* and for his encouragement through the years.

Thank you to Loralee Denny, Rob Williamson, Dr. Ken Lebensold, and Dee Cseh for their work on formatting and the final edit of the book; to Ginnie Ward, Cate Griffiths and Gayle Shirley for editing earlier version of the book; to Ken Urquhart for his work on permissions for the book; and to Chris Many for is help in naming the book.

Thank you very much to Tami Dever at TLC Graphics for her wisdom, blessings, coordination, and skill to produce a lovely book inside and out. Praise for her staff – Marisa Jackson for her stellar work on the cover and Erin Stark for her aesthetic eye to make the inside appealing.

ACKNOWLEDGEMENTS

Thank you to Terri Gamboa, Jocelyn Callard, Nancy Many, and Laurel Davar for their ideas, work, and support in the early phases; to Susan Johnson for giving substance to the initial writing by transcribing one of my university classes. Thank you to Michael Berkes, PhD for helping laying out the plan for the book.

I am grateful to Abagayle, Rosie, Chris Loukas, Kokoman and Aesha Clottey, and Kima Douglas for their personal stories.

Thank you to the myriads of people through the years who said, "I need that book!" when I said I was writing a "how-to book" on forgiving. You kept me writing.

Thank you to the SW Florida Writer group whose support was priceless through difficult times while writing the book, with particular thanks to Hana Whitfield who got me into the group and helped me on editing. Special thanks to our teacher, Ginnie Ward, who was so enthusiastic about my initial work that she renewed my own enthusiasm. You all helped me become not only a better writer but also a happy writer.

Thank you to my students and clients through the years. Your willingness and success to move beyond your upsets and find peace and freedom kept me persisting to write this book. Your stories make it rich.

A special thank you to the forgiveness researchers around the world who are making forgiveness more accepted in psychology and the scientific community, to the legal professionals who are calling for its use to resolve hurtful situations and to the therapists, spiritual advisors and church leaders all over the world who encourage its use every day.

PART I

Opening to a
Different Way

The first steps to gaining knowledge
and skill in forgiving

"There is one elementary truth the ignorance
of which kills countless ideas and splendid plans.
That the moment that one definitely commits oneself,
Providence moves too.
All sorts of things occur to help one
that would never otherwise have occurred.
A whole stream of events issues from the decision,
raising in one's favor all manner of unforeseen incidents
and meeting and material assistance, which no man
could have dreamed would have come his way.
Are you in earnest? Seize this very minute.
What you can do or dream you can.
Begin it!
Boldness has genius, power and magic in it.
Begin it now!"

GOETHE

The Opening

*"To forgive is to set a prisoner free
and discover that the prisoner was you."*

DR. LEWIS SMEDES

What is most important to you: being happy; having more love in your life; satisfaction in your relationships; contentment in your work; peace in your heart? We all have these goals, but even when we reach them, they are often short-lived. This book will show you why.

Forgiveness is not only the key to achieving all of these goals but also the way to make them a permanent part of your life. I am going to provide you with proven methods to help you forgive—even the seemingly unforgivable.

Forgiveness is letting go of resentment, grudges, negative attitudes, and upsets that occupy your mind, sap your ability to love, and destroy your peace of mind. It is not about turning the other cheek to be hurt again, or reconciling with your victimizer, or condoning what they did. These regrettable interpretations have given forgiving a terrible name.

Forgiveness is universal, common to all religions, and integral to the human experience. It is the most significant tool we have in this time of war, terrorism and crisis around the world.

Most people I have met admit they know forgiving is the right thing to do, but they say they don't know *how* to do it. Now, for the first time in history, we have made immense progress in learning how to apply this timeless lesson.

Neither psychology nor religion adequately addresses this subject. Yet, understanding your mind, emotions, and spirituality reveal vital aspects of yourself that can be used in forgiving. Your mind enables you to use your whole brain to control your stressed brain reactions; your emotions give love, compassion, joy, and feeling for life and others; and your spirituality can bring wisdom, and inner resources in difficult times.

Over the past fifteen years, I've collected over forty methods that people may use in forgiving. I've taught these in universities, colleges, hospitals, churches, public workshops, schools, and individual counseling, and I continually watch lives transform.

The question of forgiving, though, is not only "What methods help you to forgive?" but also, "What keeps you from doing it?" A book of methods provides little value if you don't also address the blocks in your mind and in your attitude that prevent forgiving, and then identify what resources are available to get past your barriers. To get past these blocks, I provide effective methods from psychology, religion and my own experience of doing this work in the trenches, as a therapist and forgiveness teacher.

The Issue of Evil

There are people who seem to be quite evil. People who show no emotion or regret for violence they have caused, who will probably do it again, and who blame their victims. This cannot be denied. The prisons are full of them.

You might have been the victim of one of them.

This book is for you and your healing, not theirs.

Stages and Phases of Forgiveness

Forgiveness is a complex subject in our world and for us as individuals. Each person is different, and each will forgive in a unique way with his or her own timing. What works for you may not work for another.

The Very First Step Is

Willingness — Without being willing to do this work, nothing will happen. You, of course, are willing in some way or you wouldn't be looking at these pages. If you are thinking of others who need to have this work, keep reading because you will understand why people do not forgive. With this understanding you can help them to be willing to let go of their upsets.

Some people will find they do this work more easily in a group, some with only one other person, and some together with an aspect of the Essence of Life.

In studying and teaching this subject, I have noticed that forgiving is a skill developed through stages with increasing levels of awareness. By observing how people progress through these steps and stages, I've carried many all the way through the process of letting go, freeing them from the pain their situations once caused, as you will find for yourself.

> "We may not know how to forgive, and we may not
> want to forgive; but the very fact we say we are willing to
> forgive begins the healing practice."
>
> LOUISE HAY
> from YOU CAN HEAL YOUR LIFE

In the first chapters, various questions, information and insights are given so that you will not only understand the essential aspects of letting go of resentment and hate, but also have practical methods to help you along. Each section builds on the last. Often, people experience relief from an unforgiven situation just by reading the book. Though various readers like to jump around in a book, I recommend first reading this book in sequence.

The book is organized to carry you through the stages just by reading it and doing the small exercises, which are mainly questions for you to consider. Any of these are exercises, which I've provided from easy to more difficult, can independently bring about forgiveness.

The book has five parts:

Part I, Opening to a Different Way, helps develop knowledge and skill in forgiving.

Part II, Taking It Deeper, deals with situations that are more difficult.

Part III, The Truth Behind the Resistance to Forgive, goes into aspects that prevent forgiveness, so that understanding and compassion increase.

Part IV, Doing the Work, presents a working model to apply what has been learned.

Part V, After the Process, looks at how to maintain and strengthen the positive effects from doing this forgiveness work.

By doing the suggestions, questions, and exercises, forgiving another person or yourself can bring astounding results. I call this work "Power Forgiveness." For, while it can be used for an isolated situation, it can also be used to heal a lifetime of guilt or resentment.

After attending my first forgiveness class, a dear friend asked me for a summary of steps on how to forgive. Through the years, no summary has been adequate. Instead, what I've found works—proven by trial and research—is a series of questions that cover all the bases in the most effective sequence. The whole route is *The Power Forgiveness Process.*

The heart of Power Forgiveness is letting go of your own regret, guilt, and self-blame. Self-forgiveness and self-compassion hold the key to releasing any kind of upset permanently. Self-forgiveness is necessary because guilt and shame keep you trapped in your negative thoughts and feelings, which keep you convinced that you don't deserve better. YOU DO.

A Transformation

In July 1993, while I was driving through the redwood trees on my way home, I realized that my life was no longer worth living. It looked okay on the surface. I had a pleasant home in the northern California wine country, a lovely daughter, a master's degree in counseling and a supportive community of friends. Yet I felt that I had utterly failed to become the person I had dreamed of being when I was young. And, my spirituality—so essential to me for years and a source of security and peace—was gone.

I had studied different psychologies and healing methods since 1968 and even taught them in graduate schools, but could not help myself. I didn't know how to start. I'd lived with anger, hate and resentment for years and thought them normal. Even when my life hit rock bottom, I didn't think those emotions were a problem. I accepted the same old ideas commonly used to justify not letting go of the many traumas and abuses experienced earlier in my life.

At this point of utter despair, I finally saw that my anger was really destroying me rather than being a source of effective energy. In my search for help, I read the introduction to *A Course In Miracles* from The Foundation for Inner Peace and realized, quite clearly, that to have an experience of Divine Love, which I so wanted, I must forgive.

In fact, forgiving *every* upset seemed the only way out. The skills I had developed from doing inner work for so many years came forward, helping me understand how to forgive—not only others, but also myself.

After many hours in seclusion, I let go of every upset and trauma that I could remember. With them went all of the resentment anger and hate I had accumulated in my life. The change was miraculous. My happiness and appreciation for life returned. My soul felt free. Love radiated to and from me, and was available constantly for the following eight years.

In discussing his book, *By The River Piedra I Sat Down and Wept: A Novel Of Forgiveness*, the famed author, Paulo Coelho, related a similar forgiveness process he went through:

> "One morning, going from Death Valley in California to Tucson in Arizona, I made a mental list of everyone I thought I hated because they had hurt me. I went along pardoning them one by one; six hours later in Tucson, my soul felt so light and my life had changed much for the better." [1]

Search for What Works

This began my journey of helping others let go of their anger, resentment, and hate. When I first started teaching these principles in 1996, I thought I could change the world through the process I had experienced, but most people didn't understand what I was talking about. From this disappointment, I began my quest to find out what works to help others to forgive.

In the summer of 2000, I went on a two-month trip across the country in a camper van with my lovely, smart, talented, thirteen-year-old daughter, Erica. We had a great time together—starting from the Redwoods of California, going to Las Vegas, exploring Texas caverns, playing at water parks, and touring New Orleans. We visited Grandma and Grandpa in Florida, went scuba diving in the Florida Keys, and spent two weeks in New York City. We even had the good fortune of having a fabulous view on top of the World Trade Center.

At the end of that vacation, before returning to my work as a school psychotherapist in Hawaii, I was thinking about the trip and wondering about my life. Suddenly, but peacefully, my mind opened to a vision of the earth. I saw it as if from God's view— seeing the whole planet *and* the individuals all over it. As I watched, people started helping each other forgive. Slowly love and peace filled our world.

All over our planet, I saw one person help another forgive, one after another letting go of their resentments in coffee shops, offices, churches, homes, and so on. Throughout this time, I kept hearing "The Forgiveness Foundation" and seeing local centers that helped this healing activity to spread. Eventually the earth filled completely with harmony and love. While I was viewing this brighter, softer world, I heard, "Do you want to take this on?" I decided, as we all have in the Foundation, to make that vision come true.

A few months afterwards, the book began when I realized that a complete guidebook was needed for those who want to forgive and for those who want to help others forgive. My passion and mission since then has been to provide everything that works to aid a person stuck in anger, resentment, hate, or guilt.

The Forgiveness Foundation was registered as a non-profit teaching charity in 2002. The Forgiveness Foundation is the publisher of this book. Its profits go to forwarding the vision of a more harmonious world through people's helping each other forgive.

I kept giving classes in forgiveness at universities and in public seminars besides focusing on it in my private counseling. I continued to learn what worked (and did not) in the act of forgiving. I read all the research, books, and articles I could on forgiving. After the first three years of working on the book, I noted in my class brochures that my book would be out in the next season.

I had no idea that it would take six more years to collect all the methods and perspectives to help a person let go of their upsets and then to put the whole activity of forgiving in an order that works most effectively.

The Power Forgiveness Process is the most complete system available at this time to help people let go of residual anger, resentment and fear from past hurtful experiences. This book, with its viewpoints, case studies, and exercises will carry you through to forgiving even the most terrible things. Though the book and *The Power Forgiveness Process* may be used for a single difficult situation, it can also transform your life by helping you letting go of *all* your known resentments, grudges, hates and upsets in a relatively short time. The systematic activity found in this guide will lead you to full forgiveness.

It's *power* forgiveness because this ultimate forgiveness workout can renew your life. There have been miracles in every class I've taught and with clients in all age groups, from young children to senior citizens and from all professional levels.

Real life successes and examples of the different ways that enable a person to forgive are included throughout the book. I am grateful to all of my students and clients. You will read their stories and learn what worked for them and what may help you. To keep their anonymity, I have changed names and exact circumstances; nevertheless, all of the situations are real.

Over 120 references for data and research are cited in the bibliography at the end of the book.

Facing Deep Trauma

If the situation you wish to deal with was deeply traumatic, you must go slowly. Dr. Richard Guyton in his book, *The Forgiving Place: Choosing Peace after Violent Trauma*, gives helpful suggestions about how to proceed in such situations. Years ago, when Dr. Guyton, a psychologist, was with a client, the police called him out his office to tell him that his wife and secretary had just been brutally stabbed to death at his home. He had to manage his own shock and be a comfort and support for his three children before he could forgive.[2]

Dr. Guyton advises that trauma generates special circumstances of shock, grief, and fear. It may lead to complete exhaustion, so it is crucial to take breaks now and then and return to the laughter and joy of normal life, even in the midst of grieving.

Similarly, in forgiveness work, don't force yourself to let it all go if it does not seem natural. Take an emotional break before moving to the next stage or incident. Accepting where you are is central in the healing process. Resting, remembering, and releasing go in cycles in healing. Be patient with yourself. You will learn methods in this book to move you through the detours, such as denial, depression, alcohol or drugs, and blaming, until you feel you can face the situation, and forgive.[3]

You will learn how to take care of forgiving traumatic incidents later in the book. Remember though that all of the earlier chapters are important to gain the most from the later ones.

"If you're going through hell, keep going."
WINSTON CHURCHILL

In Summary

This book makes forgiveness possible because it uses proven methods from psychology, time-honored spiritual practices, resources and perspectives that allow a person to move past the emotional obstacles that prevent forgiving. It also addresses brain patterns and emotional defenses to be able to gain a deeper understanding of why forgiving is difficult and how to make it easier. Reading this book in sequence enables you to learn how and why the mind holds onto harmful ideas.

Your chief action is to answer the questions provided. Then the pain of a lifetime will be gone and you will have a freedom you have not experienced for years.

> Forgiving is the ultimate choice that brings us closest to the human and divine ideal of love and peace. Likewise, not forgiving can bring us to despair.

Forgiveness is necessary not only spiritually and emotionally, but also socially. It could even be the magic pill for many social ills, like violence and addiction, especially in situations involving anger or guilt.

It raises our ability to remain in control of our thinking and to reach our highest abilities, awareness, and spirituality. It is necessary to life itself, because the ability to let go of upsets enables us to continue to be part of a deeper social and spiritual core, and brings us (and those around us) a healthier, happier life.

By using the perspectives and methods in this book:

- You will let go of anger, resentments, negative feelings, and attitudes of ill will.
- You will have more peace of mind and joy in your life.
- Your life will get better because you will understand how, when, and where to forgive.

May all your deepest dreams come true. I wish you an enlightening and rewarding journey as you read these pages.

CHAPTER ONE

How It Works

Forgiveness is the most powerful action you have to change relationships and heal your own life. The forgiving mindset engages tragedies and trauma at a higher level so that you can heal.

I've read that hunters catch small monkeys by putting peanuts into a gourd with a hole just small enough for the monkey to reach its hand inside. Then, the gourd is tied to a tree. When the hunters return, they find monkeys trapped by their unwillingness to let go of the peanuts to free their hands. This is exactly what holding onto our resentments and unforgiven hurts does to us. We hold onto the little peanuts that imprison our mind and heart, preventing love, peace, and joy from being in our life. By letting go, we free ourselves, and at the same time free those around us.

Why do we hold onto the peanuts of resentment and hate, which ruin our lives and the lives of others? What are these demons – the negative thought patterns and emotions that keep us from forgiving? Why do we listen to them? If we can answer these questions, we will have the tools to forgive.

The Best-kept Secret

Luckily, recent years have seen a blossoming of research on forgiveness. MDs, sociologists, and psychologists have published hundreds of research articles in professional journals. Overall, they have demonstrated the considerable emotional and even physical benefits of forgiveness.[1] Brain studies meanwhile have pointed to systems and patterns that can slow or prevent forgiving. Psychology has revealed the mechanisms in the mind that keep in place old, inhibiting patterns and emotions, such as resentment and anger. We have gained good knowledge on how the mind works and how it sabotages us. Finally, we have the perspectives and tools to help us forgive more easily.

With all of the new understanding about forgiveness and its notable results, psychology in general still ignores the power of forgiveness. Dr. Carl Thoresen, a retired professor of psychology and psychiatry at Stanford University and researcher for the Stanford Forgiveness Project, has called forgiveness "one of the best-kept secrets" and notes that he and his colleagues "have come across few people who understand what forgiveness is and how it works."[2] The few therapists, psychologists, and researchers who advocate forgiving amount to little more than a small cry in a wilderness of resentment and revenge.

Why is this? There is speculation on this. But, basically, in the middle to late 1800s, most psychologists, Freud in particular, rejected church control and interpretation in matters of mental health. I believe with other researchers[2a] that psychology in general, sharing this attitude, rejected forgiveness because it was associated with "The Church" and its doctrine. As a result, forgiveness was lost to the professional therapy community, and remains so today.

Finding a therapist or doctor today who understands forgiveness is not easy. One of the reasons I've written this book is to assist professionals and lay people to do a better job of helping others to learn to forgive.

Because religion has not done much better in helping people to forgive, I also hope this book helps clergy and pastoral counselors in assisting people to forgive. For centuries, clergy and priests have demanded forgiveness without giving clear ways to achieve it. Demanding doesn't work. What works is using the many forgiveness methods that are available today, which are brought together in this book.

The Types of Forgiveness

For some, it is easier **not** to look at all of the negative influences in a situation and just decide to forgive. That decision, a difficult one, I call *direct forgiveness*. It is often influenced by accepting a belief in Divine Love and Forgiveness, or the non-blaming condition of Nature. But, many of us are not able to make that direct decision to forgive; it doesn't even seem possible.

If a person experiences great emotion around an upset, forgiving is often too difficult. Merely deciding to forgive can open you to *false forgiveness*, where you have the intention yet still hold resentment and may even seek retribution in some way. Initially, if you decide to forgive without going through some sort of inner work, often the decision must be repeated frequently due to the emotional turmoil that has not been released.

Today, the majority of research, therapy, and spiritual counseling tries to get the person to the point of deciding to forgive.[3] This book and its exercises are for those who are not able to make that decision easily. It addresses how to deal permanently with resentment and guilt. You will find as you read that your upset will change and forgiveness will just take place.

The Myths of Forgiveness

As a first step, several significant university studies on forgiving dealt with the false ideas that prevent us from forgiving. In Chapter 3, I've gathered all of these wrong and harmful beliefs that give forgiveness a bad reputation and prevent its use.

Three of the most detrimental myths would have you believe that forgiving:

1. Condones harmful acts,
2. Causes you to be hurt again because you must "turn the other cheek."
3. Requires you to reconcile with the person.

In our culture, we agree with these, but they are untrue. Forgiveness does not condone evil or wrongdoing, nor does it ask for your injury. In addition, it is not about reconciling if you do not want it. Instead, it requires letting go of upsets that harm you, and setting limits on yourself and others—limits that keep you safe.

> "Forgiveness is not the misguided act of condoning irresponsible, hurtful behavior. Nor is it a superficial turning of the other cheek that leaves us feeling victimized and martyred. Rather it is the finishing of old business that allows us to experience the present, free of contamination from the past."
>
> JOAN BORYSENKO, PH.D., *FIRE IN THE SOUL*

True forgiveness frees your heart, soul, and mind. Should an abused woman forgive her husband and let him go on hitting her? Of course not! In the rest of the book, we'll be going over what works and doesn't, as you learn *how* to forgive difficult situations.

To overcome these misunderstandings, it is useful to recognize that there are two opposing aspects of human survival: attack those who threaten us, the enemy, and care for those who are close to us—family, friends, and lovers.

These categories, however, are not as stable as we might wish. Sometimes a friend or spouse is seen as the enemy. Without forgiveness, the "enemy" category keeps getting bigger. Popular sentiment is to withhold forgiveness when a friend becomes an enemy, as in a legal problem or divorce.

The Forgiveness Battle

The debate to forgive or not has been going on for eons. Revenge, not forgiveness, fills our TV screens and movies. This is due to the two parts of the survival drive discussed above, it is really the split between our highest and true self, vs. our basic survival-self. Both are part of us. The former gives us our highest vision and goals of community, peace, and kindness. The latter protects us by setting limits, but when it is in control it keeps us small, depressed, and vengeful.

To get past the basic, survival-self you need to understand its mechanisms so that your highest or authentic self—that part of you that enjoys life, thinks clearly, loves others, and is peaceful—can be prominent in your life.

My strong background in medicine and science drew me to study recent research on the brain. This research provides groundbreaking insight and understanding into why we do what we do and say what we say, particularly in high stress situations.

For many of my students, it was easier to achieve full forgiveness by having a basic understanding of the brain's stress reactions. I provide this information because it is crucial, not only in forgiving, but also in understanding what might be going on in your life. It is vital for anyone dealing with people who are upset.

If you go down the river not knowing where the snags, boulders, sandbars and old shipwrecks are, those hazards will inevitably hurt you. This book is a chart you can use to navigate the rough waters of life to arrive at a destination filled with satisfaction.

The Effects of Trauma and High Stress

Through the years, I have found when someone can't forgive, often he or she is suffering from the effects of trauma and/or intense stress. These effects need to be tackled for your forgiveness work to be entirely successful. Forgiving the trauma done by or to another is fundamental. For those who have had horrific experiences and need to get past them, in later chapters, I thoroughly address how to do it.

These terrible experiences might have happened years ago. Nevertheless, they still can have deep effects on life in the present. In November 2007, CBS news reported a suicide rate for Iraq veterans twice that of other Americans—"They are the casualties of wars you don't often hear about."[4] The suicide rate is higher for veterans than other Americans. The suicide rate for Vietnam veterans is higher than the combat fatalities in that war.[4a]

> "When a deep injury is done to us,
> we never recover until we forgive."
> ALAN PATON 1903 – 1988
> SOUTH AFRICAN WRITER/EDUCATOR

Understanding our Reactions

There is good reason for the veteran suicides, for the myths of forgiveness, for the controversy around forgiving, and for the difficulty to forgive in stressful conditions. To understand this, we need to look at how our brain functions under stress.

Brain research in recent years has given significant insight into:

- Why we act as we do
- How stress makes us react in unusual ways
- How to cope with stress reactions, so that we can respond more appropriately and with control.

Most people know the brain as a processor of information—the computer inside the head that deals with thoughts and body functions. This is not enough understanding to help when you are trying to forgive terrible behavior. Actually, most people's present understanding of the brain hinders forgiveness.

The impact of the brain's stress responses on us has not been acknowledged at the level that it should be. Better knowledge of stress and brain reactions can give insight and empathy for someone who has reacted in an unacceptable way, including yourself. This understanding and compassion does not justify what was done, but will help in letting go of the upset so that you can have peace of mind and heart.

We forgive all the time to offset the errors that we know happen as human beings. We have relatively smooth functioning on our roads, in our cities, and at our workplaces because people are forgiving. If they were not, we would have full-blown chaos and violence. Forgiveness is a normal action of the human mind when it is not trapped in the reactive systems of our brain. The more strain we have, the less we are likely to forgive—more stress, less forgiveness.

Yet forgiving is essential for success in any endeavor that involves others. Self-forgiveness is essential to succeed in any personal undertaking. Learning how your survival mechanisms affect you enables you to look at negative situations in your life in a different way.

Forgiving is difficult if the stressed-brain reactions are occurring at the same time that an offense happens because all future memories of it, for example, the loss of job, property or a loved one, are trapped in the stress response. Thus, anytime that memory recurs there is a flood of terrible reactions, even years later. Naturally, you would want to avoid those painful memories.

However, avoiding is not really to your best interest because this upset remains just under the surface of your awareness negatively coloring your life. Many unforgiven, unresolved events can subtly keep your mind in a negative state much of the time. If you add to that, the on-going stress of the threat of loss of job, home, or loved one, etc. your situation could look quite hopeless. But it isn't. Forgiving is a powerful way out. You will see.

The War of the Brains

Brain research in the 1960 & 70s revealed that we have three separate brain systems operating within us. In general, these brains function in concert with each other resulting in our best thinking, happiness, and goal achievement.[5] They function together best in a safe environment. This safety enables our mind to be a symphony instead of a war zone. The war begins when we are overwhelmed by stress or fear.

Through the eons, primitive brains adapted and expanded what was already there, as opposed to rebuilding everything.[6] Thus, we still carry the reactions of our ancient ancestors and those of mammals and reptiles. These adapted early brain structures help us to not only survive, but also to have important social qualities, and even, love in our life. However, in threatening situations or in hopelessness, they can actually shut down our newest brain, the neocortex.

The neocortex, our largest brain, provides language, logic, ability to analyze solutions to difficulties, and forgiveness. When the reactive systems of the brain, shuts down the neocortex due to a survival emergency, we respond immediately by fighting, fleeing or freezing. And, we lose clear thinking, problem-solving, and our ability to speak intelligently. All of these positive aspects we rely on and expect in our modern age. In stressful times, these reactive brain structures over influence our thinking resulting in regretted decisions and actions.[7] In prehistoric times, in order to survive, we had to react and not think about what to do or say. However, in modern society, our survival reactions are often not what's needed to come to a positive outcome.

Isaac is an easy-going guy. When someone at the office is upset, he or she knows Isaac will give them an acknowledging smile and help if needed. However, when his daughter was first diagnosed with cancer, not only did his work suffer, but also he became a terror, yelling at people even for small mistakes. The office went into chaos until they found out why Isaac was acting so differently. Then his coworkers rallied around him, helping him through the difficult weeks of initial shock. Years later, he is still embarrassed at how he reacted, and appreciative of their help.

When we are thrown into an emergency, our earlier brain structures activate our sympathetic nervous system resulting in the specific body reactions that we feel as stress. Besides the typical immediate reaction of heart pounding, tense muscles, tunnel vision, etc., we also know stress by our emotional reactions, which are usually fear with the urge to run, anger with its urge to attack, or numbness or confusion with its inability to do anything. Each person has a different threshold of stress. When we reach that over-stressed point, our sympathetic nervous system is fully engaged. The earlier brains keep it engaged until we feel safe.

To regain your true self you must find safety. Then the system will calm down. However, if "safety" is not easily found in your workplace or at home, turning off this sympathetic nervous system may be difficult, resulting in the myriads of problems we have in our society today from abuse of drugs to violence. We will go over many methods to calm down to start thinking and acting effectively, and forgiving.

Quieting the Stressed System

"The snake brain" is one of the names given to our earliest brain by the US National Institutes of Health[8] researcher, Dr. Paul Mac-Lean, who brought these multiple brains to light. The name, snake brain, is appropriate because when the serpent has its victim, it either poisons or squeezes the life out of it. This is what happens to us when this stress response becomes chronic as opposed to being an isolated reaction. The snake brain holds on tight poisoning us with fear or anger. Forgiveness is *the* key choice for helping us out of this continual reactivity.

NOTE: Feelings might resurface as you look at your upsets and you might not want to continue. This is just a smoke screen put up by fear. In nature, the hunted will often turn to fight. When monstrous situations from the past hunt you mercilessly, attack is sometimes the best defense. If you are committed to slaying your demons, and face them head on, they will lose their power to frighten or harm you.

The thought of facing our most painful situations often feels as though it will kill us. But, running from our demons actually gives them power. The defense mechanisms that have protected us now hobble our efforts to become fully alive.

Fear keeps our stress system going, not only preventing forgiveness but also stopping the joy of life. We see it all around us today: fear of loss of work, fear of spending, fear of loss of home, fear of a terrible future, etc. These are all real fears. A better life, though, demands that we step out of fear. Whether or not we forgive, fear must be quieted.

You know that people do not compete well when afraid, and that showing fear will not get you the job you want. Exhibiting fear does not evoke confidence from others or entice a person to want to be with you. Some people will use food, drugs and alcohol to quiet fear. These are poor and temporary fixes. There are plenty of ways to quiet fear without resorting to the over use of substances that in themselves cause more trouble.

Your on-going stress reaction infects everyone around you. You already know that to have any kind of decent, fruitful life, your continuing stressed-brain responses **need to be stopped**. Of course, you will say "How, when there are bills to pay, children to feed, a family to support, etc?" I understand there are challenges. I am only reminding you that your stress response though seemingly normal is not in your best interest and certainly not in the best interest of anyone around you, especially children. This book will guide you through the changes you need. There is hope.

For now, remember that the complexity going on inside your brains is far more than you realize. Under stress, rationality may be too easily overcome by strong emotions and impulses, giving way to "inhuman" behavior. This is because logic, problem-solving and analysis are relatively new functions of the brain. When the most primitive brain, the snake brain, is running the show, there will be terrible difficulties. We see the direct effect of this in suicide, violence, shooting sprees, terrorism, and the trauma of war.

Forgiveness helps quiet the fearful mind, but it's not easy when the snake brain is actively in control. You can regain control over the snake brain by finding a safe place in your own thoughts or in your environment.

Several of the ways to do this are: meditation, prayer, going to a church, talking with a friend, listening to calming music, finding a way for someone else to take care of the kids for bit, doing something you enjoy, reading something inspirational, taking a shower, exercising, etc.

Note: It only takes about 20 minutes to notice a dramatic shift away from the snake brain reactivity.

Write It Down

A helpful way to calm yourself is to write down any upsets that you have. This simple action of just writing them down on paper, is a commitment to deal with them.

As you read and look at your life, upsets with others and with yourself will inevitably come up. To get the most out of this work, write these down so that you can come back to them later.

There are two reasons for this recordkeeping. 1) to have a list of past upsets to ensure that you will address them later. 2) to use these memories during the practical exercises and questions. Situations will come up that you have not thought about for many years. Originally, they were hidden as part of your mind's defenses that help to prevent mental anguish. However, if an event still upsets you, it has not healed. It will continue to affect you beneath the surface of your awareness until you take care of it.

In her book, *Molecules of Emotion: the Science behind Mind-Body Medicine*, Dr. Candace Pert, noted researcher, and author, says that studies have shown that when trauma victims write about their experience, physiological changes actually occur.[9]

In the future there will be a companion workbook to this book. But for now, keep a journal of all your work with this book. Then you will have a record of what you worked on and how you did it. And, what you realized. Sometimes I will have journal writing practices that you can do. This is important work for yourself, so buy a nice journal, something you would like to write in. Writing will help this process.

Success in Forgiving

Letting go of upsets does not come too easily to most people but we all have the ability to develop the skills necessary to forgive. As with any skill, success at forgiving difficult upsets takes work and practice. So please do the exercises.

Research has shown that married people, those with higher education and women are the most forgiving. Could this be why women outlive men?[10] Women are typically the nurturers, they use both sides of their neocortex more, so are more adept at feeling than men. However, a man is more likely to be forgiving if he is extroverted and social.[11] Some people, including myself, propose that men are more analytical and less feeling because through the eons they have been the warriors, and a warrior must cut off feelings about killing in order to be effective. I point this out as a reminder that we all come to this work from exceedingly different perspectives.

To find happiness, you must face the demons that keep you trapped in anger, resentment, and the desire for revenge. Forgiveness releases these negative thoughts and emotions. Once free of them, you have greater control over your energy, thinking, and ability to make decisions that benefit yourself and others — decisions that arise out of positive emotions.

Please note: Forgiveness is sometimes not an easy path because it can open up painful memories. For this reason, and because of the confusion of emotions connected to the subject, it is best to keep this work private until you feel secure about it. At such a vulnerable time, you do not want to open yourself to others' criticism, ridicule or unforgiven stories. You don't need these sentiments right now. Handle your own upsets before taking on others'.

I've known clergy who preached about forgiveness but couldn't actually do it themselves, and certainly never gave it the respect or emphasis it deserves. I've been told that only saints can forgive, and perhaps that was true at one time, but things have changed. Anyone can forgive. Do your own work, and perhaps others will notice and ask you about it.

It is imperative not to tell someone you have forgiven him or her unless they have specifically asked for forgiveness in the past and you had not given it. Often telling a person you have forgiven him or her may seem arrogant. You may create more trouble by telling them you have forgiven them, because they might not have thought it was a problem or they didn't see it as a situation needing forgiveness. You don't have to tell them how wonderful you are for forgiving them. The words are not needed. Your changed attitude will be plenty, I assure you.

People who oppose forgiveness see it as weakness. Actually, it requires extraordinary courage. "The weak can never forgive. Forgiveness is the attribute of the strong." said Gandhi. Nevertheless, vengeance is popular in our culture, not forgiveness. Thus, when you forgive and tell people, there might be repercussions.

An acquaintance, whose son was killed by a drunk driver, was able to get the man prosecuted for murder, not manslaughter. Later, she realized that this young man did not deserve to spend the rest of his life in jail, and that he had a mother who was grieving for him. Her choice to forgive and help him get out of prison, caused family trouble.[12]

After Sue Norton forgave her grandparents killer, friends would move to the other side of the street to avoid her. Even with this, none of the women regretted their forgiving.[13] Promote forgiveness by all means, but only when you are totally secure in your gains and perspective.

Forgiveness wipes away the damage of the past whether the hurt occurred thirty years ago or thirty minutes ago. It allows us to experience the present moment, the only time we really live.

It produces clarity of thought because it removes emotional upsets, which cloud the mind and heart. With that clarity, you make decisions that are beneficial in all areas of life.

As Picasso said about art, I will say about forgiving:

Forgiveness washes away from the soul the dust of everyday life.

I heard a story of a woman who was driving on the freeway when a driver intentionally cut her off by swerving in front of her. She was frightened yet quickly regained control of her car without a mishap, but was shaken and upset. When she noticed he was doing it to others ahead of her, she decided to let go of her upset with him because it was impairing her driving. Being practiced in forgiving, she let the anger go and even said a prayer. A few minutes later, the man cut someone off who careened into another car and then another. All of a sudden, cars crashed into one another all around her. Nevertheless, in her composure she avoided them and pulled off the road undamaged. She credited her safety to having let go of the upset so that her thinking was clear. She knew for sure that if she had not let it go, she would have been involved in the crash scene.

From a conversation with Paolo Coelho and a friend in the postscript of his novel on forgiveness, *By The River Piedra I Sat Down and Wept:*

"Those are fine words but I don't know if I am capable of pardoning ingratitude so easily."

"It's very difficult. But there is no choice: if you don't pardon, then you'll think about the pain they caused you and that pain will never go away. I'm not saying that you have to like those who do you wrong. I'm not telling you to go back to that person's company. I'm not suggesting that you start seeing that person as an angel or as someone who acted without any hurtful intentions. All I am saying is that the energy of hate will take you nowhere, but the energy of pardon which manifests itself through love will manage to change your life in a positive sense."

CHAPTER TWO

What Forgiving Really Is

F orgiveness means: "to stop blaming or being angry with [someone] for something they have done, or to ask someone not to be angry with you".

The Cambridge International Dictionary of English

This standard definition makes forgiving seem like a one-time act, but it is a way of approaching life. As Dr. Martin Luther King, Jr. said:

"Forgiveness is not an occasional act;
it is a permanent attitude."

To make it a constant approach takes more than simply understanding the nature and practice of forgiveness; we must also overcome misconceptions or myths about it (Chapter 3) and recognize benefits that inspire us to forgive (Chapter 4).

Release of a Debt

The most effective way that I have found to explain and define forgiveness in my classes and counseling is to use the example of forgiving a financial debt—letting go of money owed.

Simply said, **the act of forgiving is letting go of what you feel another owes you.**

In a painful situation, forgiving is letting go of the physical or emotional debt that you expect to see paid. When you forgive, the person or group no longer owes you what you wanted them to give, understand, or experience. They no longer owe having to feel the physical or emotional pain that you have suffered. You might even have to let go of their apologizing because, in truth, they might have seen the situation in quite a different way. This also means letting go of the spiritual debt of God punishing them or their going to hell.

The Lord's Prayer in Christianity says it quite clearly: "Forgive us our debts, as we forgive our debtors." Just as forgiving a debt means letting go of what is owed to us, forgiving an injustice means letting go of the punishment or the payment we believe our wrongdoer owes us.

It means no longer seeking an "eye for an eye," but equally, it does not mean turning the other cheek, inviting further injury.

> "If we practice an eye for an eye and a tooth for a tooth, soon the whole world will be blind and toothless."
>
> MAHATMA GANDHI

Often people change their ideas of what they need from the offender when they think about it more deeply. You have an idea of what it would take to let go of a particular upset. The problem is that you have not received it and probably never will. There could be many reasons for this, but the bottom line is that you might have to reevaluate the reality of your expectation.

An example of forgiving a debt came from Luke, a minister, who was in one of my first forgiveness therapy classes, *Teaching How to Forgive*. Though he knew the value and necessity of forgiving, his emotions prevented him from going further because someone had lied about him to his congregation. This lie had caused a rift in his church. Luke needed the man to tell the whole church that he had lied. He laughed when telling us this, seeing that the parishioner would never do this because he felt it was true. Therefore, he saw that it was quite silly to keep expecting an apology that he would never receive. He added that the rift, which was a matter of allegiance, probably would have occurred anyway because his style was different from the previous pastor.

By merely making a statement of the debt, I've seen insights arise. But, this is not an easy place for most people to get to right away. Some people, especially women, have the experience and ability to look more deeply within themselves. Luke, the minister mentioned above, had done a considerable amount of inner work. He understood the repercussions of his unrealistic expectations, and the misery they caused him.

The second part of this exercise asks the question, can you let go to gain peace of mind? This is really a basic in forgiving. You need to be *willing* to consider the possibility of not getting what is owed to you. If you are not willing to reflect on not getting what you expect, the process will bog down.

This does not mean that nothing can be done. It only means that the next step in your forgiving must be to find another way to get what you want—a way that does not involve the other person because realistically he or she might never change or have the realization or punishment that you desire.

By forgiving, you release anger, hate, grudges, and resentments held in your mind and heart, and set limits on your negative and self-destructive attitudes. It is a gift to yourself. In situations that involve values of community well-being, family harmony, or couple's reconciliation, it is also a gift from one heart to another.[1]

Forgiveness is an act of love. It's a difficult personal choice that relieves the forgiver of the effects of pain, hurt, resentment and anger around a situation that caused injury. It takes letting go of animosity and ill will, and requires stepping out of a fixed and limited emotional stance into a grander, deeper part of yourself. It is an act of courage for it requires letting go of a justified upset.

> "Forgiveness is me giving up my right to hurt you
> for hurting me." – ANONYMOUS

How Do You Know You Have Really Forgiven?

The following quote tells you what to look for and how to know you have forgiven. I have used it for years with clients and students because it is especially clear.

> "You know you have forgiven someone when he or she
> has harmless passage through your mind." [2]
>
> REV. KARYL HUNTLEY – SENIOR MINISTER,
> GOLDEN GATE CENTER FOR SPIRITUAL LIVING

When you think of the offender, does he or she move cleanly through your mind, or crash and burn?

Renowned author and theologian, Dr. Lewis Smedes, says in his book, *Forgive and Forget: Healing the Hurts We Don't Deserve::*

> "You will know that forgiveness has begun when you recall
> those who hurt you and feel the power to wish them well."

To add to this, let's look at a more precise definition and result of forgiving. Noted forgiveness researcher, Dr. Robert Enright, and The Human Development Study Group (1996) define forgiveness as the "absence of negative affect, judgement, and behavior toward an offender and the presence of positive affect, judgement, and behavior toward this same offender."[3] This is a clear result—positive feelings, opinions and actions toward the offender *and* yourself, without negatives.

Note: I've seen forgiveness occur with just the release of the negative toward the person, without the positive entering, especially with victims of abuse and torture. But, you know for sure if the positive has entered that your forgiveness is complete.

This same forgiveness research group emphasizes that self-forgiveness entails not only facing one's wrongs but also letting go of the negative thoughts, feelings and actions against the self and "replacing them with compassion, generosity and love."[4] Forgiveness toward one's self must result in positive feelings, actions and thoughts, or it is incomplete.

Questions

1. Who cannot go through your mind without crashing and burning? Note who these people are.
2. What does each person owes you?
3. Is there anything you owe them?
4. What would it take to forgive them now? And yourself?

- See if you can get clear about what would have to happen before the person can walk through your mind without stirring up any ill feeling.
- See if you can get clear about what would have to happen for you to have compassion, generosity and love for yourself.

Justice and Punishment

The question of justice usually comes up when considering forgiveness. People will say that it's not right to forgive a person because then there will be no consequence for what they have done. The unforgiven person has broken your personal, familial, or cultural rules of behavior. Where is the justice when you have been wronged, yet you have to forgive? This is all true. However, you would not need to forgive if you did not have an expectation that includes a punishment or some repentance for the offender's behavior. The emotional effect of that desire is the problem.

It seems an injustice to let a person get away with having done something to you when you know it was not right. You may want to teach the offender a lesson. That kind of thinking, though, continues to leave you in pain. I have yet to find someone happy in his or her life who is also punishing another person. The person might say he or she is happy to be getting back at the offender, but look carefully and you will find no joy in their lives. When a person wants to punish and attack another, they are being run by their reactionary brain. Joy and love are not components of it.

This punishing may continue even when the offender is not in their lives. I have known people who hold onto upsets with parents who have been dead for years. They are still attacking the parent in their minds even when the attack is painful only to themselves.

"Before you embark on a journey of revenge,
dig two graves." — CONFUCIUS

The question of right and wrong seems vital. If you feel you were wrong and the other was right, you do not need to forgive the other. When you feel right and justified in your anger, you will have difficulty in your personal and family life.

We need justice when values, rules for behavior, or ethical principles of a person, group, or country are broken. Ideals, laws, and rules maintain a culture and hold a society together. They are also the glue of family bonds and all of our relationships.

When a person or group goes against our values or breaks our rules for behavior, whether in a one-to-one relationship or in a society, the person or group is cast out in some way. When the cast out person or group makes sufficient reparation for that offense, forgiveness occurs, enabling them to come back into the social or individual relationship.

In the legal system, he or she might come back into society by fulfilling a prison sentence or public service. A personal situation might require an apology or payment for the damage. It is easier to forgive someone who has tried to repair the result of his or her act. For example, they might acknowledge their failure to uphold the values agreed upon between the two of you or society.

Forgiving becomes difficult when the person or group disagrees with your values or your rules for their behavior. How do you forgive then? How does justice occur? How do you release the pain, anger and hurt when there is no apology or repair, when the offender sees the situation differently and feels justified in what he or she did? For this, you will have many methods to work with to get relief.

Effects of Hostility

Women who scored high on anger and hostility had a higher risk of a cardiovascular event.[5] Earlier research showed that it was not necessarily Type A people who had heart attacks, but those Type A's who scored high on the hostility portion of the questionnaire.[6] (See note A for what type A means.) Dean Ornish, MD and author of *Love and Survival,* cites forty-five studies connecting hostility and coronary heart disease.[7]

A study at Duke University showed that students who scored high on a hostility test were in greater danger of dying young than their peers were. The study concluded that those students who were prone to anger were at more risk than those who smoked, had high blood pressure or even high cholesterol.[8]

If you often find yourself angry and hostile, here is something to consider. Somewhere along the way, for your own health and happiness, you might think about resigning from the job of judge and punisher.

Important Points for Effective Forgiving
Always Be Aware Of...

The Small Shifts of Heart and Attitude. The most significant discovery I've found in forgiveness work is how quickly it can occur. As you do this work, you'll find that there will be small shifts of heart and thought. The positive energy accumulated from these small shifts enables a transformation. If you feel relief while working on a question—that might be enough for the moment. Take a break or go to the next action.

These changes of feeling and attitude, I call the "felt shift." It's a sensation in the chest area of warmth, an opening of your heart, with a relaxation of the muscles around the ribs and throat, often with a realization. It is like the "felt sense" that Dr. Eugene Gendlin described in his book, *Focusing*. It's a little movement of the heart coming back in tune.[10]

The whole secret is sense of "ah ha" and often a smile – a feeling of relief. It might be because of a compassionate thought about the person, or an understanding. If you look at the shift more closely, you will see it involves a change in attitude toward the person in some way. Often that little movement is sufficient to change your whole day, or even your whole life.

With each felt shift, you regain the life energy tied up in the emotional upset. As you look at different areas of your life, gaining understanding about them and forgiving, you recover your life energy. This processing becomes easier and quicker because this extra power boosts your life and increases your ability to forgive, live, love, and heal.

> "Forgiveness does not change the past,
> but it does enlarge the future."
>
> PAUL BOESE
> 1668 – 1738 DUTCH PHYSICIAN BOTANIST

The First Essential Aspect

Throughout the book, I reveal essential actions for doing this work. The primary one is: **Hold the highest possible vision and goal for yourself that you feel forgiving can bring.**

Without this incentive, it may be too difficult to look at upsets and you will probably give up. You will do well, though, if you have a high ideal and outcome for yourself.

In my own experience with forgiveness, I have often had to choose the strength of my highest vision. In my own healing, because my highest goal was to experience the unconditional love of God, I would ask myself, "Am I willing to let this go to experience unconditional love?" It worked every time. Each time, I would have relief in my heart and joy flow through me.

Set your vision and goal, by asking:
1. What do I want in my life from this forgiveness work? Is it to experience Healing? More Love? Calmness and peace? Divine Love? A deeper connection to God?
2. What would inspire me to let this upset go?
3. Other than myself, who benefits from my forgiving?

Journal Questions: To help you at this time, I have included an exercise used successfully for centuries by Christians:

"Forgive us our debts, as we forgive our debtors."

You need to go no further with this book if you can just apply that prayer right now. Few, however, have been able to. So let's look at this idea further.
1. What does that person owe you? An Apology? Groveling on their stomach in grief? Hanging by their toes in pain for three days? You beating them to death with your fists? Electrocution?
2. What punishment do you need to see them have? Just what is it that you expected, didn't get, or don't expect to receive? That is their debt to you. {If you are working on forgiving yourself for something, you are looking for what you owe the other or yourself.}

3. At this point, write down what the person or group owes you (or you owe another). No one is going to read this but you, so let it all out. You can be as vile and vicious as you'd like.

4. After you have written all you want, look and see if this is the justice you want. How do you feel? Then ask:

    a. How likely is it that I will get the punishment or behavior change I would like?

    b. How long am I going to wait to get it?

    c. Am I willing to let this upset go?

The Major Barrier to Forgiving:

Feeling overwhelmed – This often comes from trying to forgive too much at one time. The objective of *The Power Forgiveness Process* is to forgive everything in your life that you have not let go of, not just one thing. Here is how to do it successfully: *Break it down.*

The first thing to do with a consuming situation is to break it down into smaller, workable pieces. It's too much to try to jam a whole plate of food into your mouth at one time and try to swallow it. You take bite-size pieces. It is the same with forgiving. Look at a difficult situation and see how you can break it down into smaller, more manageable parts.

Tom's upset with a building contractor entailed writing down all of the upsetting things the contractor did. He found that this calmed him. It was only then that he was able to sit down with the man and come to an understanding.

Sometimes writing all the negative experiences down at one time is too much. Marjory was upset with several doctors for mishandling her case. She became too angry writing all her upsets down. She had to take one doctor at a time, write down her upsets with that one doctor, then forgive each thing that happened. After that, she took the next doctor, and followed the same method. In the end, her anger and underlying fear of doctors was gone and she was able to undergo a procedure that helped her healing.

Dealing with Large Organizations

If you have difficulty forgiving large institutions or organization, it's because you get overwhelmed at the magnitude of the upsets. Again, breaking it down into bite size pieces makes a difference. Don't try to eat the whole cow at once.

When you try to deal with offenses committed by something big, like governments, organizations, corporations, churches, etc., you accomplish nothing by keeping the general thought of "them." Think of specific situations and then each person in the unpleasant event.

When you get to the specifics of a situation, you get closer to the truth. When you are working on offenses, you need to address all the smaller parts to achieve full forgiveness.

People form and run organizations, movements, churches, societies, political groups, governments, etc. *The people need forgiving.* So, break down the upsets by thinking of who represents that organization. As you think of one, others will come to mind.

I worked with a woman who had been in a cult for many years. She was finally able to let go of her upsets by listing all offense that had happened to her in the course of her years in the cult. At first, she thought that writing down all those upsets would be too overwhelming, but she found it is actually more overwhelming to let those upsets boil in the dark subconscious emotional sea that can create horrific storms in our everyday lives. Instead of letting these upsets swim around her mind below the surface of her awareness, she started writing them down. To her surprise, she started feeling better.

This feeling better, though, is only a good start. Forgiving those upsets must occur.

Truth and Reconciliation Commission

In 1995 when South Africa was trying to forge peace after many years of a racially oppressive government, it set up a *Truth and Reconciliation Commission* to consider amnesty for perpetrators of crimes committed under apartheid's reign. The democratic government did not give a blanket forgiveness amnesty because it knew it would not work. The commissioners gave amnesties person by person to those who came before them. There was confrontation by victims, and confessions of guilt.

The movie, *Long Night's Journey into Day: South Africa's Search for Truth & Reconciliation*, skillfully depicts part of the Commission's work. In 2000, it was awarded the Sundance Film Festival prize for Best Documentary.[11] This amnesty model, under various names, has been used in eleven other countries, when emerging from periods of internal unrest, civil war, or dictatorship.[12]

Forgiving Big Issues

Behind broad issues in history or in the world that you do not like, racism for instance, there is a person or group of people who represent that injustice in your thoughts. You might have to relax and look at your own past to find them.

Marion was trying to forgive the Catholic Church for the atrocities against women during the Inquisition in the Middle Ages. She remained upset until she saw she had pictures in her mind of the inquisitors as dark sinister men in black robes. She knew she had to forgive these priests. This put her on a journey to understand the mindset of priests of that time. Equipped with that understanding, she was able to let her upset go.

To forgive the German Nazis, Jacob thought of each Nazi soldier and supporter he had come across in his life, and gave a prayer of forgiveness to each one individually until he felt complete with each. Because certain guards were difficult, he kept on praying until he felt relief. With others, he could see how they were caught up in the lies about Jews. Then, he was able to let go of his upset. Though this was a long process for him, he noticed that after awhile it became easier.

Margaret was in a particularly difficult court suit. After years, several lawyers, and no resolution, she was even more upset and almost broke. While she needed to get on with her life, she could not forgive the legal system, much less the person against whom she had the suit. She went through the *Power Forgiveness Process* in several counseling sessions where she forgave each legal representative she could remember on both sides of the suit. After the series of forgiveness sessions, she had a new perspective that enabled her to forgive the person and quickly resolve the suit to her satisfaction.

The Key Question

Breaking down the situation often brings up a key question about what happened or about the people involved. Answering that question often takes looking at all the pieces of the situation and forgiving each person involved to bring full resolution.

It took Gilbert and Kaitlin a year after their divorce to sit down and talk about what had happened. Both shared their experience. Gilbert found that he really had only one question. "Why did you stay with me when I was so terrible to be around and our life was so bad?" Kaitlin's answer stunned him. "I didn't mind it. The kids were doing okay. The place was nice. And you weren't as bad as you think." For someone else, a completely different answer would satisfy her or his question.

Gilbert was lucky. Often a person does not get a chance to have the key question answered directly. It helps to talk with someone about your upset, especially if it is someone who can provide insight without necessarily taking your side and agreeing with you.

Forgiving God

"How do you forgive God for allowing the terrible atrocities that people do to each other every day? I cannot and will not forgive a God that allows brutality and the decimation of peoples and cultures in his name!" Harvey said. To resolve this conflict with God, he had to look at his concepts of God, God's role, and where and when he learned them.

He also had to look at the atrocities he attributed to God. In the middle of this questioning, Harvey looked around the room shaking his head saying, "This is not about God but about the actions of men in fear and hate. And, many times, they even thought they were doing right! God does not do these things, we do. There is nothing to forgive God for."

Forgiving God seems self-centered. It is. That is exactly why we need to forgive. Our perspective is always self-centered when we see only from our own eyes.

Forgiveness requires that we walk in the other's shoes, as much as we can. That includes God's shoes—if we are to forgive God. This often requires us to reevaluate the God of our childhood. This relooking at our old concept of God can bring us understanding, a deepening of our faith, and often humility.

Adam, a young police officer, went down his list of gripes with God when he was in a personal crisis. He felt better, but it brought him to a basic question of theology. He told his pastor: "God should change the minds trapped in evil ways." Many have had this deep question of the nature of God and man.

He told me later, "I was stymied when my pastor asked me about the importance of free will. In our discussion, I finally understood that without free will we are just trapped robots. Our free will gives us our life." With this insight came immediate understanding and forgiveness.

Journal exercise: To forgive God, as with any other big upset, you must:
1. Break down the upset,
2. List all the upsetting things you feel God has done, then
3. Answer the key questions that come up.

Spend time now looking at your upset or upsets and see if you can break them down as far as possible.

The First Hurdle

By understanding:
- what forgiveness is;
- what you need to let go of to forgive;
- getting past the biggest barrier,
- knowing the essential awareness of the small shifts, and
- focusing on your highest vision for yourself,

you have passed the first hurdle to forgiving.

You are not expected to forgive this soon. But, some have. If you have, keep working on the next people to forgive.

Initial research on forgiving was in forgiveness training classes at universities. There, students were taught what forgiveness was and wasn't. Often significant forgiveness results were obtained just through this step. You are doing much more than that here.

> "It should be clear that continuing to haul around a heart full of bitterness <u>will not get you what you want</u>. Therein lies the power of forgiveness. Something did in fact happen to you, but you still, in the interest of yourself must lay it down and move on."
>
> DR. PHIL McGRAW, TV PSYCHOLOGIST,
> FROM HIS BOOK, *SELF MATTERS*

CHAPTER THREE

The Blocks to Forgiving

The Myths of Forgiveness

I n addition to the stressed-brain reactions, people resist the
idea of giving up their upsets because of persistent misconceptions about forgiving, which I call *The Myths of Forgiveness*. Sadly, these myths continue even when we know they are not true. Here are some of the most common ones. They are not in any specific order of importance, as they are all important to be aware of.

Myth 1 – The person is deceased or no longer around, so forgiveness is not needed!

You might think, "out of sight, out of mind." But, if you still carry the upsetting emotions and ideas, then the injury remains alive in you. At some level, harboring any resentment, large or small, affects your life and interactions with people. Though forgiveness may be an act of compassion for someone who is gone or deceased, it is mainly to relieve you of the self-inflicted torture of hate and anger. I have frequently had students and clients forgive their long-gone parents and then experience major changes in their lives. In one of my forgiveness groups, after a woman in her forty's forgave her father for abuses in childhood, the pain that she had had in her legs for years went away.

Myth 2 – I don't have to forgive because I never want to see them again!

Forgiveness does not mean reconciliation. Reconciliation, which is the reunion of two upset parties, is not necessarily the outcome of forgiving. A person may forgive and still choose to protect him or herself from abusive behavior by never seeing that person again.

For effective reconciliation to occur, forgiveness of the offense must have occurred. Extensive research with couples who have experienced infidelity attests to the positive healing power of forgiveness first.[1a]

Regarding reconciliation, Rick Warren, the noted pastor and writer who gave the invocation at Barack Obama's inauguration in 2009, tells us that the Bible teaches that three things are essential to resume a relationship that's been broken: repentance, restitution and rebuilding trust. "In fact," he stresses, "trust is something that's rebuilt over a period of time. It must be reearned." [1b]

Myth 3 – If I forgive, I will be condoning or justifying their offense.

Forgiveness is not condoning a bad behavior or justifying an offense. As Dr. Fred Luskin points out in his excellent book, *Forgive for Love: The Missing Ingredient for a Healthy and Lasting Relationship,* if we condone, we think that what was done is OK, thus forgiving is not necessary. Forgiveness is needed when we are hurt and grieving in some way about how we were mistreated.[2] The family of a drug abuser may forgive him or her for the behavior, but does not approve of the drug misuse and will probably do everything they can to stop it.

Though a child may break something and be forgiven, that does not mean the parents condone what the child did. In fact, the child might receive a consequence appropriate for his or her age. The consequence, however, is given with love and understanding, so that the child learns. Giving it with anger just instills fear and fosters resentment. Studies show that consequences given without anger are more effective.

When I worked as a school psychotherapist, I often saw that parents felt guilty at the prospect of hurting their child's feelings and possibly losing their love and approval, so they would not follow through with enforcement, and consequently the child didn't learn the lesson. Ideally, when a rule is broken, there is an understood and pre-established consequence. Our legal system is based on this process.

Myth 4 – I've tried, but I can't.

There may be many reasons why you can't forgive but that doesn't mean it can't be done. You are gaining the tools now not only to take it on again, but also to be successful. Sometimes a person will forgive and then regret it. That happens because of reactionary brain activity. Just by going through this book you will no longer regret any type of forgiving you've done and will have much better control over earlier brain reactions.

Myth 5 – I'm just too angry! (or too hurt!)

It's essential in forgiving to be aware of your feelings. You can see the effects of too much emotion in the violence caused by anger. Each time you bring up anger and hostility your whole physiology goes into stress, which continues to activate the reactive brains.

Allowing anger and resentment to remain by not forgiving is a temporary fix that doesn't work. Being assertive and being angry are not the same; you can learn to set limits without anger.

The ability to set limits without anger comes from a perspective of strength and peace as opposed to anger and resentment. Forgiveness has its timing. You need to calm down to do effective work. Meditation, Tai Chi, prayer, contemplation, massage, yoga, exercise, talking with friends, are all useful calming ways.

Feelings under the Surface

Becoming aware of emotions other than your dominant one will help deal with any kind of upset. Most often, a person is angry at what happened. When I facilitated groups of men who were abusers, anger was the predominant emotion. We always noted, though, that anger for these men was the easy surface emotion.

Mike saw this when we worked on his upset about his girlfriend. He knew that he controlled her with his anger. The show of anger is central in most mammalian behavior to establish dominance, and it is no different with us.

One day, Mike became extremely angry with his girlfriend, Susan, for a small thing that she did. As he said later, "it was really nothing." Nevertheless, he blew up and broke something he was working on. Of course, in his mind it was her fault. In our anger control group, he went on and on about her.

One of the men in the group, Nick, remembered that two weeks before, Mike's buddy had died. Nick knew quite well that the first response of many men to emotional situations is anger. Moreover, he knew that there were always deeper emotions under the anger. So, he asked Mike if his anger was really about his friend's death and not his girlfriend's mistake. Mike's eyes teared when he looked at that possibility. The grief was right there. The upset with Susan was completely gone. He even said later that it was easier to cope with the anger than to feel the loss and sadness around his buddy's death.

We saw this often in the anger control groups. As a result, I tended to call anger a false emotion for these men. Anger was too easy for them. It covered deeper, more uncomfortable emotions.

In forgiveness work, there is often an emotion below anger. Changes occur by contacting that emotion, perhaps fear or grief. Likewise, where anger is not an acceptable emotion, which is more often the case for women, being aware of the anger beneath the surface might be what creates movement toward resolution of the upset.

Myth 6 – They do not deserve it!

You may believe that a person doesn't deserve forgiveness. You might be right, they might not. Nevertheless, you are forgiving for yourself, for your benefit, and for your relationships. I've seen compassionate people forgive a person who doesn't deserve it because they felt the person needed love somewhere in their life. In fact, Dr. Everett Worthington, noted forgiveness researcher and author includes giving "the gift of forgiveness" as one of his forgiveness steps.[2a]

We see the effect of this gift in a true story told to me by Aeeshah Ababio-Clottey, one of the authors of *Beyond Fear – Twelve Spiritual Keys to Racial Healing*. The story occurred in Ghana in the hometown of Kokoman, Aeeshah's husband and coauthor.

A trouble boy was bullying other children in school. Obviously, everyone disliked him. The principal decided to punish him on stage in front of the whole school assembly, so that the other children would feel justice was done. Kokoman's sister was a teacher at the school and had taught all of her students about forgiveness. When the troublesome boy and principal were on stage, the students in Kokoman's sister's class started chanting, "Forgive him!" Soon the whole school was chanting, "Forgive him!" The principal stopped and let the boy off stage.[2b]

The story does not end there. The children's loving act toward the bully transformed him. He became a kinder person and good student. That act of compassion changed the whole situation at the school. In later years, the Clotteys heard this story first hand from a man who was that boy. He was working for the Attitudinal Healing Center in Ghana.

Attitudinal Healing Centers, which are located around the world, promote forgiveness as one of their principles of healing.

These principles have helped people for over 30 years. See Appendix E for these powerful guides. The renowned psychiatrist, Dr. Jerry Jampolsky, started them. He and his wife, Dr. Diane Cirincione, have authored many excellent books on healing that emphasize the importance of forgiving.[A]

> "Your attitude is everything and determines how you experience every aspect of your life. You cannot always control what happens to you in the world, but you do determine how you react to it many times a day by your attitude."
>
> JERRY JAMPOLSKY, MD AND DIANE CIRINCIONE, PhD

Myth 7 – I just want to forget about it.

> "In forgiving, people are not being asked to forget. On the contrary, it is important to remember, so that we should not let such atrocities happen again. Forgiveness does not mean condoning what has been done. It means taking what happened seriously not minimizing it; drawing out the sting in the memory that threatens our entire existence."
>
> BISHOP DESMOND TUTU[3]
> from NO FUTURE WITHOUT FORGIVENESS

Forgetting about an injury might not be forgiveness but denial. The negative results of this denial impinge insidiously under the surface of your mind. Remember—you know you have forgiven when he or she has harmless passage through your mind.

Rick Warren, the noted pastor, reminds us that forgetting is not the intention of forgiveness. He emphasizes, "The only way you can forget something is to actually refocus on something else."[4]

Forgiveness allows the upset to fade in the mind because it is no longer run by the upset and can refocus on the positives of life.

Myth 8 – Before I forgive, I need an apology!

You may wait forever and not get the admission of guilt you want. The person who caused the upset may have a different perspective of what happened and feel that an apology is unnecessary. In fact, he or she might expect an apology from you. If you are able to let the upset go by forgiving it, you will regain your own happiness and peace of mind, and not be dependent on the actions of another person. And, you will stop being the victim of them. Even if they do give you an apology, it might not be heartfelt if it comes at your insistence. Forgive without the apology and save yourself time, energy and heartache.

Myth 9 – There is too much to forgive!

Sometimes, a person is just too difficult to forgive because he or she did so much. The principle mentioned in chapter two applies. Break it down. List all the offenses the person committed.

Anna Marie said she came out of her marriage "abused and broken." "It is impossible for me to forgive the years of abuse I suffered from my husband." Her rage at him had carried on for six years. One wrong look or comment by any man demanded that she attack him verbally for his disrespect. Of course, people avoided her.

The few friends she had left told her she had to forgive and get on with her life, which is why she came to my class. "How do you forgive that many years of hurt?" she asked. Her task was first to write down each hurt from her husband that she could remember, then start forgiving the small ones. Because she did not like the person she had become, she was determined to do this. In far less time than she thought, she reached a place of peace.

Questions: If you are having difficulty forgiving, see if your situation is too big. Spend time breaking the situation down to its smallest level, and then forgive each person involved.

Is there someone or a set of people who represents the organization to you? I call this "Finding the who."

Here are further questions to help find out more about the general situation.

1. Who are the people you think of when you see this upsetting situation?
2. What is it about what they did that upsets you?
3. What does their face look like, what did they specifically do?
4. Was every person similar to "them" doing the same thing?
5. In your experience, have all of "them" been the same way?

Myth 10 – I cannot forgive because they keep doing it!

If a person continues to hurt your feelings intentionally or even unintentionally, out of habit or because they do not know any better, forgiveness can still be beneficial, although, admittedly, it is more difficult. Forgiveness wipes away the effect of the hurt even if it occurred 15 minutes ago or repeats 15 minutes from now.

Physical abuse is a completely different situation. You must protect yourself. Even emotional abuse needs to be stopped. But if there is no option, and sometimes there isn't, forgiveness can help. For example, inspirational author, Dr. Bernie Siegel, tells us in his book *Prescription for Living*, "Forgiveness is at the heart of a healthy and happy life. Forgiveness protects relationships. It also protects the person who does the forgiving."

He relates the story that psychiatrist and author, Dr. Robert Coles, told in his book, *Children of Crisis: A Study of Courage*, about Ruby Bridges, the first African-American child to integrate a Southern elementary school.

In 1960, federal marshals had to escort Ruby every day through a crowd of adults who spat at her and called her terrible names. Dr. Coles was puzzled by the amazing fact that this five-year-old girl did not seem to be emotionally damaged by the ordeal. He discovered that Ruby prayed every day asking God to forgive her persecutors.[5]

Letting go of an upset, even if it is still occurring, also involves self-forgiveness. By refusing to be respectful to yourself, you stay in the loop of "what goes around comes around." So, you will continue to get what you've been getting. To change the situation you have to take action and stop the destructive cycle by first removing yourself from being abused. This inner work might take professional help.

At a teen forgiveness group, I talked with, Cristy, whose previous good friend was spreading vicious rumors about her. Her life was deteriorating because she was depressed by the unfairness of the situation. She could not let her hurt go. When we did the forgiveness process, her attitude changed toward the other girl. Even her body language changed. This resulted in her sending a different non-verbal message in school. She began to feel less like a victim. Not only did she feel better, but also the ex-friend perceived a softening in her attitude and backed off her attacks. Ultimately, Cristy forgave her former friend and, as a result, improved her relationship with her boyfriend and others.

Myth 11 – They will just hurt me again if I forgive!

Fear keeps the reactionary stress system going. It is true that "love is letting go of fear"[6] because both cannot occur at the same time. When our basic survival system become activated by fear, what we consider "higher" functioning drops away and we are into only saving our life. This self-protection is important, but it can be a strong block to forgiving especially if we fear being hurt again, a big objection to forgiving as I mentioned in Chapter 1.

Forgiving does not mean turning the other cheek to allow the offense to occur again. Jesus' original meaning of "turn the other cheek" was to show your strength in your faith. Its broader meaning includes forgiveness, but is not limited to it.

The controversy around this statement has unjustly harmed its use. You can forgive someone completely and still hold him or her to a standard. Similarly, you can forgive a business associate for doing something damaging and warn him or her that if it happens again it might result in the ending of the business relationship.

The fear of being hurt again if you forgive is real, but when fear drives your life you are only at basic survival. As I said in Chapter Two, fear must be controlled. This might take outside help. Meditation, prayer and faith help. So does a walk in nature or listening to your favorite music. There are many methods in this book that can help. When you've quieted the fear for the moment, do some forgiveness. Do anything you can to help you out of the reactionary fearful mind. Remember, you can forgive and set limits so that you won't be hurt.

The major complaint and fear about forgiving an abusive domestic partner comes from a real concern that the abused person will bring the abuser back into her (or his) life and the violence will happen again.

When a person does forgiveness work, love often returns to the relationship. When this happens, the partner will go back to the abusive person feeling healed. **WARNING:** The returning partner is often abused again because the abuser has not completed the inner and outer work on his or her own anger. Without doing work on this anger, the abuse will probably occur again.

Abusers, men or women, don't recognize that their victims are not the cause of their anger and do not deserve to be hurt.

Because abusers have a short fuse and explode quickly, they need to learn methods to help them remain calm in stressful situations. Until an abusive person acquires these skills, he or she is not safe to be around in stressful situations. If you want to be with the physically abusive person make sure that they do an extensive anger control program, not just a short 10 week course for one night a week.

With deep forgiveness work, a person being abused in a relationship may actually find it easier to end the connection. In *The Anatomy of Peace* by The Arbinger Institute, a woman tells a story of an estranged, abusive husband who frequently visited to see their daughter, but was really trying to get back together. On one occasion, she was convinced he was about to commit suicide, and was elated at the prospect of his being out of her life. The next morning, very distraught, the man returned. He had intended suicide, but a freak power outage distracted him. He tried to persuade her it was a sign they still belonged together. She became furious, and decided to be as mean as necessary to get him back into a suicidal state.

This woman, who had done forgiveness work, was shocked at her own willingness to goad another human being into suicide, no matter how cruel he had been to her. Compassion welled up, and she put her arm around him to comfort him. She was also able to see that she had been trapped by the idea that feeling love for him meant she had to stay with him. When she realized that forgiveness, and even love, did not require this of her, she was freed from her anger and resentment, and with it her attachment to the relationship.[7]

In general, I have found that the most efficient tool for lowering the threshold of anger is forgiveness. A perceived hurt often drives anger. For an abusive person, that hurt is far deeper than the present upset. Dealing with the pain of the past lowers the level of anger for the quick-to-anger person. Healing the wounds takes in-depth work. If an abusive person is not willing to work on his or her anger, he or she will probably abuse again.

Forgiveness does not mean letting the person back into your life to abuse again. A person might forgive an abuser and still put out a restraining order with the police to protect her and the children involved. An abuser must learn self-restraint no matter how emotionally upset he or she is. Limiting harmful behavior actually helps the abuser because he or she is caught in the stressed-brain reactions. The chronic abuser needs to learn to have continual inner discipline and practice to stay above the snake brain.

When a relationship has reached the point of physical or emotional abuse, it is in deep trouble. **Outside help is needed.** Limit setting on the abuse is urgent. Working on a domestically violent relationship requires at least a psychotherapist trained specifically in this area. **It is not work you do alone.** Groups on abuse, domestic violence and anger control are effective, not only because they teach good methods, but also because the abuser must learn to find other ways to have satisfaction in his or her life other than just through a spouse or partner. And, of course, so that the abused person can be safe.

Myth 12 – God will deal them, I don't have to

It's not true that you don't have to do anything, because you will still have the upset there affecting you while you wait for the person's divine punishment. This doesn't relieve you of the upset.

Though we may speculate on how God might judge someone, in reality, we cannot possibly know God's perspective of a situation because we are unable to take the 360-degree God's-eye-view of that person or situation. We cannot see the past, or often, the present situation that made the person decide to do what he or she did. We cannot know all of the dynamics involved in their life. We often do not see the forces involved in our own lives that caused us to make a particular decision. Thus, all we can really do is our own work, and let God do God's work. In our own life, forgiveness *is* up to us.

You can of course ask for Divine Help. You can say prayers for forgiving or meditate on the person asking for an insight. You can do much with the Inner Help that is always available to you. Throughout book, many different ways are presented to get this help and to use it.

- **Look at** your present concept of God to see if your perspective is still influenced by views from childhood that are no longer accurate.

The Myths of Forgiveness Summary

There are concepts about forgiveness that are *not* correct and cause problems when people attempt to forgive another person. When we look at what forgiveness is and is not, we reveal these myths. Forgiveness is:

- Not condoning a bad behavior, justifying an offense or turning the other cheek.
- Not reconciliation with the offending party.
- Not the same as, out of sight, out of mind.
- Not dependent upon an apology.
- Not dependent on the other person being alive or in contact with you.
- Not dependent on whether the offender deserves it.
- Not losing, or the easy way out of a situation.
- Not forgetting and not lack of responsibility.
- Not dependent on a belief in God.

Myths of Forgiveness Detection: To assist your forgiving, complete this exercise.

- Bring to mind a situation in your life where you have been unsuccessful in forgiving another person.

- Look and see if one of the Myths of Forgiveness stands in the way of your being able to forgive. Write down the myth.
  1. Would dispelling that myth allow you to see the situation from a different perspective?
  2. Could you forgive the other person now?

God as a Block to Forgiving?

A strong influence on people forgiving is their particular concept of God, or a Higher Power. Some people are trained to see God primarily as a judge and condemner. With this perspective, they may justify their condemning and harming of others. They will also condemn themselves, which then justifies their own suffering, depression, and lack of peace, love, and forgiveness.

I mention this because people raised with this negative concept may have difficulty forgiving until they change their idea of God and themselves. If you have feelings of unworthiness, then self-forgiveness will be a vital area to work on. Gaining compassion and understanding for yourself will be crucial.

Self-Forgiveness

There is a problem with *love your neighbor as yourself.* If you have no love for yourself, then there is often no love to give to your neighbor. To follow the truth of this principle in its full meaning would be first to regain self-esteem, love, and worthiness. You do this by gaining self-forgiveness.

As author Paulo Coelho says:

> "Pay attention to every moment because the opportunity — the 'magic moment'—is within our reach, although we let it pass by because we feel guilty." [9]

I use the term, "gain self-forgiveness" because you cannot always do your own forgiving. You have to see how you feel.

Sometimes you need to make amends for what you did, as in the 12-step programs. Or, you might need to turn to a Higher Power for help in releasing your heart from self-torment.

To gain forgiveness from his dead father for the way he treated him through the years, Simon did a daily ritual from Judaism for his father. At the end of two months, he felt a significant change. He continued this ritual because it continued to help him deepen his connection with life, love, and God.

Ruth felt that her anger in her mother's last months was unforgivable. Even though she knew the forgiveness process, she couldn't find relief. My suggestions were of no help. Her choice was to pray regularly at a beautiful cathedral. Even though she wasn't Catholic, her mother was. At a service she went to, she said, "I felt a change inside and felt my mother's love and forgiveness."

Sometimes we need to **get** forgiveness from those we have hurt to feel right about ourselves. This often takes at least an apology. In her book, *The Power of Apology,* Beverly Engel gives us a fine three-step method for giving a meaningful apology:[9a]

1. State your regret for causing situation.

2. Accept responsibility for your what you did.

3. Give a way to repair the harm done perhaps a pledge or act..
Her book gives plenty of helpful ideas on doing these steps.

For some, gaining self-forgiveness might mean looking deeply at their family of origin to gain some objectivity. For others to regaining their self esteem, it might be donation to or working for a cause they feel is import. You won't know what will work until you are in the process. Sometimes the most powerful action you can do to gain self-forgiveness is to ask for inner spiritual help with deep sincerity.

In Appendix C, there is a helpful prayer by Dr. Masaharu Taniguchi, the founder of a spiritual movement in Japan called

Seicho-NO-IE. The prayer, though affirming reconciliation, is really about gaining self-forgiveness. Try it.

Is It True That Only God Forgives?

Some religious factions teach that people are incapable of forgiveness because humans are inherently evil and thus only God forgives. Twenty years of research shows, however, that people of all lifestyles, religious or not, forgive regularly, much to their benefit and the benefit of others. Those without any religious orientation can enjoy the same positive benefits from letting go of old hates and resentments as a religious person.

I've worked with atheists and people from many different religions, all of whom have experienced radical changes in their lives through forgiving. Forgiveness is a movement of the mind and heart toward compassion, kindness, and love. It is an action of peace, which results in joy for the forgiver, regardless of religious belief.

"Only God forgives" may be an excuse used by clergy unable to help people forgive. While historically, Jesus brought a tremendous focus on the subject, it is no longer true that the church (and God by their extension) holds sole control of forgiveness. That is a falsehood that continues to help condemn forgiving even today. It is given by anyone to anyone, and anyone can help another to forgive. We have the methods and outline of how to use them. We have only to do it.

One of my students, Jean, a psychotherapist and an atheist, was quite offended when I said that people with a religious background might find it easier to forgive. She cited instances in her own life of supposedly religious people who were quite unforgiving. She knew many people and clients with no religious perspective who were kind and forgiving people. And she had forgiven a tragic abuse from her past. People who are raised with strong love and kindness carry this into their adulthood.

However, if you feel you were not raised with enough love, this might be the time to let that upset go. No matter what has happened to you, you have the capacity to find the Highest within and around you to regain any love you might have missed in the past. Forgiveness is a good way to do this.

Awareness of Feelings

In Myth 5, we talked of feelings under the surface, and that lack of awareness of other emotions concerning a situation can keep us from forgiving. When we carry old hurts and trauma they affect us below the surface of awareness in our subconscious mind. Have you ever been driving and noticed all of a sudden that your neck hurt and felt tense? It did not seem to hurt a minute before. Nevertheless, when you thought back, it had been hurting for awhile, but not in your conscious awareness. Once you become aware that you have been holding onto the tension, you feel the pain. Then you can do actions to alleviate the pain.

Our subconscious protects us from the emotional pain of old injuries by putting them out of our consciousness. Although the old events may be out of our awareness, they can still be harmful. They may appear as physical symptoms, irritability, or general anger, which can explode and cause serious harm in our life. These old injuries and the negative attitudes from them continue to affect us destructively in the ways we interact in the world.

Awareness of our emotions is a key in letting go of an upset. Remember, if you are not aware of it, you cannot deal with it. Just finding the emotion below the surface of an unforgiven situation, such as sadness, grief or hurt, can change the reaction drastically.

"Here I am 42 years old and I never knew we had so many emotions!" Jake complained at an anger control group after receiving a list of emotions. "Why haven't I been shown this before? Why didn't they teach this in school?" he said. I was amazed at his statement and through the years have supplied emotion lists to help people see exactly what they are feeling. See Appendix D.

Valuable Points to Remember Concerning Feelings

- Forgiveness is not only an intellectual course of action. Strong feelings will surface.
- Feelings are the entry point for forgiving.
- Feelings are often multilayered, particularly anger. Often feelings of fear and grief drive anger.
- Avoiding difficult feelings is normal but not helpful in this work. You can't let go of something that is hidden.
- Being willing to feel what might be underneath the surface and not resist it, takes honesty and courage.

Help in Awareness of Your Emotions: In the Appendix, you will find the page: *How We Are Likely to Feel When Our Needs Are Not Being Met.* I have also included *Feelings Likely To Be Present When Your Needs Are Being Satisfied.* These are from the excellent communication work of Dr. Marshall Rosenberg, the author of *Nonviolent Communication – A Language of Compassion.* He found that people communicate better, and are heard better by others, when they say the emotion that is affecting them in the moment.[10] I highly recommend his book and work.

Here are some things to do to help you understand what you might be feeling other than the typical anger, hurt or resentment. Often by knowing the deeper or more accurate emotion, people are able to understand the whole situation better.

1. Think of an upset you are working on
2. Go down the list in Appendix E: *How We Are Likely to Feel When Our Needs Are Not Being Met.*

3. Notice how your experience changes when you come upon feelings involved in this situation.
4. Write about these in your journal, and if anything has changed for you around the situation?
5. Go through the list in Appendix E: *Feelings Likely To Be Present When Your Needs Are Being Satisfied.* Notice how you feel better just thinking of these emotions. Do this anytime to feel better.

The Second Hurdle

By identifying the major barriers to forgiving, and by being aware of emotions under the surface, you have passed the second hurdle to forgiving. You know the best way to handle a difficult situations and you have cleared up the misunderstandings about it. This might not have brought you the justice or satisfaction you were looking for, but for many this information is enough to bring about forgiving. I hope that you have achieved some relief through understanding and awareness.

"To carry a grudge is like being stung to death by one bee."
WILLIAM H. WALTON

CHAPTER FOUR

The Proven Benefits of Forgiving

The Mind Transforms through Forgiving.

When you let go of the bitterness of the past, mental, spiritual, and physical energy becomes more available. How much life energy returns depends on how much energy you expended holding onto resentments from the past, and how much letting go is completed.

By becoming energized through forgiving, you will notice that it actually takes more energy to be in the lower brains than in your heart and newest brain, the neocortex. When the energy trapped in the lower brains releases, the world actually does look different. We will address this later in the chapter but for now look at all the remarkable results from forgiving.

Research Results

Research conducted at prestigious universities shows that forgiveness results in an increase in cardiovascular functioning, lowering both blood pressure and heart rate. Findings also include an increase in psychological and emotional well-being, less anxiety and stress, reduction in depression and hopelessness[2], less anger, more confidence, and higher self-esteem.

When held too long, grudges and resentments damage the heart and blood vessels. All age groups noted these effects. The gains remained long after the forgiveness training ended. In both short-term and long-term well-being, people who were more forgiving had fewer chronic conditions and physical symptoms of illness, and more vitality and emotional resiliency. It seems there is no negative outcome from learning to forgive.[3]

In his bestselling book, *Forgive for Good, A Proven Prescription for Health and Happiness,* Dr. Fred Luskin, of the Stanford Forgiveness Project, tells us that researchers have found that just the idea of forgiving someone allowed some people to feel better psychologically and emotionally. Conversely, if the participants in the study imagined themselves as unforgiving, they had negative reactions, such as high blood pressure. Solely the idea of forgiving is helpful.

He also cites that forgiveness research has revealed these general results:[3a]

- People who are more forgiving report fewer symptoms of stress and health problems.
- Failure to forgive may be more significant than hostility as a risk factor for heart disease.
- Even people with devastating losses can learn to forgive and feel better psychologically and emotionally.
- On the other hand, people who blame others for their troubles have a higher incidence of illnesses such as cardio-vascular disease and cancer.

Forgiveness training in scientific studies has been shown to:[3b]
1. Heal relationships
2. Increase hopefulness, personal growth and self-confidence
3. Decrease depression, anger and anxiety
4. Improve compassion, spiritual well-being and quality of life.

Forgiveness Therapy Results

Drs. Robert Enright and Richard Fitzgibbons have a textbook on the benefits of Forgiveness Therapy called *Helping Clients Forgive: An Empirical Guide for Resolving Anger and Restoring Hope*. Their studies show that Forgiveness Therapy can be beneficial for treating: [4]

- Anxiety disorders, including generalized anxiety disorder, separation anxiety disorder, panic disorder, social phobia, obsessive-compulsive disorder
- Post Traumatic Stress Disorder (PTSD)
- Depression, including Bipolar Disorder
- Children with conduct disorders, such as Oppositional Defiance Disorder, Attention Deficit Hyperactive Disorder (ADHD), and impulsivity
- Substance abuse and eating disorders
- Impulse control disorders, such as gambling, pyromania, and kleptomania
- Personality disorders, such as paranoia, borderline, histrionic, and narcissistic
- Any condition were strong anger is involved

Increased Energy and Uplifted Spirits

Unforgiven situations can cause depression by keeping your life energy low. Upsets and resentments do not remain in your mind without effort. You are investing your own life energy on upsetting thoughts. When you let them go, you regain zest and life.

On a relaxing summer trip across the U.S. a few years ago, I decided to review my life year by year using the Power Forgiveness method to clear up any remaining upsets. I reviewed all of the people I had known, and all of my negative events. If I noticed an upset, I would look at it, apply the work of this book, and let it go. I was astonished at how much my energy increased each day that I drove. Not only did I enjoy the trip more than I expected, but it also opened me to a deep vision for my life a week later.

Salesmen who had a one-day workshop on forgiveness and emotional competence and regular telephone forgiveness coaching over a six month period sold two and a half times more than their co-workers who had none of this training.[5]

Changes in Others

Years ago, a friend's daughter and the daughter's fiancé were brutally murdered. The murderer was found, convicted, and sent to prison. My friend, Aba Gayle, who was miserable for years, finally said, "I just can't hate like this!" She needed to find out why he did it, so she went to the prison to meet the murderer. In hearing his story, she realized she had to forgive. Over time, she made friends with him. Although she never attempted to get him out of prison and always believed that he killed her loved ones, she was moved by his humanity.[6a]

Her reaching out changed him. While she was visiting him on death row, she would also talk with the other inmates. She tried not to see them as they saw themselves, or as others saw them. These men all wanted to be in her presence—all because she learned to forgive.

Happier Relationships

Forgiving improves relationships because you are able to be emotionally present and communicate a deeper level of love. In intimate relationships, you and your partner are more in tune with each other. Loving thoughts can come forward releasing upsets more easily. When there is an upset, there is more compassion for the other, rather than a determined defense of your own position.

My dear friend, Kima, sent me this note after I asked her how she and her husband, Michael, had managed to remain so happy in their marriage for 35 years. Whenever I'd talk with them, they'd say, "Our relationship hasn't been better!" Here's what she wrote:[6b]

"After several years together and things not going well, we spent many days going over situations where our feelings were hurt. We looked at our relationship from every angle, talked about every one of our upsets, and let them go. These were not big things, but when they accumulated, they caused big hurts. From that forgiveness work, we have managed to build a rock solid platform for our marriage.

So, I want to say that when you are dealing with couples, what is left unsaid can be a vicious sting later down the line, especially if it seems silly embarrassing to one person. Those things come up later to harm the relationship."

This was intense work, difficult for couples to do without help. Michael was a psychotherapist. They both knew the value of doing this "cleanup work." I would recommend getting a counselor initially to help you to get to that level of communication.

Positive Results with Children

Paul was quite angry after his divorce. He was not loving toward his three children because they reminded him of the painful divorce and of his financial troubles. He did not behave rationally or tenderly toward them. Of course, they did not want to be around him. Yet Paul did not see how he was creating the estrangement.

Luckily, his girlfriend dragged him to a forgiveness class. In it, he finally was able to see his responsibility in the estrangement from his children. A month later in his summary paper for the class, he said that he was able to recreate a loving bond with them instead of blaming them and his ex-wife.

Dealing with Marriage and New Relationships

Statistics show that second and third marriages are NOT likely to be more successful than first marriages. As with computers, old programs from parents and failed relationships are still in our conscious *operating system*, disrupting the new relationship until it is *cor-corrupted*. The problems will, in reality, increase until the system *crashes* in another ruptured relationship, or a health problem.

You owe it to each new relationship or life endeavor to look for and clean up anything that might contaminate it. Forgiveness presents an opportunity to change destructive family patterns.

In order to install a new operating system, you have to uninstall the old one. You are doing that with Power Forgiveness. To *install* a better inner system for higher possibility and happiness, remove as many old resentments and grievances as you can. Look at the *Power Forgiveness Process* as an antivirus program, removing vicious incidents that are ruining your life.

Physical Healing

Research published in the *Journal of General Psychiatry* showed that hostile marital interactions slowed physical wound healing and caused an increase in an inflammatory protein in the blood. This data also shows "hostile or abrasive relationships affect physiological functioning and health."[7a] Chronically high levels of this "hostile" protein can contribute to cardiovascular disease, arthritis, certain kinds of cancers, and other conditions.[7b]

> "There's something called the 'physiology of forgiveness.'
> Being unable to forgive other people's faults
> is harmful to one's health."
> HERBERT BENSON, MD, NOTED AUTHOR, RESEARCHER AND
> HEAD OF THE MIND/BODY MEDICAL INSTITUTE

Julia came to a weekly forgiveness group for two months. Life was getting better for her, but she still had trouble forgiving her abuse as a child. On the fourth week, the group gave Julia the whole evening to work on the issues she still had with her parents, who had been dead ten years. She felt good after the session. Two or three weeks later, she revealed that the pain in her knees, for which she had treatment for years, was gone. She said it all went away that night when she finally forgave her father.

When Hank felt miserable and hopeless from a fever and sore throat, he decided to look for an unresolved upset that could have caused the illness. After looking for only a few minutes, he said, "I remembered an assistant at work had demanded a salary equal to my own even though he didn't have the years of experience or skill. I was quite upset with him." Hank used the forgiveness process outlined in the workshop.

Later he said, "When I realized that the guy was just being himself and really did need a raise, I felt fine about him, and all of a sudden, the sore throat started clearing up and the fever started coming down. I was well in less than three hours. That was amazing." Although this result is unusual, it is clear that mastering forgiveness can help maintain better health.

Chris Loukas

Even the devastating effects of trauma heal faster with forgiveness, often miraculously. Chris Loukas, a deeply spiritual man and old friend, lives forgiveness. One night, years ago, a drunk driver collided with Chris' van. For six weeks, he lay in a coma suffering from multiple fractures. When he regained consciousness, the doctors told him he would never walk again.

With the prayers of many and forgiveness for the fellow who hit him, he did walk again.

When he recovered, Chris not only befriended the young man who caused the accident, but treated him as a son, helping him to get off alcohol and find work. Chris held no resentment. His forgiving attitude not only facilitated his physical recovery, but also left him with peace of mind.[8a]

After my workshops, some people are so convinced of the benefits of forgiveness, they check to see whom they haven't forgiven when the first symptoms of illness appear. Often, the symptoms will clear up quickly and sometimes go away within a few hours of performing this action.

When you find yourself sick, ask yourself:[9]

1. When did it start?
2. What was going on in my life at that time?
3. Who do I need to forgive?

Hope

Hopelessness, which is a sense of uselessness and negative expectations about the future and one's personal goals, is also a factor contributing to depression. Research has show that hopelessness is strongly related to adverse cardiovascular outcome.[8b] Actor Christopher Reeve, paralyzed from the neck down after being thrown from a horse, continued for several years (until his death) to be a vital public figure and vigorous activist for research into spinal cord injuries. Even though he felt like a physical burden on others, he gave strong credit for his continual good spirits and will to live, to the fact that he had never blamed the horse for his injuries, not even during and right after the incident.

Experiencing Deeper Spirituality

All of the above research and examples show the mental, emotional, and physical benefits of forgiving. Even more significant are the spiritual benefits.

Spiritually, the clear and forgiving mind can sense The Divine and Sacred of life. In letting go of upsets, life becomes full, the heart becomes peaceful, and the mind, calm. Joy is then a natural consequence, love is renewed, and true self-esteem is reestablished.

Then we experience the truth of who we are through the connection to the Essence of Life.

Those people who live the forgiving way of life, the way of letting go of upsets, tell us and show us that Love is an essential part of our natural state of being.

Some people have deeply religious experiences after forgiving. They say that they have a deeper understanding of life, love, and God. Lewis Smedes, in his book, *Forgive and Forget* suggests:

"When you forgive the person who hurt you deeply and unfairly, you perform a miracle that has no equal. Nothing else is the same. Forgiving has its own feel, color and climax, different from any other creative act in the repertoire of human relationships."[10]

Forgiveness work is effective in changing our lives because we are realigning our mind with the Primary Principle of Existence—God, Higher Power, Allah, The Great Spirit, etc. This empowers us to go beyond thinking about:

1. the way things should be, and
2. what happened to us.

This act of quieting our self-centeredness and realigning with the Highest Power within and around us calls forth a higher magnitude of healing power.

Because something was terribly negative or continued for a long time does not mean its release must be comparably difficult or drawn out. Psychotherapy is often caught in this false thinking. In Power Forgiveness, we are talking about a different approach. Standard psychotherapy often addresses the issue from the level and mindset of victimhood. In forgiveness counseling, the practitioner and the person working on his or her upsets are attempting to hold the mindset of the Highest Potential available.

"No problem can be solved from the same level of
consciousness that created it."

ALBERT EINSTEIN

The highest potential perspective will bring our thoughts back
to our highest capacity. Holding grudges, resentments, anger, revenge thoughts, obsessing about a hurt, or avoiding someone are
all manifestations of lack of love and lack of connection to the
highest within us. By the mere willingness to realign to our highest
potential or power, we call forth resources both personal and universal to assist us.

The Real Consequence of Holding on to Upsets

Sometimes people believe there is a benefit to not forgiving. So
let's look at this. The first thing to look at is **the payoff** for not
letting go of the upset. Generally, people have a good reason for
doing not doing something. Even though a decision we've made
might not seem to be in our best interest, if we look deeply, we'll
find a belief that the choice was the best one possible at the time.
Often, we are influenced by lower brain activities and stress.

Ask yourself:
    A. What do I get by keeping the upset going? Write down
       any benefits. Who benefits and how?
    B. Is being right more important than being happy?

Sometimes you don't notice how much the upset affects you.

Here are questions to ask:
    1. What am I really getting out of this upset? List the negatives
       and the positive.
    2. What is happening to the people closest to me by holding
       onto the upset?
    3. In my life, how strong are love, peace, and joy?

4. Could forgiving this situation increase my happiness and those around me?

The following are questions about being a victim:
   a. Have I seen myself as a victim of others?
   b. How long have I felt victimized?
   c. How long is it okay to let others be in control of my happiness?
   d. Am I a possible contributor to the problem, not just the victim?

The Seldom Used Act That Brings Big Results

Prayer for Inner Help – Even though many people have a religious or spiritual perspective in their life, they seldom pray for help in forgiving. We do have deep inner help available. It can show us a different way of viewing any negative situation and can unburden us if we are willing to accept it. I call it Divine Help because it seems to have much greater wisdom and honesty than I have. Accessing this Power beyond our small unforgiving-self is effective. You are empowered by realigning with the Creation Principle of the universe—opening your mind to possibilities and perspectives other than your own.

To connect with this Divine Help:
   1. Take time to relax and contemplate the highest in yourself as you do this forgiveness work.
   2. Take a moment now to ask for inner Divine support through a prayer to assist you in forgiving.

Note: Ask for help to see your situation in another way. The prayer, **"Please help me to see this in a different way,"** is extremely useful.

If you bog down at any time during this work, be silent, and make a sincere request for Help. *Have faith in Divine Love.* When you have done all you can do, let the struggle go and listen. I cannot tell you how this help will manifest or how it will occur, but I know that it is there to assist you.[11a]

Writing Dialogue: Writing about what is going on with you now concerning a specific incident or person is an effective tool in forgiving. I use what I call the *Dialogue Process.* It is a writing technique, which helps you to get underneath the upsets and gain a different view of it. This shift in viewpoint is critical in the whole process of letting go.

To do it, talk with yourself in writing about your upset until you come up with the next logical question. For example, if you are upset with your husband, you write about how upset you are until a question comes up. Perhaps, "How could he do that?" You then write, answering that question until the next question comes up, as "Was his mother like that to him?" This goes on until understanding, or compassion arises.

This is a valuable method. The questions and answers never fail to surprise. If I start out with a prayer for guidance and help, I find the help always comes. When emotions come up, accept them and keep writing, or ask another question, like "what's behind this emotion."

The Simplest Forgiveness Practice

At first, I was skeptical of Rosie's forgiveness beads and prayer. When I met Rosie Rodriguez, a sweet and spiritual woman in Santa Rosa, California, she had been teaching her work and having people make her "pay-it-forward beads" for over a year with terrific results. Rosie had a vision of these beads in her meditation from the Angel of Forgiveness.

There are 490 beads in all, resembling Catholic rosary beads. This number comes from the Bible (KJV)– Matthew 18:21-22:

"Then came Peter to him, and said, Lord, how oft shall my brother sin against me, and I forgive him? Till seven times? saith unto him, I say not unto thee, until seven times: but, until seventy times seven."

To my amazement, none of the forgiveness methods and exercises I had been collecting and teaching for almost ten years are as simple as this one. The first time I used the beads, I tackled a big forgiveness issue that was bothering me. I simply prayed "I forgive," with strong prayerful intention on each of the prayer beads. After ten beads there is a gratitude bead where I said something I was grateful for from that situation. At the end of that session, the upset was gone and never came back. [12a,b]

Self-forgiveness is usually the most difficult inner work a person can do. So, I decided a few months later to tackle an area of my life where I felt guilt and needed self-compassion. Again, I used Rosie's method. Again, I broke down the big upset into bite-size pieces. On each of the smaller upsets with myself, with strong intention, I just prayed, "I forgive" repeatedly with a grateful thought after ten to twenty repetitions. I was pleased with the changes from pain to relief that I had within five to seven minutes on each small issue. I continued for 45 minutes until there were no small upsets. I felt great—the big upset was no longer there.

In my workshops and counseling, I teach this method early on. It has been effective for people with both large and small upsets.

Hope for Humankind

Our highest self comes forward in a calm, unthreatened state of mind. Then, our brains begin to synchronize making sense of our lives and giving meaning to our actions. Forgiveness makes that state of mind stable so that we can function at our highest level and fulfill our deepest dreams.

Forgiveness, then, is the hope for humankind, because forgiving readily brings the highest function of the mind and heart to the forefront, assisting us to let go of unreasonable expectations, fears, and attack. It enables us to undo the chronic primitive brain reactions, fear and fight, allowing the highest functioning of the brain to occur. In addition, we have the connection to the Divine, enabling us to reach our highest capacity.

Forgiveness is not the highest function of the human mind. It is, however, the most powerful way you have to quell the storm of emotions and primitive stimulus response mechanisms that you experience. Through a forgiving mind, you can function at a higher level of kindness, peace, problem-solving, and openness to the highest creative power available to you—a state to which humanity aspires.

The Third Hurdle

By being convinced of the power of forgiveness, you have passed the third hurdle in forgiving. You know what it can do in your life and what not forgiving has done to you. This might not have brought you to forgiving your main upset, but for many this information helps sway the thoughts of forgiving toward the positive. By this time, you should have found excellent reason to forgive, and, have worked on forgiving some people in your life.

All of the results from forgiving can easily be attributed to your mind and heart finally returning to their natural state. This "natural state" is more than a release of control by the lower brains, it is also spiritual. That spiritual connection is influenced by the functioning of your brain systems working in concert. We will look further at the implication and potential of your brain in the next chapter.

In further chapters, we will be going into many other effective methods to deal with upsets so that your healing can occur.

At the core of most methods is:
1. increased awareness of what is going on inside you concerning the upset, and
2. the **willingness** to let go of your upset.

"Forgiveness does not mean that we suppress anger;
forgiveness means that we have asked for a miracle:
the ability to see through mistakes that someone has
made to the truth that lies in all of our hearts.
Forgiveness is not always easy.
At times, it feels more painful than the wound we suffered, to forgive the one that inflicted it. And yet,
there is no peace without forgiveness.
Attack thoughts towards others are
attack thoughts towards ourselves."

Marianne Williamson
Illuminata: A Return to Prayer

PART II

Going Deeper

From a Buddhist story:[1]

"A man is struck by an arrow from an unknown assailant. Rather than tending to the wound, he refuses to remove the arrow until the archer is found and punished. In the meantime, the wound festers until finally the poison kills him. Which is the more responsible for this death: the archer's letting go or the victim's foolish holding on?"

from COLIN BERG

AMERICAN AUTHOR/TEACHER

CHAPTER FIVE

Making Sense of Our Thinking

Our Complex and Amazing Brain

The greatest accumulation of nerve cells in our body is in our brain. Surrounding the outer edge of the brain, closest to the skull bone, is the gray matter. It is only a quarter of an inch thick, yet in this gray quarter inch (6 – 7 mm) there are 100 billion nerve cell bodies. The nerve cell, or neuron, is made of the cell body and its arms, which send and receive messages to and from other nerve cells, muscles, and organs. Each nerve cell body can have up to 10,000 connections to other cells. The white matter of the brain, which takes up the most volume in our skull, is where the arms from the gray matter cell bodies connect.

The number of these interconnections is astronomical (100 billion times 10,000). If you spent fifteen hours a day tapping your finger on the table every second, without any days off (not even to go to the doctor for your finger), it would take you 50 years to do just one billion taps.

All that you learn and do creates new neural connections in the brain every second until you die. The hundreds of trillions of nerve pathways enable you to access all of your memories, skills, and life activities from the womb to death.

Look at these connections as your brain's highway system for your thoughts, emotions and actions. The impulses around the brain go at 200 miles per hour (320 kph). There, you have everything from ten lane highways to walking trails to map your experiences.

Why Habits Are Hard to Break

What you do most, generates the highest number of nerve connections. These would be akin to a freeway or major city highway artery. Lesser-used responses have fewer nerve cells involved.

To become a habit, anything new that you try will take effort. It's like following a well-worn path through the woods. When you try to create a new trail, it is initially difficult, but becomes easier each time you take it. At first, you will need to remove branches and rocks that are in the way. As you remove the obstacles to the path, and continue to use it, your way becomes easier. Eventually the thing you are trying to learn develops a large enough nerve pathway and becomes easy.

When you do something repeatedly, you create a neuron *super-highway*. This is a habit. Habits can help you function better and do your work more efficiently. For example, you drive your vehicle out of habit, barely aware of what you are doing. This is helpful for many activities, but not for what you want to change.

If you spend forty years rehearsing resentment about someone, you develop a nerve *freeway* to that resentment. As long as you are speaking or thinking of a negative situation, you are reinforcing that negative pathway in your brain that will not only consume your thoughts, but can also cause physical problems.

Though habits keep you in ruts you do not like, changing them may be frustrating. Repeated attempts to change will normally bring success unless the stressed brain reactions are active.

What's behind Your Thoughts

In order to deal with and make sense of all the information we receive, we sort and catalog incoming data according to our past associations and experiences. In addition, the mind stores and retrieves data through a personal symbolic shorthand—a code—known only to us based on our own experiences. You can't really know what another person is thinking because you don't know their code, and they usually don't either because this all takes place below conscious awareness.

Since we associate our experiences in unique ways, problems may occur because every new experience we have, integrates with an *already formed* group. The most probable nerve pathway that already exists incorporates the new experience. This merging is also dependent on the most activated pathway at the time.

The new piggybacks onto the old. Thus, each person takes in his or her new experience differently.

A girl raised in a loving family might connect her new boyfriend with loving family experiences and feel secure about their relationship. The woman with a terrible family relationship might also connect her boyfriend with her *family neural pathway*. If her family security was nonexistent, she will probably expect abuse similar to that given by her father or ex-husband and thus, not trust the boyfriend. This is a formula for failure even though the boyfriend might be a fine person.

The Triune Brain

As I mentioned in Chapter 1, our brain is really three-in-one. Evolutionarily, earlier brains adapt the structures already there into new functions and structures. As the amphibian line moved into the mammals, so did the brain. As that mammalian line developed into the primate line and into the human line, so did the brain.

A way to represent these brains would be to picture a golf club, which is the reptilian brain; then put a golf club head cover over that, which is mammalian part, the limbic brain; then put those two inside a watermelon, which is the neocortex. That is the physical representation.

Dr. David Linden, a professor of neuroscience at Johns Hopkins University, says in his book, *The Accidental Mind*, that functionally, our brain is like an iPod built around an eight-track cassette player. It's certainly not ideal.[1] And, a cruel joke if this was planned. Psychologically, consider a lion tamer, as the neocortex, the lion, as the mammalian brain/limbic brain, and an alligator, as the reptilian brain, all in the same cage. As long as each has their food, water, and sleep, the situation will go okay. Now take away the food. That is what happens to us when we get overwhelmed.

The neocortex in the front part of our skull, the Pre-Frontal Cortex, mainly differentiates us as humans. Some say that this is even the fourth brain. Brain studies have shown that this area seems to be where forgiveness occurs.[2] Each side of the prefrontal cortex is responsible for controlling the responses of an earlier brains. The right side managing the reptilian functions and the left, works to control the Limbic system. Magnetic resonance shows that when a person is depressed, the limbic system is overactive and the left prefrontal cortex is much less active.[3]

The Neocortex

The brain most people are familiar with is the neocortex, which is the main storehouse of our information and memories. It,

- Generates our ideas, gives us our capacity for concentration, and uses symbols to produce our ability to read, write, talk and do math.[4]
- Helps us to be not only logical and systematic, but also intuitive and imaginative. [5]
- Overrides and suppresses unacceptable social responses of the lower brains. [6]

In its highest functioning, it is not only the agent of invention and creativity, but also influences prayer and the spiritual experience.[7] Even if we didn't have all the wonderful forgiveness research results, you can see that just functioning in the neocortex more would be a positive result in itself.

This newest brain enables us to:

1. Give meaning to our life and world.
2. Analyze different perspectives and alternative possibilities to make choices among them.
3. Coordinate with the lower brains – enabling us to have empathy and better judgement.[8]

Our Emotional Brain

In the center of the brain is our emotional center—the limbic system, which is a series of interconnected structures the size of a walnut. With the development of the limbic system in birds and mammals, our nurturing and loving connections became established:[9]

- Enabling the nursing and better protection of offspring and family
- Creating activities like friendship, love and affection, laughter and playfulness
- Controlling aggressive behaviors

It gives our life and language interest, and even passion.

"Emotion is the messenger of love," Drs Lewis, Amini, and Landon tell us in *A General Theory of Love*. They add that emotions carry the signals of our heart to one another. And, that for many of us, feeling deeply is one and the same with being alive.[11]

This sounds good doesn't it. The problem occurs when this love is stopped for whatever reason. Then other strong emotions like misery or rage, to name a couple, can take hold and cause terrible reactions and consequences.

(Because there is controversy among neuroscientists as to which structures are part of this system, our concern with the limbic system and forgiveness is the fear mechanism and the amygdala, the structure that activates fear reactions.[10])

The limbic system gives feelings to our life events—feelings through a whole range of emotions, from terror and grief to excitement, joy, and passion. These help us remember both positive and negative events because our memories always have emotional content.[12] In fact, greater emotional stimulation around a learning event increases a person's retention of that event.[13]

In stress and emotional turmoil, the control of aggressive behavior decreases, and anger, revenge and jealousy can increase, causing even more difficulty. This turmoil is capable of shutting down "rational behavior". In the legal system, this is *temporary insanity* and in society *crimes of passion*.

Ralph was disappointed in himself about not being able to forgive his sister for a hurtful comment she made at a family gathering. When we discussed how he felt, he said, "Feelings have nothing to do with this; I should still be able to forgive her." Difficult unforgiven situations always have strong emotions tied to them. Avoiding how he felt prevented real forgiving. I'm not saying wallowing in feelings is good, but, acknowledging how you feel does help your letting go of an upset, as I mentioned.

Ongoing trauma or tension enlarges the amygdala, the instigator of the fear response, which then predisposes it to creating more fear in that person's life. When this response goes on long too long the person is said to have Post Traumatic Stress Disorder (PTSD). We will go into this in Chapter 12.

Remember: Forgiving may take time because of intense feelings that may be present.

The limbic system sets the tone for our response to events and our enjoyment of life. It is the switchboard that coordinates all the information from the external and internal world. Either it feeds incoming data to the neocortex for conscious thought, planning, or problem-solving, or it feeds the data to the reptilian brain for a survival reaction. It decides which way to send the messages by immediately comparing the present conditions with similar past experiences.[14]

This information switchboard creates problems, however, when a person is emotionally upset. At those times, all data coming in is classified as unpleasant even when, normally, it might not be. Then, when the limbic system compares new information coming in with the distorted information already gathered, there is inaccuracy and the new data is reacted to or classified as dangerous. A person in chronic pain or in an ongoing threatening situation will have an enormous store of negative memories and probably be in constant reaction mode, feeling quite upset, and being unpleasant to be around.

Alex, a therapist, was not able to forgive his father for his childhood abuse and for harshness towards him even into adulthood. Their relationship had always been strained. When Alex started having work and physical problems, he came to forgiveness work. Though he was able to forgive everyone else in his life, he couldn't forgive his father. Because of this one major unforgiven thing, his work and physical condition were getting worse. I was unable to give him perspectives or processes to help him to forgive his father. Finally, after two months of decline and struggle, he remembered that his father had been in continual pain all his life. With that insight, he understood why his father had been so angry and mean all those years. Alex's forgiveness was automatic, and his work and physical condition started turning around within a week.

We learn two key lessons from Alex's forgiveness work. The first is—**just one unforgiven person is enough to prevent healing.** The second came from Alex several months after forgiving his father. He visited his dad and told me that they had a better time together than they had ever had. In addition, they had no arguing or disagreeing. His father was even friendly. Alex saw that **his own negative mind-set had affected their relationship.**

With that attitude gone, replaced with compassion and understanding, his father acted differently. "We even had a peak experience one night just chatting and listening to music. Dad even said at the time, 'It doesn't get any better than this!'" The second lesson is: *we affect our relationships by our subtle attitudes toward one another.*

> "Who you are speaks so loudly
> I can't hear what you are saying."
>
> RALPH WALDO EMERSON

When the negative memories become stronger than the positive, over-activation of the limbic system can cause: [15]

- moodiness, irritability, clinical depression
- increased negative thinking and perceiving
- decreased motivation and drive
- flood of negative emotions
- appetite and sleep problems
- decreased sexual responsiveness
- Social isolation,

Sadness, hopelessness, and an overabundance of automatic negative thoughts also occur. [16]

Psychiatrists Lewis, Amini, and Landon in their book, *A General Theory of Love,* point out that we cannot direct our emotional life as we can our muscles. We cannot force ourselves "to want the right thing or to love the right person or even to be happy after a disappointment or even to be happy in happy times." This is not because we have a shortage of discipline, but because *will* is limited only to the newest brain. "The emotional life can be influenced but not commanded," the doctors say.[17]

There are spiritual teachers as well as brain scientists who maintain that people can learn to direct their emotions, but this still requires serious practice. Thus, if the person you are trying to forgive has reacted emotionally and you are condemning her or him for not changing, you must understand that they might not be able to change in the time and in the way you would like them to.

Martin was a responsible man; he took care of his family quite well. He was devoted and worked hard for them, even doing work he didn't like. He did it because he wanted to provide a decent home for his family. However, because he did not like his work, he was often grumpy and tired. After a few years of this, his wife became fed up and asked for a divorce. He went crazy, and almost killed her. Here we see how emotions can drive us in positive and negative directions.

In a similar example, Rick not only disliked his work but also hated the city in which he and his family lived. He stayed there because his wife, Natalie, liked it. When she tired of his lack of enthusiasm for her and for his life, she decided the marriage was over. When she took the kids and filed for divorce, Rick was lost in his emotional upset and tried to kill himself. Natalie could not understand his grief and upset at all. She said, "He never showed much interest in me or the kids when he came home."

In the first case, Martin could not forgive his wife for years because he could not understand how she did not see that he was sacrificing for the family doing work he didn't enjoy. In addition, he felt she had no regard for what he went through every day at work. In the second case, Natalie could not understand how Rick could get so upset when their marriage seemed to be nothing. When she examined the relationship from his point of view, she understood.

Our emotional circuits can drive us to behave in bizarre and irrational ways in the name of love (and hate). This is because the emotional system develops before the neocortex, our ability to analyze is the last to be developed, and is often less used. In teenagers, the neocortex is not yet fully developed. Overall, they seem more emotional, and they are, due to incomplete brain growth. Full development usually take place by age 21.

The limbic system is also involved in alcoholism, drug addiction, impulsive gambling, and compulsion for sweet foods.[18] This is why a person cannot just decide to quit addictions, but must make a strong, ongoing, and concerted effort to do it. Because we are social beings, working with addictions in a group can have great results. A fact, the Twelve-Step movement found long ago.

In summary, the limbic system gives passion and interest to our lives. It decides how we will react to events, and even colors those events with emotions. In coordination with the neocortex, it adds a richness to our lives and memories. On the other hand, when it activates the earliest brain, the snake brain, we may go for a very rough ride.

The Reptilian Brain

Our earliest brain, the R-Complex, also known as the reptilian brain or snake brain, is quick acting, set up for self-preservation, and is the foundation of our physical and species survival. Its structures include the brainstem and cerebellum. Bodily, it deals with mechanical functions like muscles, digestion, respiration, circulation and reproduction.[20] It never sleeps, but we are the least conscious of it.

Through the years, Dr. Paul MacLean who did extensive research on the three brains gave us a quality description of the workings of this earliest brain.[21] In addition to its physiological actions, here are the basic life activities that this brain affects:

- **Domination and control of territory** – Our space is our empire, our territory. Here is the source of reaction to strangers or people who are *different*. This starting place of prejudice comes out of our basic need to protect what is ours. Under stress, it becomes "I will attack any stranger who enters my space." In driving, we see this in road rage, which often results from a violation of one's space or "territory."

- **Courting and mating behavior and displays** – These actions guarantee survival of the species. This includes sexual aggression and submission. The answer to why a woman sometimes submits against her better judgement to sexual aggression, and why men and women may become overwhelmed with sexual desires, is here deep in the reptilian brain.

- **Control of interaction with others** – This is the drive for social maintenance and dominance through establishing a *pecking order*, a chain of command. At the deepest level, we are social beings. This is why we have a tendency to follow the crowd and its standards, and have awe for authority.[22]

- **Ritual behavior** – Following regular rituals and having ceremonies is valuable in keeping people part of the social matrix and having them feel included as part of the group.[23] Thus, routines and patterns give us a basic sense of security. This is why we organize. Here is the force behind religions, governments, and institutions.[24] Under stress these rituals and activities may become compulsions where the person become obsessed with doing them, and even become fierce about forcing these routines on others.

This level of the brain usually keeps our social and group interactions at a priority. At its highest influence, it is the impetus for forgiveness; at its lowest, it is violence and fascism.

Out of this desire for social interaction and control comes imitating, copying, and deception—all in order to be part of the group. The fashion industry is built on this drive.

Change in any of the above areas can bring about strong reactions. Fear drives the reactive responses. It produces our basic fear reflex which is displayed as aggression or submission.[25]

The reactions of Reptilian Brain (or Snake Brain) is the main reason we resist forgiving. Though the amygdala in the limbic system, initiates the fear signal, it is the brainstem of the reptilian brain that carries out our responses to the fear.[26] The snake brain becomes our enemy and sabotages us if we let it have control for too long.

It doesn't incapacitate us on purpose, it's just doing its survival job. It's really what causes a person to attack, be violent, run away, or withdraw. It can makes a human a victim. The program it follows is survival and all it knows is its reactions when it perceives threats.

Make no mistake about it—this is not you! It's normal for a person to misidentify these stressed-brain reactions as one's own. They're not. It's like calling a computer program the computer. The program might be faulty, and cause trouble with the computer's functioning, but the program is not the computer. They are both quite different.

Realize also that the program can be repaired to function properly. We are a complex mixture of mind, body and spirit not a ancient programmed reaction.

Additional responses of the reptilian/snake brain when it is in reactive control include:[27]

- nervousness and panic attacks
- ongoing prediction of the worst that can happen
- conflict avoidance or aggression
- low or too much motivation

Discomfort with change and maintaining the status quo are the hallmarks of this basic brain. It repeatedly does the same behaviors, never learning from past mistakes.[28] Action without rational thinking is its drive under stress. Its key motto then may become, "Might makes right!" Yet for another, the motto could be, "Hide!", or for another, "Run!"

Rod seemed to be stuck at this level of brain function. He could not work out situations too well or solve problems. He was in fights regularly and had been in and out of jail since he was an early teen. He abused his wife sexually and physically. He controlled her money, where she went, and whom she met. He wanted immediate compliance with his orders. She submitted to all of his demands for her the safety of her young child. But when he started becoming controlling and violent to the child, she realized the terrible danger they were in. She sought help through a women's counseling center and left him to hide at a "safe house." He did all he could to find her. Luckily, he was unable to locate that women and children's shelter.

When he talked about his early life, I was able to understand how he ended up as he did. His father was an alcoholic who beat him with a belt or his fists as early as age two. He never knew when his father would go into a rage and beat him. By hearing this, I realized why he lived his life as he did. He had known no other way to be than in his snake brain—the source of psychopathic, sociopathic and antisocial behavior.

If I had worked with his wife, I would never have recommended she go back with him, but I would have counseled her to try to understand why he was the way he was, so that she would not hate him, or herself for having been with him. What he did I don't justify or condone, nor would I ask her to. I would encourage her, through forgiveness work, to release her rage so that she could heal, move on with a positive outlook on life. Thus, she would avoid traumatizing her child and others with her negative attitudes and actions.

Note: People who have not dealt with their deep trauma are more likely to react from the snake brain because it has had control for so long. They often have not learned any other way to respond when they are under pressure. Even respectable people when placed under constant stress, like being in a war zone or a cult, may start reacting from this lowest brain more and more, and do acts they would not have normally done. This is crucial to know if you are trying to forgive yourself for terrible ways you might have acted when you were under unending, awful strain.

The Reptilian/Snake Brain's reactions and the Limbic responses can overwhelm a person. The survival function of these earlier systems are powerful. Given enough ongoing stress/fear, I believe anyone may start manifesting on-going snake brain behavior squeezing the life out of themselves and others. That said, don't use it as a justification for continued reactive behavior. Luckily, there are many tools to assist you to come back to your true self. Forgiving is an indispensable tool that can move you out of being trapped in basic survival and into full joy of life and human functioning.

Management by Fear

By understanding the stress reactions of this brain level, we see why *management by fear* is the least effective of all management styles. It may create results, but in the end, it not only sabotages the employees but also the company itself.

If you were part of an organization that used fear or had a manager like that, it is vital to realize that the people you are trying to forgive were likely functioning at their most stressed level. It's possible you were too. Cults and some religious sects function at this level. They might even profess, "God is love" but, they certainly don't live it; they live and promote fear. Keeping people in fear and under constant pressure is part of brainwashing and may cause the victims to do things they wouldn't do normally.

To avoid being controlled by this brain, you must be willing to look at your behavior as an observer—as if it were not your own.[29] In truth, it is not you. From that detached perspective where you are not reactive, you can ask questions of yourself and understand what might be creating the reaction. I recommend doing this with another or others who can hold an objective viewpoint with you. If you get reactivated they can help you out.

Distinguished educator, Dr. Elaine De Beauport says that this basic brain resists against any new desire from your limbic brain or any new decision by your neocortex. She feels that this resistance is why willpower alone, "however strong or well intentioned" is not enough to significantly change behavior.[30]

In summary, this brain affects our behavior concerning:
- Our immediate physical domain,
- Mating
- Social contact.

Change in any of these areas can bring about strong reactions. Fear drives the reactive responses. It produces our basic fear reflex, which is displayed as aggression or submission.[31]

- Now, look at your own unforgiven situation more carefully and see how this information helps you to understand the person in a different way.

How the Brain Works Best

Given the number of stimuli and reactions that occur each moment, the brain's ability to orchestrate our life into a symphony of action and decisions is incredible. Our brain structures intermingle and communicate, yet they differ in structure, properties, and chemistry. Even though they have separate structures, research has shown quite clearly that they do not work independently.[32] Our exceedingly complex brain has many levels of interaction all occurring at the same time. They function best together in a safe environment which enables our mind to be a symphony instead of a war zone.

As I've said, built into our nervous system are survival functions that do not always allow us to be the perfect functioning individuals we wish to be. Survival in dangerous situations depends on the quick action of these mechanisms, which developed over hundreds of thousands of years. In the high stress of threat (fear) and hopelessness, the earlier brain systems, can more easily take over control, and we lose our compassion and our ability to think through our difficulties clearly. Fight, flight, or freeze are only a few of these survival responses. When they occur at the wrong time in our modern and highly complex society, they can cause embarrassment and social disapproval, and can even have legal consequences.

Note: Since the brain does its magic best when it is not threatened, make sure you put yourself into a comfortable environment when you do this work or any time you have an upset. Then your emotions can calm down and your higher thinking abilities can work in harmony to deal with your unforgiven stressful situation.

We often seem to be imprisoned by our stress reactions. And yet, it is this same brain that can bring us our best times. The next chapter will examine better ways to manage frustrations, anxieties, and unforgiven areas in your life.

CHAPTER SIX

Breaking Out of Prison

"Hold no one prisoner. Release instead of bind, for thus are you made free. The way is simple. Every time you feel a stab of anger, realize you hold a sword above your head. And it will fall or be averted as you choose to be condemned or free."

A COURSE IN MIRACLES- LESSON 192

Dealing with Emotional Pain

This stressed mind can often seem like our jailer, punishing us and others. In this chapter, we will look at ways to put the snake brain to rest.

The Overlooked Aid for Empowering Yourself

Finding Outer Support – The value of external support in helping to forgive is often overlooked. Help from others in forgiving moves us more quickly and easily through it. Surrounding yourself with those who practice forgiveness assists you to forgive. Seeing others who are skilled in forgiveness helps you learn how to do it.

Group or individual help can be surprisingly useful when you are stuck and cannot seem to progress. Often you are not able to see the patterns in your life, particularly if these patterns go back to your earliest years.

Is there a support group, therapist, counselor, or minister that could help you cope with a negative life situation, so that you can be more positive about your life? 12-step programs are excellent. Find the one appropriate for you. If you belong to a church or meditation group, take advantage of the support to continue your work in forgiveness.

Dr. Donald Hall's research at Vanderbilt University showed that social support and contact have an effect on: [1]

- How well people to cope with stress in life. And how happy and content or depressed or lonely, they are,.
- How effectively the body's immune system functions and survival when a person faces with crises or serious illness.

He says that social contact is even a predictor of how long a person lives.

> "Love and intimacy have a powerful effect on our health. Social support and interaction are as powerful in improving health and longevity as are not smoking, exercising, and eating healthfully."
>
> DEAN ORNISH, MD [2]

- Is there someone you can talk with to help in your forgiving?

Our Comfort Zone

When we are forced to move away from what is familiar, our brains give us uncomfortable signals we call stress. We all have different thresholds of stress. Some people can comfortably handle running a company of hundreds of employees or more. That same executive might be extremely anxious in intimate settings. Others cannot stand being responsible for even one person, but are comfortable in intimate settings.

Being in our comfort zone allows us to feel safe. Threatening environments cause discomfort, fear and even panic, removing our ability to think clearly. Thus, the best learning environment is a non-threatening one.[3]

Our comfort zone, however, is not always the healthiest place for us, but it is the most familiar. For example, because of familiarity and comfort, people who live in war zones sometimes go back to their home even though the situation is dangerous and they are more likely to be harmed there. Often, we think we are doing the best thing when we actually put ourselves in danger by going back to familiar family patterns and old ways of acting even though they did not work originally.

A friend gave me a personal example of this. "Walking across a bridge with a railing, I noticed that my fear of heights made me list toward the traffic side of the walkway instead of the railing. If my foot slipped for some reason, I would fall into traffic rather than the railing. Even though I felt certain the traffic was a greater risk, it still took strong effort could I keep myself in the safer place."

As a child, Mario hated being hit by his father for not obeying. He hated his father and left home at a young age. He became upset when anyone yelled. Yet when his son disobeyed, Mario would hit him and shout at him just like his father had. His outbursts made him not only feel guilty, but also depressed because he had no idea why he did this or how to change it.

In stressful situations, strong emotions, earlier events and defenses attack us below the surface of our awareness— subconsciously. Thus, we *must* consider the role of stress in situations that require forgiveness of others or our self.

We have a high level of complexity in our society because forgiving is built into our highest functioning as human beings. Yet, when we are emotionally upset, for example, depressed, overwhelmed, angry or resentful, we are not able to function at our highest level. At these times, forgiveness is essential though more difficult.

Making Sense

An interesting activity of the neocortex is to even out our visual impressions. From the reptilian function of the brain, our eyes actually make tiny jumps as they sweep across a field of view. The points <u>between</u> where the eyes land are blurry. Nevertheless, the neocortex creates a coherent perception out of them, filling in the gaps of the jerky feed, so that what you see is continuous and smooth. But in truth, it is not.[4]

Though it works well for jumpy eye movements, there is a problem with this fill-in-the-gaps work of the neocortex.. In his book, *The Accidental Mind*, Dr. David Linden, a professor of neuroscience at Johns Hopkins University, tells us that the this creative brain can also take the raw material of memory, and in the same way, weave it into a consistent, yet bizarre story.[5] Thus, each person at a crime scene or accident can have a different story as to what happened.

We see this in stage hypnosis where the person is given a post hypnotic suggestion to do a certain behavior, when he is brought out of hypnosis and then acts on the suggestion, he will make up all sorts of excuses why he is acting as he is. The excuses are the neocortex trying to make sense out of what is happening.

Depending on how your stress system is activated, the neocortex will use what you see and the "facts" to create a story incorporating all the factors to have a smooth flow. The neocortex uses the data available at the time but often through the lens of emotion at the time. A person caught in a fear response will see fearful circumstances and justify their response even when the response is bizarre.

The implications of this in forgiving are critical. The story you tell yourself, from what you saw and the "facts" you have, might not be accurate. It may easily be a story created by the neocortex to smooth out the events. We like to think we see clearly and think clearly, but in truth, we don't. Our brain functioning and clarity of thought is not as accurate as we suppose. There are gaps. We have a brain not built on reasoning but on reaction. This must be taken into account not only when you are forgiving others but also yourself!

How Our Outer World Reflects Our Inner One

The world we see is often upsetting. But, in reality, what we really see are just particles or waves of light in patterns. Physiologically, this light comes through the eye and registers on the retina, which then sends these light patterns through the optical nerve to the brain. The brain then has to interpret those patterns before we know what we are seeing. To do this, the brain must access its "experience and information data stockpile," which provides not only an interpretation of what it sees, but also the emotions tied to it.

In our first years, we rapidly fill our information stockpile. We learn to identify our surroundings initially from the first people in our lives. They teach us what things are and what they do. In addition, they also give their emotional bias about those items. We interpret all our other experiences through our first teachers— Mom, Dad, siblings, and others close to us, and our experiences with them. Our mother is actually our primary emotional and information source; this information is even transmitted through the womb.[6] Therefore, your initial teachers have a tremendous influence, not only upon **how** you see and feel the world, but also on **what** you view and sense.

Even something as simple as color may create a strong emotional reaction. For example, if a mother hates red because of a trauma she experienced, she will pass that bias along to her child. The child does not have to be told red is bad. He or she will pick it up in voice inflection and facial expression.[7]

A child raised in an abusive household will often see the world as unsafe, to be feared. Similarly, a child raised by a paranoid parent often will be fearful of people and surroundings. Because of the fear that the parent and child have, their lower brains are more active. Hence, there is less opportunity for rational thinking and positive emotions. As a result, fear will be constant and joy absent.

Conversely, a child raised with love feels safer and sees the world as a safer place than one who is beaten or abused in some other way. The child who feels safe will think better and be happier. Many studies have shown that children raised in their first year of life with no touch tend to die, and if they survive, they have poor emotional responses to people and life.[8]

What is going on inside of us determines how we see the world, because *how* we react to what we see comes from our parents, our family members, our original religion, and native country. People from different cultures and families often respond differently to the same event. The stressed-brain reactions are influenced especially by our familial, cultural and religious teachings and bias.

Oddly, we still accept and use our early programming from persons we do not respect or agree with. Therefore, to change a habitual reaction, you have to look at your original indoctrination and make a strong effort to transform it. This is not easy because this early training and emotional reactions have been a part of you for many years and often come from the earlier brains.

Nevertheless, the freedom gained by examining your behavioral rules and expectations of others is invaluable. Psychotherapy can certainly help in this examination.

At age 55, Allen was discouraged about ever finding a partner to care about and grow old with. He was a professional, good looking and smart, yet had never been in a long-term relationship. In class, he had a hard time forgiving his mother. Because of his difficulty, he decided to look deeply at all his original training from his mother—he called it "brainwashing." He especially searched for her subtle messages and rules.

"This was the toughest thing I've done in my life," Allen admitted. "I hated the way my mother treated me as a kid. She was too protective and too concerned about everything I did. She was hurt when I didn't give her enough attention. What surprised me when I looked at our relationship is that I expected other women to give me extraordinary attention. When they didn't it was obvious they didn't like me." He added, "No wonder I have never been in a long-term relationship. I never gave anyone a chance. The truth is, I didn't want to ever be smothered again, and even worse, I felt I could never do enough for any partner. I saw women as a bottomless pit. That was unfair to every woman I went out with." He understood why his mother was that way, and forgave her, but as he said, "It looks like I will probably never have a decent relationship. That's what's sad."

This shows us how Allen's outer world was a reflection of his inner world. Women were not interested in him because he judged them. Allen's ability to see how his early programming ran his life was profound, as were his insights. It had taken him many years of inner work to be able to look inside himself with skill. Because our paths crossed socially, I was aware that within a year, he developed a loving relationship that seemed to be leading toward marriage.

> "We don't live outside ourselves; life goes on within us,
> and our thinking determines the experience."
>
> JIM ROSEMERGY,
> AUTHOR & UNITY MINISTER

In children, we often see this example of negative programming. Again, the outer world reflects inner beliefs. A person who is taught early on that another race is bad and evil will always see those people in a certain way until there is a different set of messages put into the brain. We are given many prejudices and negative responses in our early life. These continue to run us even as adults because we can only interpret what is going on for us with the information we have.

The forgiveness process enables us to change our habitual response so that we can pursue truth more effectively.

Possibly, you have had the experience of driving through a town when you were hungry. If you are hungry, maybe the lack of restaurants influences what you think of the town. If you are angry, you might only see the unfriendly people and problems. Another person in the car might be affected by something else and have a different reaction to the town. When asked about the town, each person in the car will have a different response, some, even strongly emotional.

Changing our Responses

Because our survival responses are habitual, changing them takes real examination and reevaluation. What you are feeling and seeing is only your reaction and may not be reality. During an upset, if you can remember this, you might try to relax, breathe deeply, and perhaps say a prayer to help change your experience. If you do not like what is going on in your life, you have the capacity to look again and shift your reaction.

The best understanding can do is bring humility. It carries with it the humble insight that there is another way to view what you see. Yours is not the only way. This opens the door to peace and to forgiveness, which will bring the emotional shift you seek.

Our Standards

We can hold others and ourselves to unrealistic standards due to of our expectations of perfection. Identifying our standards and re-evaluating them is central in forgiving and to being content.

The noted Stanford Forgiveness Project researcher, Dr. Fred Luskin, calls these our rules. Effective Communication expert, Dr. Marshall Rosenberg, calls them our values. Both are useful words to enable us to go deeper in looking at how we judge people. These judgements are what keep us from forgiving.

Though we like to think that critical analysis helps us to function better, in reality we often misuse this analyzing to judge and condemn. Thus, we keep others and ourselves in the debris of failure instead of enabling us to get up, brush off, and move on.

We need standards, values, and rules for living because these are important to the fabric of our social, religious, and personal development, expression, and expansion. The problem comes when our judgements lead to condemnation and attack of our selves or others.

Our attacks, whether in our own mind or in the world, bring unhappiness at the least and tragedy at the extreme. Just look at the decimation of peoples and cultures in Rwanda and Bosnia in recent times, and the ongoing threats of jihad and terrorism.

I am not advocating lowering standards, but looking at where your standards come from and if they are truly appropriate. I am promoting being less judgemental toward yourself and others when those standards are not met. If the standards are valuable, keep using them.

The original meaning of "sin" is from Greek and actually means—**to miss the mark**. When you miss the mark, you keep trying to do well and keep practicing until you hit where you are aiming. Forgiveness through reevaluation of your unrealistic expectations and focusing on your valuable targets is the key to attaining what you want.

Unrealistic expectations come most often from the opinions of other people. Members of Murder Victims against Capital Punishment are sometimes harassed, and even receive death threats because they have forgiven the offender and chose not to be a victim of hatred.

Try this: To find out how others influence your decision to forgive, look at family and friends' opinions about any situation you are finding difficult.

    1. What are they saying that prevents you from forgiving?

    2. What will people think of you if you forgive?

Addressing these questions will allow you to go deeper into the social and cultural assumptions that keep you from forgiving.

The Deadly Rules, Judgements and Expectations

If you do not like the world you see, this section is indispensable. One of the ways to have the subconscious affect us less is to be aware of the attitudes that run us. As we mentioned in the previous section, under the surface of our action and thinking are rules, judgements and expectations that are often driven by the survival mechanisms of the lower brains.

As I mentioned, much of the difficulty we have in forgiving comes from the emotional and survival rules taught to us as children by our family, religion, and society in general. From these, we make our judgements about people. These judgements and the rules behind them determine our standards and whether or not to forgive. Under intense stress, our perception and understanding of these rules become more distorted, even when the rules are valid.

Our family, peers, teachers, society, religion, and country all have emotionally influenced:

    A. What we value,

    B. How we should act, and

    C. What we expect of others.

Note Well: Not all of what we are taught is necessarily the truth or of value. Religious and social values may be extremely different from family to family—even in the same country. These differences are even wider between countries or cultures. Thus, it is up to us as responsible adults and citizens to reevaluate what we were taught as children, especially when we have expectations that are not being met.

When people break your rules and you get very upset, you can be pretty sure that the emotion behind that reaction has not come from the highest place within you but the lowest. I'm talking here about strong reaction, probably anger and the desire to attack and harm others when a person perhaps only voiced an opinion or did something that was socially okay with others. I'm not talking about the abuse or violation of person or property, but even then the level of our reaction can get too extreme.

Emotions give you zest for life and people. But, when they are running your life and making it unhappy, then, it is essential that to reevaluate your rules, expectations, and judgements with an eye toward forgiveness. The function of the neocortex is to control these earlier brain attitudes and acts. You must set limits on the emotions that are ruining your life.

Ned's mother had always told him, "You are just like your father." This was a negative image for him to carry because Ned was not like his father. For many years, Ned said could not see his father's goodness. Then, in a guided forgiveness meditation, he remembered that his mother's opinion of her own father was terrible because of abuse in her childhood. Ned realized that this experience had polluted her opinion of *all* fathers, and all men in general. This understanding of her perspective enabled him to forgive her for her constant criticism of him.

Forgiveness often entails taking a different perspective than your habitual one so that past associations can change. Rules for behavior may come from negative sources. Reevaluating these rules lets you see how useful they actually are to you now.

Mary was an only child raised in the country and had spent most of her time alone. Pete, from a large Italian family, was raised in the city. At first, these differences were exciting to them. Mary loved being with his large family. Pete saw that she brought peacefulness into his life by creating personal time for them alone. He was also comfortable having his family around. After a while, she resented not having her own personal and private time and started criticizing Pete whenever the family was around. Pete attacked back. Soon they felt their differences were irreconcilable.

Then Pete discovered forgiveness training. When Mary was upset with him, he just tried to let go of the upset and find calmness within himself in an effort to save the marriage. Instead of reacting, he found that by remaining calm, he began to understand Mary. "Finally," he said, "when I started listening through the 'ears of forgiveness', we were able to come up with helpful solutions to our differences and save our marriage."

Pete had the good sense not to stick to his way as the only way. Thus, he didn't try to go to all the family gatherings, though he wanted to. Mary appreciated that he did this for her, and became more willing to go to the gatherings. During this work of reconciling their differences, they agreed to leave the family functions much earlier than they had in the past. Mary noticed that in leaving early, she did not mind being there. In the past, she had been upset staying with the family so late at night. By going through this process, they gained understanding.

A journal process for you:
To deal with the validity and reality of others' rules and your own:
1. List the values, laws, rules, or moral codes that you feel your offender has broken.
2. Looking at each, ask:
    a) Where did this rule come from?

b) Is it a valid rule or code? Or one that needs revision?

3. Then ask:

    a) Do I have an unrealistic expectation of another to follow that law, value, or rule, especially if I have done the same thing in some way to others or myself?

    b) Do I have an unrealistic expectation for myself to obey that law, value, or rule?

The Letters Practice

This practice of writing three letters is one of the best early tasks I've found to help in forgiving. (You will use the third letter later in the book.)

Communication is fundamental to our existence. Babies in Communist Romania who had little human contact either died or became overly withdrawn and even antisocial. When we look at unforgiven situations, often a communication problem was usually hurtful, rejecting or needed. Even if you don't want the contact reestablished, you must to look at what happened with it, because the way we manifest our upset is often through communication or the lack of it.

I first came across a similar letter sequence of Dr. John Gray from Robert Plath, the Founder and Executive Director of The Worldwide Forgiveness Alliance. Bob is a caring lawyer who has dedicated his life to having forgiveness used more in the world. One of his primary goals is to establish International Forgiveness Day as a globally celebrated holiday.[10]

The origin of these letters is really from our own human experience. It is how we often interact when we're upset. First, we confront the offender. We might get angry and tell the person why. Then they respond. Ideally, the upset is cleared up, and the connection reestablished.

The Hurt Letter

Because forgiveness is an emotional action, we first need to be aware of the feelings involved, and to release them.

Write a letter to the person you wish to forgive. In the letter, spell out **exactly** how this situation hurt you and how you feel about the person now. Use the letter to vent all your feelings and thoughts about the person and the situation. Do not give him or her the benefit of the doubt in this letter. Just write down how upset you are.

This is where you voice all of your distress and disappointment with the person. You say just how displeased you are. It is crucial to write all of this down so that you don't fall into emotional attack or overwhelm that may occur if you happen see the offender face to face. or, even think of them.

Make sure that you look at these questions:
1. How did they hurt you
2. What are the things in this situation that are unforgivable?
3. What in my past reminds me of this?
4. Is there something about this that robs me of the strength or willingness to consider forgiveness?

Write down the feelings that come to mind. You may find these questions helpful:
1. What do I feel when I picture the person involved in the situation, for example, sad, depressed, angry, guilty, hurt, anxious?
2. Apart from the main emotion, are there others, such as embarrassment, humiliation, or shame, beneath or mixed up with the main one?
3. Am I willing to engage these feelings and not avoid them?

In the middle of this letter, if you remember a similar but earlier situation you had with that person or someone else, it's valuable to immediately write about what happened in that earlier time. Remember, the earlier distress may often hold the later one in place because the later event is most likely neurally connected in the brain to the earlier one.

In this *emotional* letter, you keep writing until there is nothing left to say. Reread it to see if there is anything to add. Then, put it to the side. Some people have made a ritual of burning the letter. Though you might want to send it, hold off. It is not from the first letter but from the second that understanding arises.

Now move onto the next letter.

The Response Letter

I learned the effectiveness of hearing the other person's viewpoint not only from my training in marriage and family counseling but also in my work in Hawaii in a family healing process and ritual called *Ho'o Pono Pono*. This is an ancient traditional Hawaiian practice where family members come together when there are relationship problems and disharmony in their immediate family. This may be a large family gathering up to 20 people or more.

In *Ho'o Pono Pono*, each family member, from child to elder, says how he or she is affected by the disharmony and by any offense that took place. Forgiveness is expected all around and harmony is reestablished. The sharing can become involved and may take a long time, even days, so that everyone has their time to say how they feel, sort out what happened, and be willing to forgive all integral to the reestablishment of harmony and goodwill. [11]

Write the second letter from the offender's point of view. Use it to answer each of your upsets, but with his or her experience as the primary one. Write the letter to yourself as if it came from the offender. You are being that voice, saying exactly what happened and why, from that perspective solely.

Somewhere in the letter, after they explain and justify their past, write what you would like to hear from them. Have them explain how your grief or upset affected him or her. It is important to get what you want. If you want an apology, write it. If you need the offender to have an insight, hear it from that person in the letter. Though this is a wishful letter, you might be surprised how insightful and useful it can be.

Even though you know it is from you, something often happens in writing from another's perspective. I have had several students say that the person would never say that. In realizing this, they recognized the futility of wanting what they would never get, and let it go.

To assist at this level, I have done hypnotherapy with clients. I have them picture themselves getting what they want. You can do this yourself by relaxing, and picture in your own mind receiving an apology or whatever you would like to have. This is powerful because research has shown that the mind does not often know the difference between what happens in the hypnotic state and in reality. Thus, giving yourself what you prefer in a deeply relaxed state of mind enables you to feel better about the situation.

To truly understand a person's worldview, **walk in their shoes.** Here are guidelines that might help:

1. Write down what you believe to be the governing moral code that this person lives by and that should have influenced their behavior in this situation.
2. How do they see the world? What do they fear and love, like and dislike?
3. What was it like growing up in their family?
4. What was it like to come from their culture or time?
5. What were their issues?
6. What is their emotional intelligence?
7. What was their expectation of you, of others?

If you cannot answer these questions, then you do not know enough to condemn this person.

Relief will often come as you write. Understanding always brings a decrease in emotional turmoil. Compassion brings forgiveness.

If you don't seem to be able to let go, that is all right, just go to the next chapter. Forgiveness work has snowballing results. As long as you do your best at each stage, you will move through the process. Then all of a sudden, there will be a shift and you will let go of the upset.

The Fourth Hurdle

Your reaction to the world and people in it comes from your own programming in your own mind. When you look for the truth, you can take control of your life. You now have tools to do it.

This is a major hurdle because you can stop blaming others for your condition and you can take control of your reactions. This is not easy, but is more rewarding than anger and resentment. When bad things happen, you do not have to look outside of yourself for ways to deal with them. Rather, the problem becomes a challenge and an opportunity to get past your early training, see the situation in a different way and forgive.

> "Forgiveness is a method of giving love.
> It is a way of saying, 'I am going to let go of
> the wrong you did; I am not going to be bitter
> and I am going to go on loving you anyway.'"
> BERNIE SIEGEL, MD, *PRESCRIPTION FOR LIVING*

CHAPTER SEVEN

Making Forgiving Easier

"He that cannot forgive others breaks the bridge
over which he must pass himself;
for every man has need to be forgiven."

GEORGE HERBERT (1593 – 1633)

Find Meaning in Forgiving

It's essential to find meaning in your forgiving. Here are two stories that show its power.

Amy Biehls

During the apartheid violence in South Africa in 1993, a young black man killed Amy Biehls, an American Rhodes Scholar and exchange student. Her parents, who had supported her apartheid protests, came from the U.S. to visit the family of the young man who killed their daughter as a way of paying tribute to her and her ideals. They forgave him and then testified in court on the young man's behalf so that he would receive a pardon. They said they were only able to do this because they knew it would be their daughter's wish. [1]

Her parents were able, out of love for their daughter and her highest vision, to shift their perspective and embrace her point of view. This meaning enabled them to forgive.

Wild Bill

George Ritchie, a psychiatrist for many years at the University of Virginia, wrote a profound book, *Return from Tomorrow,* in which he relates the following powerful story.

Before he became a doctor, Ritchie was part of a small medical team sent to a newly liberated Nazi concentration camp. There he met Wild Bill Cody, the nickname of one of the Jewish prisoners. His eyes were bright and he worked along with the American soldiers 15 – 16 hours a day without showing weariness. Though the soldiers showed fatigue, his strength seemed to increase."His compassion for his fellow prisoners glowed on his face," Dr. Ritchie reported.

It seemed obvious to the Americans that Wild Bill had not been in the concentration camp too long. When Ritchie discovered records that showed Wild Bill was imprisoned there in 1939, he was shocked. He asked Wild Bill how he had kept his vitality for six years when everyone else was barely alive. Here is what he said:

"We lived in the Jewish section of Warsaw, my wife, our two daughters, and our three little boys....When the Germans reached our street, they lined everyone against a wall and opened up with machine guns. I begged to be allowed to die with my family, but because I spoke German they put me in a work group. I had to decide right then whether to let myself hate the soldiers who had done this. It was an easy decision, really. I was a lawyer. In my practice, I had seen too often what hate could do to peoples' minds and bodies. Hate had just killed the six people who mattered most to me in the world. I decided then that I would spend the rest of my life – whether it was a few days or many years – loving every person I came in contact with."[2]

Man's Search for Meaning

This is the title of a book by Dr. Victor Frankel, who was also a Nazi death camp survivor. He survived because he was able to find meaning in his life. He noticed that those who did not have some meaning in their life often did not survive.

A whole therapy came out of his work helping people find meaning in their life. He felt that our primary drive in life is doing what we find meaningful. Amazon says that in the 1990s, his was considered one the ten most influential books in America.

Finding meaning is a vital lesson not only for forgiving but also for living.

- What in your life would inspire you to forgive?

The Best Strategy for Dealing with Difficult Situations

In reality, you do not know how experiences will be associated in anyone else's brain or even in your own. A new difficult situation or problem might connect to a dozen different thought patterns and experiences and twice as many different rules and judgements. This is why the best strategy in doing forgiveness work is to break down the upset (Chapter 3). If you are still having difficulty with a situation, break it down further.

A Technique to Make Forgiveness Go Faster

Look at earlier events that are similar. Each new experience we have attaches to an *already formed* group of experiences in the brain. Thus, we see the importance of looking at earlier situations in our life that might be similar to the one we are dealing with presently. I've found that forgiveness can deepen as you look at and work on the earliest people and situations in your life.

Remember, your appreciation of life deepens as you mend the upsets of your family, religion, and culture you were raised in.[3]

In forgiveness counseling, you make the sessions go more easily by looking at earlier situations that are related to the current one in some way. When a person can't forgive a spouse who is similar to a parent or sibling, drop working on the spouse for the moment, and work on the parent or sibling if the situations are alike. When you handle the earlier person first, the upset with the spouse or partner becomes much easier to handle.

If you are having difficulty forgiving someone, ask yourself:
1. Is there someone earlier in my life who has done this same or a similar thing to me?
2. Have I done this or something similar earlier in my life?
3. Have I been in this situation before? If so, identify the earlier time.
4. Work on that earlier time and if you are still having difficulty ask again if there is an even earlier situation to look at. For example, an upset with husband-2 might be similar to one with husband-1. If the upset doesn't change much, you might look even earlier.

Concern for Fairness as a Block to Forgiving

Strong desire for fairness can negatively affect willingness to forgive. Often, from our viewpoint, what another did was unfair especially if he or she has not apologized or recognized how what happened affected us. There might be many reasons for the lack of apology, but often we will not consider them because we believe we are right. What's fair is tough to agree on because others see differently. We think this difference should not be, but it is. That is why we use courts of law to determine what is fair. Socially we create laws to decide fairness, and still they aren't fair. This complaint starts in childhood and never ceases: "No fair!"

Even though it is tempting to idealize how it would be if people were fair or really valued you, the other person hardly ever sees it your way. You end up just causing yourself a lot of upset, sometimes over nothing. Fairness is often a masquerade for personal preferences and wants. *Fair* is what I want, but what the other person wants is not as legitimate. Consequently, each person locks into his or her own point of view. The result is each fighting for what is theirs and experiencing mounting resentment. Most importantly be fair to yourself. [4a]

With this false fairness thinking, we often see conditional beliefs based on inner laws, as, "If he loved me, he'd do the dishes." "If he loved me, he'd make sure I had a nice car." "If he cared at all, he'd come home right after work." "If they valued my work here, they'd give me a raise." "If she loved me, she wouldn't bother me when I come home from work." As the authors of *Thoughts & Feelings: the Art of Cognitive Stress Intervention*, Dr. Mathew McKay, Dr. Martha. Davis, and Patrick Fanning, point out, you can undo the fallacy of fairness by recognizing that what is "fair," is often not agreed upon. It is more helpful to say what you want, need or prefer. Without the presumption of unfairness, you become honest with yourself and the other person. [4b]

Getting Needs and Wants Met

Expressing your needs and wants, as well as having them satisfied, is difficult. Without a willingness to at least hear the other person's perspective, your needs probably will not be met. Even then, it takes excellent communication skills to express those desires to another.

Dr. Marshall Rosenberg has spent his life teaching *compassionate communication,* which helps people understand themselves and others better, so that they can get their needs and wants satisfied more easily. His excellent work is described in his book, *Nonviolent Communication: A Language of Compassion.*[5]

Our needs and wants often arise out of the subconscious. The rest of this book will enable you to look more closely at your true needs and wants from a deeper level, so that forgiving can occur.

The Secret Attitude That Aids Forgiving

The secret that makes forgiving less difficult is humility. It may take a person quite awhile to understand the power of this attitude. It enables us to step back from that part of us that always needs to be right, and look more objectively at the situation. Humility, doesn't mean weakness, timidity, submissiveness, or groveling. It means having enough inner strength to say, "I don't know it all!"

Above any other attribute, it opens us to forgiving because it enables us to let down our defenses and bring in the compassion to try to understand another's situation. It quiets the snake brain. It allows us to step back from the defensive part of us that needs to blame and attack to feel protected. Humility asks us to step away from playing God, thinking we know everything.

Humility enables us to admit that we, too, have done harmful things to others and are not so high above the other whom we cannot forgive. It also allows us to forgive ourselves by stepping down from the pedestal where we play God and admit our shortcomings, not as our condemnation, but in the admission, "There, but for the grace of God, go I." In this statement, we admit we are not that different from others except for circumstance. It helps us to let go of defense and attack, and come back to our birthright of peace, joy, and love.

How to See the Truth

To see the truth in a situation honestly, most often requires us to step back from our strong desire to always be right. Being humble is a difficult coat to put on, but when we do, it increase our joy, peace, and love. For many, humility brings the recognition of The Sacred and Divine in our life.

Anger, fear, or any expression of lack of love requires our humility to enable us to say, "I don't know what is really going on here." Then, we can possibly step into that higher aspect of us, allowing a flow of love, life, and peace to occur. Here is true rightness from which forgiveness flows.

Not only does humility ask us to step away from playing God, thinking we understand everything, but we may even need to take the hand of God. In that act, if we ask for the truth, we will see it because we will be looking through the eyes of love.

Developing Your Power of Decision

Another essential in forgiving is your ability to *decide* to forgive. In this section, decide is used as an active verb, rooted in the present, rather than a plan for later. The words *willingness* and *intention*, by contrast, focus on forgiving at some future time. The decision to forgive, therefore, may need to be continually renewed.

Early in the book, I talked about the difficulty of deciding to forgive. The decision to forgive can be powerful and comes easier when understanding is present. As you keep reading this book, you are gaining enough understanding of your unforgiven situations and enough compassion for yourself and others to decide sooner to let upsets go. It might have happened already in one situation and you are working on others now.

The qualities of willingness and intention help in making a decision of any sort. Although you are gathering information by reading this book, your accumulation of data is influenced by these two qualities. Inspiration increases willingness and intention.

Willingness

When we hold the highest vision (the first essential to forgiveness, Chapter 1, we are inspired to be willing to forgive. This willingness is the primary element in forgiving. All else comes from the movement of our will.

Questions to ask yourself:
1. Am I willing to work on this?
2. Am I willing to face my own demons?
3. Am I willing to let this go?
4. Am I willing to be completely honest with myself?

Intention

Prepare for the *Power Forgiveness Process* with this intention: "Forgiveness has great power, and will free me." If your intention is strong, you can stay in the process until you feel an inner shift. Then the decision to forgive will be easier. It might take time, particularly if there are old wounds to heal, but maintaining that core intention to let the upset go is the foremost step.

At rock bottom in my own life in 1993, I tried to figure out what was going on. I read the preface to A Course in Miracles, which basically said that God is unconditional love, but to experience this love you must forgive. My highest vision, experiencing God as love, ignited. As I read the preface further, my willingness, and then my intention, to forgive increased. When I realized that to experience this unconditional love, I must forgive, I made the decision to sit down in my reading chair and not get up until I forgave all that I could. Many hours later, I had let go of every upset I was aware of at that time in my life.

This seems an unbelievable feat, but it was not. I had been doing inner work for thirty years and was quite familiar with psychology and spirituality. These came together to help me.

After that major letting go, the experience of Divine Love was available to me for seven straight years.

This overall intention, along with the decision, highlights that there are always several levels of commitment in what we do. I committed to the overall process, but on individual upsets, I sometimes became stuck.

We see this same pattern in marriage. The commitment and decision to be in the marriage remains, but there may be problems in the relationship causing conflict. If the struggle to remain together continues without inspiration to make the relationship better, the desire to be apart might become stronger than being together. Then the commitment to the marriage may fail and the couple will decide to end the relationship.

Deciding to Forgive

Sometimes you must make a conscious decision to forgive while you are in this process. This decision is an act of will made as a solid commitment to your highest self, which will carry you through difficult emotional terrain. Openness to forgiving occurs by recognizing that anger is not working. In making the decision to forgive, you are taking back the power that the offending person or situation has stolen from your life.

Questions on Making the Decision to Forgive: In your journal, write down your answers to these:
1. Am I willing to work on this difficult situation?
2. Why do I want to forgive this person?
3. Am I committed to freeing myself from the negative consequences in my life that this situation has caused?
4. What prevents me from deciding to let this go?

The Overlooked Brain Function

The ability of the brain that we often overlook in our modern computer-focused society is the use of our *intuitive power*—a feature that is quite useful in our work in forgiving. This is often associated with the functioning of the right side of the brain.[7]

Accessing Your Intuition – In forgiveness work, we have inner resources to help us heal. Being open to creative input and other sources of wisdom and knowledge is a key in the higher functions of the human mind. We all have a natural ability that goes by many names: intuition, hunches, inner guidance, and so on. This ability has been recognized in significant historical people through the ages. Some develop it more than others, but it is available to all.

> "The mind can proceed only so far upon what it knows and can prove. There comes a point where the mind takes a higher plane of knowledge, but can never prove how it got there. All great discoveries have involved such a leap."
>
> ALBERT EINSTEIN[8]

Thomas Edison was a firm believer in this intuitive sense and used it often. When he struggled to find a solution to a problem, he would try to sleep in a chair while he kept the area under question in his mind. In his hand, he would hold his keys. Once he fell asleep, his keys would fall, waking him. He would then remember what he was dreaming. Often in that dream, there would be an answer to his problem.[9]

Accessing intuition requires being open to trying something new. When we face an apparently unsolvable problem or dilemma, what we really need is a perspective outside our normal way of thinking; this is often called "thinking outside the box."

A quiet, calm environment and mind assists in our search for this creative part of us. For me, it is most often available in the early mornings, just before waking up completely. A friend, Neal, a building contractor, would design projects or work out building problems in these early hours. {Many say that this is also the best time for meditation.} He often would become aware of mistakes he had made the day before that needed correcting.

Peace and calm keeps the more reactive and emotional parts of the brain deactivated, enabling the problem-solving and intuitive parts of us to be available.

While you are working on forgiving, make sure to use this powerful source of help.

In the following passage, Pantajali, a sage scholar of the third century BC, tells us how and why our intuition works:[10]

> "When you are inspired by some great purpose, some extraordinary project, all your thoughts break their bonds; your mind transcends limitations, your consciousness expands in every direction, and you find yourself in a new, great, and wonderful world. Dormant forces, faculties and talents become alive, and you discover yourself to be a greater person by far than you ever dreamed yourself to be."

Changing Old Thought Habits

By holding resentments, we are unable to hold the thoughts of peace, much less a Higher Power. Effective thinking ability is lost under undue stress. Survival mechanisms and reactions can take over making us incapable of those higher thoughts.

Please note—To assist in relieving stress, **Stop and focus your mind.**

More than thirty years ago, Dr. Herbert Benson of Harvard Medical School created *The Relaxation Response* to help people deal with stress and its negative effects, such as high blood pressure. He studied meditators from around the world to incorporate their methods into his valuable relaxation method to help people feel better and to change their negative thinking patterns.[11]

There is a great deal of data from neuroscience and cognitive studies showing the power of thoughts and beliefs. Here again, forgiveness plays an effective role. If many negative thoughts are roaming through a person's mind, he or she often will not find relief from them until they are viewed and each put to rest.

Another way is to raise the mind to a higher state through *ongoing* meditation or contemplation. Either way, forgiveness is critical.

The Power Forgiveness Process does this well. The person cleared of their victim and guilt thoughts will be in a more positive place to have peace, joy and love in life. Until this happens, the deepest spiritual and life potential cannot easily be accessed.

How to Change Your Inner Experience:

Using your imagination. Recent hypnosis research is fascinating on the subject of changing our inner experience. The New York Times reported in November 2005, "What you see is not always what you get, because what you see depends on a framework built by experience that stands ready to interpret the raw information." This is a restatement of what we went over in the previous chapter. The article explained that when people who were hypnotized reviewed an event in their past and then changed it, the brain acted as though the changed event was real. When the event was recalled later, the brain responded as if the new experience from hypnosis was real.[12]

We have known this for a long time in hypnotherapy, but now science confirms it. Guided meditations also allow us to reinterpret and often change the experience of a trauma. Professor Charles Figley of Tulane University and Florida State University, a pioneer in trauma research and responsible for the establishment of the Green Cross Foundation and the Academy of Traumatology, acknowledges the Visual Kinesthetic Disassociation (VKD) hypnosis method as valid in helping relieve people of traumatic incidents.[13]

Whenever you relax, breathe, and picture yourself, perhaps at a beach, or in the mountains, and make the picture and feelings seem real, the mind will act as if it is true. Doing this can change your upsetting experience in minutes. It takes practice, of course, but in a short while, you will find the relaxation and the mind shift that you are seeking.

Maria was ready to quit work when she came to see me. "I hate my boss and so does everyone else," she said in tears. Her boss had been unkind to her in front of other employees. She could not forgive him. With hypnosis, I had Maria picture herself having the boss apologize. Then I had her picture forgiving her boss. I did not ask her to forgive, but only to picture it as if it had occurred. The session was 20 minutes, but at the end of it, she felt fine about her boss and felt she could be at work again. A month later, she was enthusiastic about her work and was getting along fine with the boss.

This is an example of the power of imagination in forgiving. Though this situation was done through hypnosis, you can do the method itself anytime. It is called by many names—creative visualization and self-hypnosis are the most common. It is a skill we all have; it only needs developing and practice.

A Forgiveness Visualization: The first step in any mental picturing is to take a break and relax.

1. Close your eyes.
2. Relax any tensions you are aware of as well as you can. For just this exercise let go of other concerns and focus on becoming calm.
3. Imagine love pouring into you in any way that you can, perhaps from a Divine Source or anyone you can think of real or imaginary who can send you love. This in itself may be quite moving.
4. When you feel love filling you, imagine the person who upsets you. Send love to them (You might even hug them in your mind.) Continue until you feel something positive change in yourself.

5. You'll notice that the more you give love the more you feel it. You will not only feel better, but also more forgiving.
6. See yourself walking in the other person's shoes and what it was like for him or her in life.
7. Imagine forgiving them. What would that feel like.

You will be surprised what this activity can do for you. We often see the negative scenarios very well. But, picturing the positive is so much better.

Do Positive Affirmations Work?

Positive affirmations are optimistic statements that people repeat during day. Imagination is behind their power. As you repeat these constructive assertions, you convince yourself of their truth instead of the negative ones you might be saying to yourself. By taking a breath and relaxing, you help these statements go deeper into your mind. These positive statements may eventually move out the negative ones. However, it is similar to painting a wall that has a stain on it. The stain can often continue to seep through. Forgiveness is crucial to make sure the old stains in your mind will not destroy your positive declarations and intentions.

The secret behind positive affirmations and creative visualizations is not especially the words or what you see, but your positive emotional responses behind them. The optimistic emotions are what carry you out of the snake brain mentality and give the confidence needed to make the words or visions happen. The words are not magic, but the uplifting emotions are. As long as you let the survival-self, control your life with its negative emotions, you will not have the life you want because you are only living in the lowest part of your brain and thinking.

In psychology, Cognitive Therapy targets the negative statements you say to yourself throughout the day. Often, you are not aware of these judgments on yourself and others because they are rooted in our childhood. Nevertheless, they sit there, just under the surface of your awareness, condemning what you do. This "negative self-talk" is devastating and must be changed to achieve happiness and the ability to forgive. Distorted thinking patterns ruin lives.

Alicia came to class furious with her sister-in-law, Janet. All day she thought about how Janet hurt her. Not only did she replay the upset, but she also made statements throughout the day that kept her anger going, like "that ungrateful ..." She was a wreck emotionally, and also admitted that she had made comments against herself, like "No one cares about me." In addition, she started saying things to herself against her husband.

This is mind *poison*. Negative self-talk destroys. By the end of class, she was able to look at the unreality of what she was saying to herself, and forgive. Then she replaced the negative statements about herself and her family with positive ones.

The quest for a positive frame of mind has a four-fold action:
1. Becoming aware of the negative statements that you have been saying to yourself for years
2. Stopping each one, every chance you get.
3. Making positive emotional declarations to replace the negative ones.
4. Forgiving yourself and others.

The first three actions will enable forgiving thoughts to take hold because you are lifting yourself out of the control of the snake brain. This brain with its survival functions is meant for crisis, not ongoing perception. If you find yourself caught in long-lasting fear or anger you are letting your lower brains have too much control. Do the four steps above. Live the life you were meant to live.

A Summary of the Essentials

Through the chapters, I've pointed out essentials to do in forgiveness work. These are the key points on which to focus. Keep them in mind whenever you do this work.

1. **Hold your highest vision** – Remain inspired to forgive.
2. **Find meaning in forgiving** – Use a core value or principle in your life, as Wild Bill did in the concentration camp and Amy Biehls' parents in South Africa.
3. **Ask for Divine help**
4. **Commit to the process** – Be willing to forgive. Intend to forgive. Decide to forgive.
5. **Feel the feelings** – Look for the feelings under the surface.
6. **Find the truth** – Be honest – The truth will set you free!

The Secrets of Forgiveness Work

I've been doing a range of counseling work since 1968. Through the years of doing forgiveness work, I've found the following counseling wisdoms to be significant in helping people forgive. Because so few people in general are aware of these, I call them secrets. They are:

1. **Break down the situation** – Analyze it piece by piece, person by person.
2. **Use your intuition**
3. **Get support from others**
4. **Use your imagination**
5. **Look for earlier events** – Search for experiences in the past that are alike or similar to the one you are working on now.
6. **Let go of being right and open to humility**

The Fifth Hurdle

You have now passed the fifth hurdle. You know what makes forgiving easier. You continue to gain information and skill at forgiving. You might even have reached forgiveness for your original upset by now and be working on others.

The essentials, secrets, and exercises will all come together for you as you go along. There will be a summary of the first part of the *Power Forgiveness Process* in Chapter 9, and then a full summary of the whole process in Chapter 14 and a concise summary in the appendix. With these, you will see how it all fits together, and so that you can use it in any other situation.

Forgiveness has remained in the realm of religion because it sometimes seems to take an act of God to help us let go. An acceptance of some sort of Higher Power does help in dealing with those things that seem to have great power over us—where we seem powerless.

> "When we harbor negative emotions toward others or toward ourselves, or when we intentionally create pain for others, we poison our own physical and spiritual systems. By far the strongest poison to the human spirit is the inability to forgive oneself or another person. It disables a person's emotional resources. The challenge ... is to refine our capacity to love others as well as ourselves and to develop the power of forgiveness."
>
> CAROLINE MYSS, www.myss.com
> from ANATOMY OF THE SPIRIT

CHAPTER EIGHT

The Power behind Forgiving

"Everyone who is seriously involved in the pursuit of science becomes convinced that a spirit is manifest in the laws of the Universe—a spirit vastly superior to that of man."

ALBERT EINSTEIN[1A]

When we speak of forgiveness, we are speaking of the key for gaining happiness and love after deep hurt. Letting go of *all* upsets, the goal of Power Forgiveness, truly can open us up to a completely different connection to love and to the inspiration and creative principle of life – the Healer of woes.

The Core of Our Being

The power of forgiveness may be viewed in a myriad of ways, *but at its core is love and compassion*, even biologically—love is built into the system. In his well-researched book on living systems, *The Self-Organizing Universe,* Scientist Eric Jantsch tells us: "Since the earliest aggregation of cells of primitive organisms is the capacity to go beyond one's self for the community." [1c] This is love in its essence.

Love is at the core of the dynamic tension of life, our will to selfhood versus our will to community. Love, to me, is that sense in our heart of goodness, kindness, and compassion towards others and life.

All of life flows from the foundation of love.

> "We must be saved by the final form of love
> which is forgiveness."
>
> REINHOLD NIEBUHR

In many world religions, love or compassion is the foremost point in their philosophy, beliefs, meditations, and theology. Since love, personally, extends from us to others and the outside world, we could even say that love is a fundamental part of the uniqueness of life. This sense of going beyond one's self is integral to forgiving.

At the spiritual level, we understand the true power of forgiveness. Through forgiving, love returns the mind and the heart to its Truth. Love is vital to our being. It is our center. And, the most powerful and significant emotion we have. (By spiritual, I mean a level of life beyond our physical, mental, and emotional survival and functioning. Focusing on our spiritual level of being not only gives our lives purpose and meaning, but also helps us rise above our bodily and emotional problems. Religion is an organized attempt to make sense of and bring about a spiritual experience and perspective.[2])

The Heart – the Altar of the Divine

We feel love in our heart. Even though we talk about our sense of the Divine or Higher Power, or God, the experience is in our everyday life. People with no religion still know what it means to be heartfelt and loving.

With only a small shift in our perspective, we can see the reason for peoples' actions from the perspective of love. Our heart and love that drives us in what we do, whether it is sacrificing our life for family or country, or killing another being to protect our own loved ones. Even hate is driven by a distorted sense of love. The spirit of love and integrity infuses our lives whether we accept it or not and whether we seem to experience it or not.

We feel guilty when we act against the Principle of love and life. This guilt seems to move us away from the highest within and around us. It moves us out of our highest thoughts and goals, seeming to block us from feeling joy or peace. Letting go of guilt is our path back to the Divine Principle of Life, and back to reexperiencing love, peace and joy. This is the reason for forgiving, and gives forgiveness its ultimate power in the path back to happiness.

"But seek first his kingdom and his righteousness, and all
these things will be given to you as well."
JESUS - *MATTHEW 6:33*

Love and Forgiveness

Love brings a joy that fulfills our life in infinite ways. It makes forgiveness indispensable. Without love as the foundation in our life and heart, we succumb more easily to afflictions, loss, and lack—making life unpleasant and often unbearable.

Why forgiving others and ourselves works so well and heals so quickly is simple. Underneath the complexity of our emotions and reactions, and beneath our survival mechanisms is a purity of spirit, of heart and of honesty. That is our essence, and why forgiving is so powerful in changing our life.

Overall, I believe most people are honest. We are decent people who punish ourselves for our wrong doings. Forgiveness of others and gaining forgiveness for ourselves bring us back to our highest functioning. Just doing an unloving act itself sets up a reaction inside us creating guilt. This is basic to why forgiveness works. It brings us back to a more real and authentic self and state of being.

Martin Luther King, Jr. told us: "We must develop and maintain the capacity to forgive. He who is devoid of the power to forgive is devoid of the power to love."

Our Healthiest State of Mind

To explain this authentic, positive state further, consider this example. Imagine your mind and heart being like a large, loose circular rubber band on a table, no tension, but filled with thoughts of fulfillment, kindness, and love. Imagine also living your life in that state of mind. Perhaps you can feel peacefulness in your daily affairs and working at a higher level because of your clarity and heartfulness.

If you start to pull on that rubber band, you create tension. In our example, that tension could be resentment or guilt. As you know, just a little tension will remove all of the space inside that rubber band, which was your true way of being. The more tension put on the rubber band, the more effort it takes to hold the tension in place. Thus, any way that you can relieve that tension allows your mind and heart to go back to its natural position—a space of fulfillment, power, clarity, and love.

Through the ages, forgiveness has been a powerful force because it opens the mind to healing through a Source far greater than our survival self. This Source has many names: Love, Nature, God, Allah, The Great Spirit, etc. Beyond all the names is what activates our highest thoughts, goals, and our maximum potential. By letting go of any resentments, hurts, and pain of the past, we loosen the tension of our mind and heart so that we can more easily have a sense of our Highest Power, allowing us to function at a happier and more creative, fulfilling level.

Nourish your heart with this:
Here is a method that opens people to a deeper sense of love.

1. Put immediate concerns to the side and go through a relaxation process. Let go of tension in your body, starting with your head and working down, letting those tensions drain out your feet.

2. Now, be aware of with a sense of love in your heart. Increase it and feel that love extending out from you into the room.

3. Feel it naturally moving outside of where you are into the neighborhood or area surrounding where you are.

4. Expand that love to fill your city. Have it fill the area surrounding your city, extending to loved ones, other people, the trees, countryside and to other towns until your whole region is touched by love.

5. Allow it to fill your nation, and then other nations.

6. Now see and feel love filling the earth and everyone on it.

7. See the love you are sending benefitting all of life.

8. Come back when you are ready.

Real Healing

If you have a leg wound with dirt in it, it will not heal until you remove the dirt. Even then, a blemish might be there for a while. Nevertheless, it may look and function well. Before the full beauty of the leg can come forward in the healing process, the dirt needs to be removed and time is needed for the blemish to disappear. When you remove resentment from your mind, the memory is still there, but it can now finally heal instead of festering with the poison of anger or guilt.

Likewise, if you do prayers, positive affirmations, or meditation with resentment and guilt in your heart, your positive intentions will not easily take hold. You must remove the dirt. When you remove the upset, healing takes place. Otherwise, the affirmation, prayer, or meditation will have to be redone on a continuing basis. The dirt will not allow healing or your highest vision to occur.

When I meditated before my forgiveness transformation, I could get to a "pretty good" state of mind. I even taught meditation, having meditated on and off since I was sixteen. After that forgiveness transformation, my mind was much calmer and cleaner, and, my meditations started at a peacefulness that before forgiving would have taken much time just to get to.

This experience of healing is the result of a simple principle of the mind: **Your thoughts cannot go in opposing directions at the same time and get anywhere.** Resentment, guilt, anger, and fear take the mind in the opposite direction from love, happiness, and peace. Until you are willing to let go of these resentments and fears, deep change cannot occur.

Because love is the essence of our being and, by extension, the highest functioning of the brain, when we forgive all upsets, the mind undergoes a change, a transformation, where there is much more love, peace, and joy.

When this occurs, a positive outlook naturally occurs. The end goal of forgiveness work is to re-pattern your thinking so that love, joy, peace, patience, kindness, integrity, faithfulness, gentleness, and self-control are more available each moment.

> "When you examine the lives of the most influential people
> who have ever walked among us, you discover one thread
> that winds through them all. They have been aligned
> first with their spiritual nature and only then
> with their physical selves."
> ALBERT EINSTEIN[4]

The question in forgiveness work becomes: "Where are you putting your mind and do you want to keep it there?" Several forgiveness methods are available to assist in this:

- Put your mind on love and send that love to the offender or offenders and yourself.
- Send prayers to them and yourself.
- If you want peace, keep your mind on peace and send that to them and yourself.

These are all ways to clear the upset and have a happier outlook. Feed yourself what you need. If chaos reigns, choose peace.

> "Therefore confess your sins to each other and pray for each other so that you may be healed. The prayer of a righteous man is powerful and effective."
>
> JESUS - *JAMES 5:16*

The Twelve-Steps

"If you have a resentment you want to be free of, if you will pray for the person or the thing you resent, you will be free. If you will ask in prayer for everything you want for yourself to be given to them, you will be free. Ask for their health, their prosperity, their happiness, and you will be free. Even when you don't really want it for them, and your prayers are only words and you don't mean it, go ahead and do it anyway. Do it every day for two weeks and you will find you have come to mean it and want it for them, and you will realize that where you used to feel bitterness and resentment and hatred, you now feel compassionate understanding and love."   *THE AA BIG BOOK* [6]

We can witness the power of Twelve-step programs that work with addictions of all sorts through the first three steps:

1. We admitted we were powerless over (alcohol, drugs, or other negative influence), that our lives had become unmanageable.

2. We came to believe that a power greater than ourselves could restore us to sanity.
3. We made a decision to turn our will and our lives over to the care of God, as we understood God.

A Twelve-step program is a fellowship that aims at the recovery of its members from the consequences of an addiction, a compulsion, or another harmful influence on their lives, with the help of the faith-based Twelve Steps.[5]

Being Positive

Positive attitudes about life help you to feel better. Unforgiven situations and people perpetuate the animosity in your heart. Love and animosity/attack thoughts cannot be in your mind at the same time and result in peace and positive thoughts. Thus, for your prayers and desires to manifest, forgiveness must occur.

If we maintain and harbor resentment, anger, and upset with anyone, we are maintaining and believing that we can split our mind in two and still be happy. Because this is impossible, we are actually canceling the possibility of having a joyful, peaceful, or loving life. Harboring resentment and an unforgiving attitude will bring the opposite of a calm happy life.

A clean mind and heart will experience the divine nature of life.

> "Therefore, if you are offering your gift at the altar
> and there remember that your brother has something
> against you, leave your gift there in front of the altar.
> First go and be reconciled to your brother;
> then come and offer your gift."
> JESUS, *MATTHEW 5:23-24*

Forgiveness brings back the ability to be positive, for it enables you to clean up your negative thinking. When you remove the negatives of life, you begin to maintain new and positive patterns.

Enrique was an old friend who through the years was becoming more and more negative. He did not like where he lived though it was a delightful place to most people; he was upset with his family, and he was not able to make friends. I convinced him to do the *Power Forgiveness Process*. He worked hard, looked deeply, and took to heart what I said. Within a month, he was in a better intimate relationship than he had been in for years, he had better communication with his family, and he was much happier with where he lived.

Finding the Positive in Tragedy and Trauma

Some of us have been dealt some very hard lessons by life. Most of us get trapped in those incidents because we don't see anything positive about them. Seeing the positive aids forgiveness.

But how do you gain that positive perspective about something terrible. As in the overall action of forgiving—take bite-size pieces. Start with the small things. Time heals all wounds is the old adage. But, the truth is you speed up that healing by finding small things to be grateful for that came from that negative experience.

Gratitude

Gratitude is a mighty method for change. It works any time and provides the opportunity each day to feel better.

The third largest religion in Japan, Seicho-No-Ie, holds the virtue of gratitude very highly. The founder, Masaharu Taniguchi, had an enlightenment experience in the 1920s. Afterwards, he started teaching that the most important virtues to develop to deepen one's spiritual experience are gratitude, forgiveness and reconciliation. He worked with individuals to bring these into peoples' hearts. Many miracles through the decades are attributed to his gratitude work and prayers.

Positive Psychology is a movement in psychology that finally places attention on the high-quality aspects of our mind instead of our negative pathology. Dr. Martin Seligman is the inspiration and research force behind this work.

One of his research teams compiled more than a hundred *happiness processes*, from the Buddha to Anthony Robbins to discover which ones actually works. One of the most effective ways to have happiness, they found, was to use gratitude daily. In the study, people wrote down three good things, big or small, that happened during the day. They did this every night for one week. Next to each entry, they answered the question, "Why did this good thing happen?" After three months, these people were still significantly happier and less depressed than the control group.[7]

The Third Letter of the Sequence

Mediators and negotiators have used the following method to prevent revenge from starting or continuing. Because we don't always have a mediator, counselor, or another neutral person available, the sequence of letters that you started in Chapter 6 can help. You wrote the *Letter of Hurt* and the *Response Letter*. The third is the *Gratitude letter*, which you will be composing now. If there are several people in your upset, I recommend a separate letter sequence for each.

A portion of the Gratitude letter comes from the *Honorable Closure* work[8] of Dr. Angeles Arrien, a cultural anthropologist, award-winning author, educator, and business consultant. I highly recommend her many books for anyone interested in what is common to all of us across religions and cultures.

The Gratitude Letter

At this stage in forgiving, write a letter of appreciation to the person you wish to forgive. In the letter, tell of your thankfulness for what they have contributed to your life. Release your negative feelings, as they do not belong in this letter.

1. Thank them for the gifts you have received from them through the years.
2. Tell them, if you can, *how* you matured mentally, emotionally, or spiritually from this.
3. Thank them for what you have learned from them, and express your appreciation for who they have been in your life.
4. If there was once love, *pretend* to feel this love and remember what you once loved about the person.
5. Appreciate their positive qualities and write what you admire in them.
6. How did they inspire you?
7. Speak of the love given and love received.
8. Notice the shift in your body. Write down your insights.

In being grateful, initially, you might have to "Fake it till you make it," but it will come.

Apologize only when you recognize intentional or unintentional harm you have done.

You might acknowledge the person's skills, character, integrity, strength, appearance, and what you like about them in general.

If you can see that you might have done something similar to their offense in any way, then compassion and humility can enter into your thoughts more easily, and forgiveness might occur in a flash. Then the challenge will be self-forgiveness.

Don't send the first two letters, but consider sending the gratitude one.

- What issues does this bring to mind? Write about them.

Jeanette's gratitude letter to her abusive husband started with an appreciation of his helping her gain strength to say no and to walk away from his abuse. Then she saw how hard he had worked and even had sacrificed for her so that she could have a attractive house. It ended in tears with her seeing the love that really had been there.

NOTE: I want to repeat a warning I mentioned in the first part of the book. When the love returns in an abusive relationship, the person may go back to the abuser feeling healed and may be abused again. See Myth 11 in Chapter 3.

If it is too hard to write this letter right now, then hold off until it is appropriate. The crucial point here is to be aware of the possibility of gratitude in this or any situation for there is a gift in it.

You might look at the book; *Thank God I...:Stories of Inspiration for Evryday Situations* by edited by John Castagnini. In it are stories by people who have found the positive in their greatest challenges. Some of the stories are: Thank God My Wife Cheated, Thank God I Was Raped, Thank God I Had Cancer, Thank God I Have Herpes, Thank God My Son Died, Thank God My Husband Was An Alcoholic.

An Inner Sense of Truth

If our Source is loving and harmonious, perhaps our own barriers to love and peace prevent us from experiencing our highest state of mind and spirit – love, joy, peace, and forgiveness.

By acknowledging that you might *not know* the whole truth in the situation, you open yourself up to see more deeply into the situation. For example, you might not know God's reason for this situation, or the lesson for your or another's involvement. You might not know the truth behind the other person's perspective.

Besides basic intuition, most of us have an inner sense of knowing the right thing to do. I have worked with people who have felt justified in their harmful actions toward another, but when we went deeper and became more truthful, they always admitted there was a part of them that knew it was not right. Not listening to that honest part of ourselves creates turmoil and guilt. This inner sense of rightness is conscience. This sense of truth leads us to be aware that healing can only come through honesty. Through this inner sense of rightness, we can undo much of the turmoil around unforgiven situations.

This quality within is not condemning, but wholly beneficent and wise. It might even be called the *Spirit of Compassion* within you—for you. It's available, but never controls. It's subtle but feels right. If your response is not love, peace, or joy, you have listened to the pessimistic survival-self. Agitation is a sure sign that you are *not* using your inner sense of truth.

How to Empower Yourself and Others

Connecting with this Highest Aspect of life is the best way to empower yourself. For some this seems to be difficult. I created *Effective Ways of Empowering Yourself and Others* for my workshops to enable people to work with many of the sources of inner strength that you can use. These helped people connect with the power needed to forgive. Appendix B contains the handout along with questions to help you.

Journal Questions
1. Am I prepared to be completely honest with myself and in my recollections?
2. Can I be complete and not omit or add details?
3. Can I be objective?
4. Am I prepared to be truthful about my own participation in my unforgiven situations?

CHAPTER NINE

Working on Upsets

I n this short chapter is a summary of the steps from all the previous chapters to help you forgive. This is not all the steps of the *Power Forgiveness Process,* but these can carry you quite far in forgiving.

Vital Steps and Actions to Remember

To deal with a person or situation:

1 – Make a Choice that Feels Right

Start small. Take one upset, or part of one, to work on. It might be just one of a group of people or one of many upsets with a person.

2 – Look at your Willingness

- Are you willing to work on this upset?

(If not, take another upset that you are willing to face.) As I mentioned, willingness is essential because it provides the beginning of the commitment that leads to forgiving. Your willingness to take on upsets that are more difficult will increase as you forgive. You don't have to start with the big stuff first, just take what piece you are willing to do.

3 – Focus on What Inspires You to Forgive

- What inspires you to do this work?

The essential quality in doing forgiveness work is to have continual inspiration to forgive. You need to have a worthy reason to do it. This inspired reason will take you past the natural internal resistance in the mind against forgiving. This motivation can be spiritual, emotional, or even physical.

Inspiration is the most effective beginning of any endeavor—the stronger the inspiration the greater the possibility of success.

The opening stage in forgiving is the kindling or rekindling of your desire to forgive. This initial opening through inspiration carries your spirit forward to the quest for more knowledge of the subject and, later, it carries you through emotional blocks that might come up.

4 – Deal with Feelings Effectively

- What are you feeling when you think of the situation?

Dealing with feelings is valuable in order to prevent false forgiveness. When your feelings change to positive ones, forgiving has occurred. You may find these questions helpful in looking at your initial mind-set:

A. What do I feel when I think of the person involved in this situation? For example, sad, depressed, angry, apathetic, guilty, hurt, anxious.
B. Apart from my main emotion, when I think of each situation, are there other feelings underneath, or mixed up with that main one, like embarrassment, humiliation, or shame?
C. Am I willing to engage these feelings and not avoid them?
D. What was I afraid would happen at the time? What am I afraid of now if I forgive?

5 – Find Your Needs and Debt Owed

Remember, our working definition of forgiveness is letting go of what is owed – as in forgiving a financial debt.

- What do they owe you for having to feel what you have felt?
- What do you need out of the situation? What would satisfy you?

For some, having the person go to jail will bring relief. For others, watching the person die is not enough. Therefore, the initial question in any forgiveness situation is, what do they owe you?

Here are further questions to help you in this step:
- A. Am I willing to entertain the possibility of not getting what they owe me?
- B. Can I let it go to gain peace of mind?
- C. Is it worth carrying this upset when it is unrealistic that I would ever get what I want from the them?

6 – Look at the Real Consequences of Holding on to this Upset

This step does not have to be an essay; it can be done in moments.

Payoff

- A. What do I get by keeping the upset going? Write down any benefits. Who benefits and how?
- B. Is being right more important than being happy?

Negative consequences

Sometimes you don't notice how much the upset has affected you. Here are some questions to consider:
- A. What am I really getting out of this upset? List the negatives.
- B. What is happening to the people closest to me by holding onto the upset?

C. How happy am I in my life?
D. Could letting go of with this situation increase love, peace, and joy in my life?

Being a Victim

A. How long has my victimization been going on?
B. How long is it okay to let others be in control of my happiness?
C. Am I a possible contributor to the problem and not just the victim?

7 – Handle Resistance to Forgiving

What often prevents people from letting go are misunderstandings about the nature of forgiveness.

We listed these in the Myths chapter of the book. and repeat them here to make sure misunderstandings are not inhibiting your ability to move forward.

Remember, forgiveness is:

- Not condoning a bad behavior, justifying an offense or turning the other cheek.
- Not reconciliation with the offending party.
- Not the same as out of sight, out of mind.
- Not dependent upon an apology.
- Not dependent on the other person being alive or in contact with you.
- Not dependent on whether the offending party deserves forgiveness.
- Not losing, or the easy way out of a situation.
- Not lack of responsibility.

If any of these are affecting your forgiving, look over the Myths of Forgiveness section in Chapter 3.

Deciding to Forgive

Sometimes you can make a conscious decision to forgive while you are in the process. This decision is an act of the will with full intention and a solid commitment to your highest self. The decision to forgive can occur anytime.

Questions you might ask are:
1. Can I decide to forgive right now for myself?
2. Even though they don't deserve it, can I decide to forgive as an act of compassion toward the other person and myself?

As you make the decision to forgive, you keep going through the rest of the stages. Forgiving someone is not the end of this process; forgiving yourself is, if you want to be rid of the situation for good.

NOTE: The more you decide to forgive and feel the emotional relief, the easier it will be to make a decision to forgive at another time. Power Forgiveness becomes faster as you go along because your decision to forgive becomes easier, enabling you to let go of upsets permanently. The speed of the process looks unrealistic to those who don't understand what forgiving is. The more you do it the better you become at it. When you keep on seeing the repetitive negative patterns of your mind and how they play out in different unforgiven situations, your understanding about those situations increases and the decision to forgive becomes easy.

Key questions

A. Have I taken the time to relax, meditate, or contemplate on the highest in myself while doing this forgiveness work?
B. Am I listening to the highest aspect of myself?
C. What is the highest goal for my life that this situation might be stopping, either in its existence or in my own attitude?

PART III

The Truth behind the Resistance to Forgive

Some of the significant parts of the forgiving process that we will cover in this section:
- Self-Forgiveness
- Dealing with marriage and new relationships
- Coping with stress, trauma and emotional pain.
- Effectively controlling stressed brain takeovers
- How to make forgiving permanent.

"Be not angry
that you cannot make others
as you wish them to be,
since you cannot make yourself
as you wish to be.
If you cannot mould yourself
entirely as you would wish,
how can you expect other people
to be entirely to your liking?"

THOMAS A KEMPIS,
THE IMITATION OF CHRIST
FROM THE 15TH CENTURY

CHAPTER TEN

Forgiving Permanently

*"Everyone complains of his memory
and nobody complains of his judgement."*

FRANCOIS DE LA ROCHEFOUCAULD
FRENCH AUTHOR (1613 – 1680)

We condone revenge in our novels, films and cultures. Our heroes do not forgive offenders; they find them and destroy them, making the world safer for people with decent values. So what's the problem if good values are upheld and the bad guys get what they deserve? The problem is that there are always two sides to a conflict. Justice, to be fair, needs to be carried out in a controlled situation, like a legal system.

When we judge and attack people close to us based on our own opinion of what is right, we run the risk of being wrong. This includes governments. Often, when it comes to human interaction and behavior, we do not have all the information we need to come to a reasoned conclusion, just an emotional one. Many wars started with no better justification than revenge or humiliation.

Behind the reason for not forgiving is the truth that enables you to forgive. Studying your confusion and resistance can actually increases your quality of life and ability to forgive. Compassion enables you to be *willing* to understand a person, perhaps by walking in his or her shoes. Understanding speeds up forgiving and can make it lasting.

In my forgiveness therapy classes, I have found it vital to address the deep inner factors that prevent forgiving but that can, when addressed, make forgiving permanent. In the quest for understanding, we've gone over the importance of knowing why people don't act or see the world as we do, or have the values we have. In the search for truth, we must look more deeply at our personal reactions and their effect.

As Einstein said:[1]

"A human being is a part of the whole, called by us the 'Universe', a part limited in time and space. He experiences himself, his thoughts, and feelings, as something separate from the rest—a kind of optical delusion of his consciousness. This delusion is a kind of prison for us, restricting us to our personal desires and to affection for a few persons nearest to us. Our task must be to free ourselves from this prison by widening our circle of compassion to embrace all living creatures and the whole of nature in its beauty. Nobody is able to achieve this completely, but the striving for such achievement is in itself a part of the liberation and a foundation for inner security."

To develop skill in letting go, you need to learn the deeper aspects of your mind that not only protect you, but may also cause problems and affect forgiving. From this, you will gain an even better understanding of why you acted the way you did, and why others act the way they do. Fortified with this knowledge, forgiving becomes straightforward and painless. This is the objective of this third part of the book.

How to Keep Our Stressed-Brain Reactions from Overriding Our Thinking and Creative Functions

Being in charge of our thoughts is not easy. It takes work. We make mistakes every day, some big, some small. We need forgiveness to grease the mechanisms of social and personal interactions, so that we and those around us can be happy.

The brain is programmed to react. How much influence the reactive systems have is regulated not only by how much stress is present, but also by how much experience we have in controlling these reactions.

As mentioned in Chapter 5, to forgive we need to be in a somewhat calm, non-threatening space. Meditation, prayer, contemplation, and other stress reduction methods like the *Relaxation Response* developed by Dr. Herbert Benson at Harvard, help to keep the earlier brains from gaining or holding control.

Note: You are not always able to control all of the stress responses in the body and mind, but with knowledge and practice, these reactions have less power over your life.

This became clear to me in a documentary on how Tiger Woods' father taught him to play golf in competition. His father wanted Tiger to focus on what he was doing, no matter what was going on around him. To teach him to cope with the pressure of competition, his father would drop the golf bag when Tiger was in the beginning of a swinging, or otherwise create tension so that Tiger's practice would remain calm and focused even under high stress. Succeeding in competition demands this degree of focus and calm, as does succeeding in life.

People who have not learned how to manage their reactions will have a difficult time in stressful situations. Some never learn to deal effectively with stress. It takes much practice. Putting violent people who are in prison back on the street when they have not learned to deal with these powerful reactions, accomplishes little. I don't advocate for punishment, but for a program of stress management and rehabilitation, along with forgiveness training. If these trainings were done, we would see a radical change for those in prison and a lowering of crime rates.

I encourage people who have been violent or abusive to learn to work with their angry reactions, so that they will not be a danger to others or themselves. Otherwise, the violence and out-of-control reactions will continue.

Please Note: Changing behavior patterns is difficult because they often are connected to early pleasure and safety experiences. Consequently, to change them you need to make sure that there is pleasure and safety in the new pattern. If you get angry with yourself when you are trying to put in new patterns, you defeat your purpose by putting in stress rather than pleasure.

If you go to a dance and want to learn Salsa, your old patterns of other dance steps might help or they might get in the way. In any dance style, until you learn the beat and steps, you'll feel uncomfortable. That is why you learn the basics first. You start slowly so that you build on understanding and pleasure, not fear and anxiety.

If a person never learned about music, beat, and step patterns for dance, he or she might judge dancing as stupid and the people who do it ignorant. Likewise, if one's dance step is different from another's, there may be harsh judgement. This same kind of judging and condemning is what brings pain and relationship difficulties. Forgiveness then becomes a step that makes the dance of a relationship smoother.

Understanding our reactions to stress will give us insight into why forgiving is so difficult, at times passionately attacked, or equally defended.

Previously we talked of how the lower brain reactions may take away the control of our neocortex. Here are more indicators of this "take over". When a person becomes overstressed and their highest function is greatly dimmed, these problems may show up:[3]

- distracted easily and/or hyperactivity
- lack of determination
- impulse control problems
- chronic lateness and poor time management
- disorganization and procrastination

If you expect yourself or another to function well when the above signs of overstress are present, you are being unrealistic at best.

Look at your unforgiven situation and see if you can step out of being the effect of it and move into an observer role—watching yourself. From this perspective:

1. What in your past do you think makes you react as you have to this situation?
2. Consider why you think you might be having the feelings you have?

Sometimes you will quickly get an insight into what is under the surface; sometimes it will come days later when you least expect it. The point is to gain the ability to separate yourself from your reactions, and to have a deeper insight into the cause of your reactions in this situation.

Our Mind's Defenses that Prevent Forgiving

"Why do you look at the speck of sawdust in your
brother's eye and pay no attention to the plank in your
own eye? ... You hypocrite, first take the plank out of
your own eye, and then you will see clearly to remove the
speck from your brother's eye."

JESUS, *MATTHEW 7:3,5*

What we most loudly condemn in others might be what we are suffering from ourselves. Shakespeare implied this centuries ago in *Hamlet*: "The lady doth protest too much, methinks." Jesus' teaching of removing the plank from our own eye before removing the speck of sawdust from our neighbor's eye is a lesson in a major obstacle to forgiveness—our defense mechanisms.

When something is too uncomfortable for us to deal with, our mind will protect us through a set of defenses. We are not aware of these defensive responses. Like our stressed-brain reactions, these too are below our conscious awareness, which is how they are able to work and continue causing terrible trouble for us.

We often use defensiveness to respond when we are in a stress reaction or when we have made a mistake. The part of us that is concerned with our moral sense and tries to contend with reality has a hard time with the struggle to keep the snake brain satisfied and not get out of hand. Often, we make decisions and do acts that we regret. To preserve the sense of who we are morally and to feel better about our self, we adopt mechanisms to defend and justify our desires, mistakes and behaviors.

For around a hundred years, psychology studied these defenses and reactions. Many books and papers have been written about them. In fact, up to the 1970s, most psychiatrists in Europe and the US were trained in them. This approach fell out of popularity when thought and behavior changing approaches became more accepted. These new approaches did not especially agree with the concept of a subconscious and its defense mechanism.

Yet, I have seen very effective forgiveness work done through becoming aware of the subconscious mechanisms that hold us back. Some of these *ego defense mechanisms*, as they are called, point to a truth that enables forgiving to be permanent. Though they are below our conscious awareness, with attentiveness some can be seen and worked with. The key in working with them is not the awareness of them alone, but using self-forgiveness to undo them.

By understanding the basics of ego defenses, we:
- Gain a deeper understanding of the resistance to forgiving
- Find the way that makes forgiving permanent.

Note: The defenses are what we do to make us feel better and often justify our negative responses to stress. Instead of dealing with our reactions directly and quieting them before we make a mistake or react, we create an elaborate system to justify our actions and then hide it from our self so that we feel better. We would actually feel better and not put trash in our subconscious, if we just quieted the stress system and made effective decisions, but often these defenses happen in difficult situation and usually start in childhood.

The Defenses

Two primary defenses seem to have a great deal to do with forgiveness. One is to hide upsetting or intolerable thoughts, events, or desires deeply below our conscious perception. There are many subtleties and names for this hiding defense: denial, repression, suppression, dissociation. For our work, I will use the word *denial* for this general category of *hiding the upsets inside us*.

The other defense, called projection or displacement, is to put the upsetting thought outside us onto others. Here, we hide it in another person, then deny it has anything to do with us. Blaming and scapegoating are the typical result. I will use the term *projection* for this act of placing responsibility for our negative beliefs or actions onto others, and then denying our own involvement.

Jesus' scolding of taking the plank out of your own eye, points to these two subconscious methods of defense. In projection, we deny a failing in ourselves, but readily see it in others. In Chapter 6, in *How Our Outer World Reflects Our Inner One*, we examined the general action of projecting our inner perspective onto the outer world. Even though the action is natural, it still originates in our own mind first.

This has been a simplification of our defense mechanisms for forgiveness work, not psychoanalysis.

Ted prided himself on his honesty. It was a large part of his identity. Sometimes, however, he lied to his wife about their bank balance because he did not always make as much money as he thought he should. Because he could not admit to that dishonest behavior, he accused the bank of dishonesty when he received the monthly statement. And, he really believed it!

With projection, we accept these distortions as true. Hitler blamed the Jews for the trouble Germany was having after World War I and millions agreed with him. It is easier to blame than accept responsibility. The whole idea of the scapegoat is behind this mental mechanism and comes directly from the snake brain.

Making Forgiveness Permanent

Projection and denial cannot easily coexist with self-forgiveness, which is a courageous and effective alternative. Instead of defending against emotional pain, forgiveness begins by confronting it and the circumstances surrounding it with scrupulous honesty. It is completed by transforming it into something positive, even inspiring, focused on preventing rather than perpetuating harm. Psychology has overlooked forgiveness for decades by relegating it to religion.

With clients who have held anger for years, I often search for how they have projected upsets with themselves onto others. Looking at projection and doing self-forgiveness removes the reason to put it on others. Looking at projection and gaining self-forgiveness is one of the fastest ways of getting out of an upset with another.

Note: What we will go over now is for long-term resentments where you are letting go of all upsets, not traumas that were out of your control, e.g., rapes and other acts of violence or terrorism. At times this will not apply even to regular situations. This is an advanced model and awareness. I offer it because I have seen it work for people and myself. (If you are doing this work with friends or clients, don't use it if the person doesn't get it. If it works, great, if not there are plenty of other methods.)

To help another forgive permanently:

1. Help the person look at the situation to see, in any way, if they have been guilty of the same or a similar behavior for which they are trying to forgive the other person. If so, then
2. Have them forgive the other person, since they have done the same thing themselves. Then,
3. Get them to forgive themselves, if possible, or find a way that they can gain forgiveness for what they have done.

With self-forgiveness, they may not have done the offending act to the same degree, but I have seen the upset released when people see how they have done a similar thing in some way, know only to themselves.

Remember that the mind works in metaphor, which is the comparison of two unlike things that have something in common.[3a] For example, when Jesus says, "you are Peter, and upon this rock I will build My church." Peter is not a rock but the rock symbolizes Peter's strength. Or, the verse in a song, "You are the wind beneath my wings." The person doesn't have wings but the wind and the wings symbolize the person's relationship to the other. That commonality is what we are looking for in the projection. It is not literal, but might be; normally it points in a direction.

The next example shows this shared meaning. Even though I addressed a violent situation, which normally I would not, I did so because of the awareness, sincerity, and intelligence this woman had shown previously in class.

Riva, a great-grandmother, could not forgive Hitler for what he had done to the Jews and her family. She was an angry, unhappy woman. Because nothing seemed to work to move her toward forgiveness, we started talking about projection centered on Hitler. She was willing to look at this.

It was obvious that she had not killed any Jews, but when asked how many times she had killed Hitler and the Nazis in her mind, and through the years killed herself inside for surviving, she became quiet. She found the courage to look at this aspect of herself. With great honesty, she admitted that the anger and hate she carried all those years had negatively affected her family and those around her. Her children did not see her often, nor did she have many friends.

I did not ask her to condone or justify what Hitler did, or even forgive him. I asked her to forgive herself for the hate, anger, and negativity she had indirectly put on others for so many years. When she finally did that, the tears flowed for her family, and she said she felt a peace she had not felt for decades.

Janet, a friend, shared the following event with me. She and her husband were going to a lovely resort. Her husband had arranged to pick her up from her work at a certain time. But, he was delayed by a phone call from his brother, whom he had not spoken with for several months. She waited for forty-five minutes in the hot sun, and was quite angry with him when she heard that he had put a phone call ahead of their meeting.

Her anger ruined that night for both of them. Luckily, her forgiveness training enabled her to gain insight into why her anger was so strong and persistent. "Finally, in the middle of the next day, I saw that I had done the same thing to my children."

She admitted that she had left her kids waiting so that she could get her PhD. She left them home at night, and sometimes had them get their own meals—all because she felt she had something more important to do. She had *left them waiting,* just as her husband had left her. This brought up her guilt and ire because it is something in her, not his action. She did her forgiveness work right there. The rest of their stay at the resort went wonderfully.

Charlotte's situation, which follows, is an example of denial. Her mother told her that her father had severely beaten her when she was 18 months old. Her mother was in tears when relating this incident. Several years later, her mother denied the story completely: "I don't know what you're talking about. Your father would never do something like that."

Charlotte, an older psychotherapist, understood the protective function of defense mechanisms. She understood that her mother's denial was not a lie, but simply an attempt to protect her illusions about the man she had married and the mother she was. What kind of mother would allow her child to be beaten like that? People will naturally defend against being bad. It is built into the system. Eventually they will believe the defense, in this case denial.

Working with Projection

Here is an example of how you can work with projection. Suppose you are angry at a foreign dictatorship. You might have a picture of the leader in your mind. Ask yourself, "What is it I don't like about what he's doing?" There might be a whole list. Let's say one of your answer is, "Taking freedom away from people." Remembering the previous section on defense mechanisms, ask yourself if that is a possible projection by asking:

1. How do I behave as that dictator in my own life?
2. Do I take away the freedom of others, or let others take away the freedom of another?

3. Do I take my own freedom away? (This is usually the essential question.)
4. Do I tie myself to the grindstone and never take a break or vacation?
5. Do I feel imprisoned in my own life?
6. Have I imprisoned myself and feel unable to get out?

These are all questions that look at this projection from different angles. Situations that cause strong emotions may often point right back to our own mistakes and failure to forgive ourselves.

> Bo Diddley, Creedence Clearwater Revival, and Eric Clapton remind us in the song *Before You Accuse Me,*
> take a look at yourself.

Gil was a tough guy. He was big, and had been in many fights through the years, often taking on several men at a time. But, life had crushed him. He was angry, depressed, and wanted to change. During a counseling session, he admitted for the first time to anyone that he was the victim of incest. He had always hated his father but had never talked about him as a perpetrator of incest. He cried for five minutes in deep sobs.

Later, he could see how being sexually abused caused his reckless driving and his desire to fight. He saw that his fights were to punish *tough* men like his father. He also saw that he was punishing himself for feeling so degraded. As he worked with the results of his resentment, he realized that he was continuing the original injury in his own life, bringing himself alienation, humiliation, and powerlessness. Two years later his lifestyle had changed. He was working to help other men who were violent, and had stopped his drinking, reckless driving, and fighting.

Journal Activity:

1. Look at the list that you have been making. Take one offense that seems appropriate.

2. Write down any time that you have done the same or a similar thing.

3. At this point, you may notice resistance. Write down what comes up for you. Our defense mechanisms may be keeping us from the truth of the situation because they are too hard to face. Be honest with yourself and know that truth will set you free from the old patterns.

4. Look at where you feel resistance. Try not to defend yourself or attack with a denial. Pay attention to your emotions.

5. If you can see that you have done a similar thing, Forgive the person. It shouldn't be hard because you have done the same thing.

6. Now forgive yourself for that. This might be much harder. But find a way to gain forgiveness.

Note: Byron Katie has done excellent training on looking deeply at how we prevent our own healing. I highly recommend her method, which she calls "The Work." I have used this method and her book *Loving What Is: Four Questions That Can Change Your Life* with wonderful success in forgiveness groups I've led.[4]

Awareness of Defense Mechanisms Is Not Enough

Awareness of projection is not sufficient to change your life. Forgiving what the projection reveals is also necessary.

Riva, the great-grandmother I mentioned earlier, had to forgive herself for the damage she did to her own family because of her hatred of the Nazis. She saw how she continued the work of Hitler and Goebbels by clinging to her hatred. She could see why her son did not like to be around her and how her daughter had developed the same negativity.

Psychiatrists have been aware of defense mechanisms for 70-plus years, yet their own suicide rate was extraordinarily high all that time. Lack of forgiveness of self or others is a major factor in the depression or hopelessness that causes suicide.

How to Unearth Your Defense Mechanisms: To reveal your projections and denials, examine those situations that always leave you feeling offended. Your irritability is the evidence and way-shower.

Write down what you continually find fault with in other people. This can provide you with clues to your defenses, particularly denial and projection. Take particular note of faults with those closest to you.

Go to a quiet place where you will be undisturbed for at least an hour. Write down what people do that sets you off, or that you find intolerable. Try to be as honest with yourself as you can and simply record those events. You will also use this in later chapters.

Now with that list turn the situation around. Ask:

1. Have I done the same thing to another? Or to myself?
2. Is this similar in any way to something I've done to another or myself?
3. Is this similar to a family pattern or to the actions of someone else in my family?

My own forgiveness transformation came out of going down my extensive list of upsets with people and seeing how I had, in some way, done a similar thing to people. For me, forgiving the offender was easy. I needed help on forgiving myself for all of my offenses to others.

Stressed Thinking That Sabotages Forgiving

Here are three of the main ways that we sabotage our thinking and our happiness. Included, are some forgiving ways to use with them.

A. Focusing on the Negative & Rejecting the Positive

For survival under immediate threat, the reptilian brain focuses sharply on danger. This tunnel vision toward only the negative qualities of a person or situation does reveal dangers, but it also exaggerates fears, failures, and frustrations, leaving the person agitated and unhappy.

Roberta could only see the negative aspects of her marriage. She could not forgive herself for being in such a bad situation. She actually wasn't able to see anything positive until she did an exercise of writing down what was positive in her home and family when she saw them. For a week, she did this by carrying a pad with her all the time. To her surprise, her list of positives was longer than the list of negatives she had completed in session. The lesson in situations is – **Increase focus on the positive.**

Try this: In a negative area of your life, write down the positives in it. As much as possible try saying, "What is positive in this?" and "What have I gained from this?" Do this even when you think you can't. Also, see if you can forgive the negatives in that person directly, remembering that the other person might be doing the very best she or he can do.

B. Black and White Thinking

In this kind of reactive thinking, there is good or bad with no in-between and no shades of gray. One day a person is wonderful, the next he's horrible. For the reptilian brain, the simple way to sort through the great deal of input from the environment is to see only danger or safety. This kind of thinking affects relationships quite adversely. For example, daughter one is wonderful, daughter two, terrible. People, however, are not either–or, smart or stupid, good or bad, beautiful or ugly, but are somewhere along a scale.[5]

We are too multifaceted to be reduced to the black-or-white judgements of the snake brain. In this thinking, the greatest pitfall is how you judge yourself. If you aren't perfect, you're a failure – no room for mistakes. This is a major issue in self-forgiveness.

I knew an especially bright person who had been caught up in a cult when she was younger. Even though she was competent and had held quite responsible jobs, she continued to berate herself for being stupid for falling for the lies of the cult leader. Because of this mistake, she would only hold menial jobs. Her statement to herself was, "I used to be smart, now I'm stupid." In like fashion, it is quite common for women coming out of abusive relationships to consider only jobs that are below their level of competence, even though they know they had excelled before.

To overcome black and white thinking, Dr. McKay, Dr. Davis and P. Fanning, the authors of *Thoughts and Feelings*, tell us to think in terms of percentages.[6] Here are examples: "25% of her work is unsatisfactory, but 75% is quite good." Another is, "About 60% of the time he seems terribly preoccupied with himself, but there is the 40% when he can be quite generous," or "15% of the time I'm a jerk, the rest of the time I do all right."

By catching yourself in this *either-or* thinking, and by using percentages, you are being more forgiving, because you are stepping out of the judgement you have made. Self-forgiveness is essential here, as is forgiveness of imperfections in others.

Remember: When we forgive other's imperfections, we exercise the muscle of forgiving ourselves.

Try this: Make a list of all the behaviors or qualities for which you condemn yourself, and look at it realistically, using percentages. Then forgive yourself for each thing.

C. Catastrophe Thinking (Catastrophizing)

This thinking sees disaster in anything negative that happens. It is similar to #1 but more out of control. Both are common with people who have lived with tragedy and trauma. It may also be a learned response from parents. It's actually the movement of fear and hopelessness into a situation with the complete loss of rationality, faith and positive thinking. Your job loss = lose of your house = your wife and children will leave you. All of these thoughts occurring within seconds. Then the emotional response occurs with the snake brain going into a range of reactions from hiding and no movement to rage and killing others.

When this perspective becomes chronic, there is no trust that life will get better. The future is bleak. There is rage over minor events, or ongoing fear. My father, who was raised in Brooklyn, NY, couldn't play on the street when he was young because his mother was concerned that he would be "hit by a car." This is when there weren't many cars. All his buddies where out there but him. In fact, he owned the ball and bat they played with! No wonder he left home at the age of fifteen.

This type of thinking can actually create bad situations, not because of the stressing incident but because of the reaction to it, man looses job and kills coworker is obvious. More subtle is a mistake at work means they will fire me so I may as well not work as hard because they are going to fire me anyway. Or a prevalent one for people trying to forgive the termination of a relationship: I will never find another person to love me again. With this attitude, they probably won't, which is why forgiving is so worthwhile. With it, you are relieved of the pain and attitude of being a victim.

This thinking is a lack of trust of others and self and contains no forgiveness. What it needs is patience and some rational control so that the person can look at other options and possibilities other than the first one presented by the snake.

Once a stressed mind latches onto a culprit for what happened, it doesn't let go. It's like a pit bull, which especially likes the blood of its owner.

To step out of an immediate catastrophe response, first you need to quiet the stress-reacting system. Take a walk, call a friend, do the Relaxation Response, etc. Once you are calm and somewhat rational, do the exercise below.

Try this: As you re-look at these three negative thinking styles you can probably see strong similarities in them. In all, you need to observe what is happening from an objective perspective, one that is separate from your reactions.

For catastrophizing, make a list of what you think will happen because of what happened.

1. With each item, ask, "Is it true?" and then "How do I know it will happen?"
2. Look for positive possibilities that could occur for each one.
3. Note any behaviors or qualities you condemn others for or yourself. Then see if you can forgive yourself or the others for each thing. Save this list as you will use it again soon.

If you can't do these right now, carry on reading the chapters and doing the exercises.

Catastrophe/disaster thinking takes more than forgiveness to resolve. Though forgiving helps, it takes trust and faith in Life and yourself, which are beyond the scope of this book. Trust and faith take connecting with the truest part of us. That journey, to me, is our main one. Forgiveness helps to clear the way.

> "For there is nothing either good or bad, but thinking
> makes it so"   - SHAKESPEARE, *HAMLET*
> The modern version:
> "One man's trash is another man's treasure."

CHAPTER ELEVEN

Self-Forgiveness and Empowerment

"Misfortunes one can endure — they come from outside; they are accidents. But to suffer for one's own faults — ah, there is the sting of life."

OSCAR WILDE

The Keys to Self-Forgiveness

In the previous chapter, we looked at making your forgiveness permanent by viewing your defense mechanisms and doing self-forgiveness to get past them. That is not easy. Now we will look even more deeply at gaining forgiveness for yourself.

Remember in chapter two, researchers stated that self-forgiveness entails not only facing one's wrongs but also letting go of the negative thoughts, feelings and actions against the self and "replacing them with compassion, generosity and love." You know you have forgiven yourself when you have positive feelings, actions and thoughts, for yourself.

If you find that you don't have those positives for yourself, then this chapter will help.

Guilt, Pain and Punishment

People's values, rules, and moral code set the standard by which they live. When they act against their values and standards, they feel bad, knowing that what they did was not right. At those times, they will often experience a sense of guilt.

Our perceived *lack of worthiness.* keeps us from our inner power. It comes from guilt, which is anger directed at the self. Because of guilt, we feel we deserve punishment and have often concluded that at some level we are bad because of some shameful behavior. If we hold onto these negative feelings, keeping them alive with judgements and self-attack, we set up a destructive loop that may keep us depressed and believing the world is against us.

When you let go of all the guilt that you can, you restore the highest qualities within you, just as you restore your personal relationships when you forgive others. Thus, we often feel that we too are inherently good, as are most people in the world.

In his book, *Big Prisons, Big Dreams: Crime and the Failure of America's Penal System*, Michael J. Lynch shows that of the three methods for changing behavior, 1. positive reinforcement, 2. negative reinforcement and 3. punishment, **punishment is the least effective on humans**. Positive reinforcement is the most successful. Please take this to heart when dealing with yourself.

Punishing yourself is not effective to change behavior for the better.[1] Punishment has been used for eons in cultures to change behavior. Through habit, we will usually do what was done to us. Nevertheless, you need to resist this temptation because punishment only brings fear by activating the lower brains and increasing resentment, which you are trying to get rid of. Thus, it defeats your purpose in self-forgiving.

Letting go of guilt is not easy. You might have to use *many* forgiveness methods to assist you. I recommend working with someone else as opposed to doing it by yourself if you aren't noticing much change in your life.

Carl felt terrible that he hadn't cleaned up a big upset with his father who had died suddenly. He used one of the oldest methods known for help. He went for regular long walks in nature and in his own way prayed for release from his guilt. Finally, on one of those long prayerful walks, he felt the forgiveness he sought.

Guilt should only be a call to action. When we see that we "missed the mark," (the meaning of *sin* in the original biblical Greek) we only need to correct our aim and try again. Repeated self-blame does not improve behavior or skill; practice and confidence do.

Dealing with Inner Conflict

Thomas Merton, explains in *No Man is an Island:* [2]

"All men seek peace first of all with themselves. That is necessary, because we do not naturally find rest even in our own being. We have to learn to commune with ourselves before we can communicate with other men and with God. A man who is not at peace with himself necessarily projects his interior fighting into the society of those he lives with, and spreads a contagion of conflict all around him. Even when he tries to do good to others his efforts are hopeless, since he does not know how to do good to himself."

Matthew was raised as a strict Christian and was vehemently opposed to the enormous profits in capitalistic ventures. A favorite teaching for him was: "it is easier for a camel to pass through the eye of a needle than for one who is rich to enter the kingdom of God" – *Matthew 19:24 (NAB)* Yet as an adult, he made plenty of money in his business and lived quite a comfortable lifestyle. Because of this inner conflict, guilt and depression tortured him.

Through his sister, he eventually did a forgiveness method of listing the positives in his life and the culture he lived in. That action led him to a deeper appreciation of the value of providing for his family and teaching his children important principles in a system that actually had much good. With this new perspective, he saw that he could use his money to help others who were not as fortunate as himself. In helping others, his guilt evaporated. As an added benefit, he was less judgemental of others. To many, his solution was obvious, but because he was trapped in such self-criticism, he hadn't seen it.

Juliette hated her father for his violence and felt terrible guilt because she could not protect her sisters or mother when she was young. Adults around her told her, "You shouldn't feel this way," and "You could really do nothing being so young." That did not change her guilt because she had to have these realizations for herself. The forgiveness process helped her see the irrational aspect of her guilt and let go of her self-anger.

Agnes was raped on a date. She felt many emotions, among them shame. In therapy, she was able to take all of these emotions apart and examine what was behind them. She saw that she felt ashamed and guilty that she had let this happen to her. Although this response was not rational because she was blameless in the attack, she nonetheless experienced guilt. When Agnes forgave herself for getting into the situation, even though she could not have helped it, not only did she feel a great weight lift from her mind, she also saw that it was her rapist who must bear the *full* responsibility for the rape.

Differing Values

We can observe that most people have values and a sense of ethical behavior. Though we might not agree with others' morals, we see that they do have values and standards. By understanding that the unforgiven person's life was quite different and dominated by different values, a humbleness can enter that says "I don't know everything." Forgiveness may then be a gift of the heart, creating a new and refreshing dynamic for them and you.

One hot summer afternoon, Lucy's life changed when she had the insight that her father was actually a decent father compared to his own father. She always resented how strict and emotionless he was, and how distant he kept himself. But she said, "When I talked with my aunt, his sister, I could see he has come a long way from his childhood, where he had been beaten often and mercilessly. He was a good father compared to the father he had." This gave her a newfound appreciation of her father, which enabled her to let go of much of her resentment for his seeming lack-of-love parenting. And she could see that it was not her fault.

How people deal with their early childhood training may be different even among family members. In an interview with two brothers, one said, "My parents were alcoholics; they got drunk all the time. So, of course, I became an alcoholic." The other said: "I saw what alcoholism did to my parents and how it ruined their lives, so of course, I never drank."

Giving and Receiving

We would all like to be happy. However, we can only be happy to the level that we can experience it. The person who can bring happiness to others has attained a skill, which often translates into his or her own life. Likewise, to get love, you give it. Can you encourage people to love you if you do not allow that love into your own life? It seems that if you can find out what prevents you from having love, you could have more of it. This is also true of joy, peace, and other positive feelings.

Don't ask the questions "Why can't I find an intimate partner or someone who will love me?" or "Where did the love go?" if you are unforgiving toward yourself or others. Love disappears in the choice to resent, to be angry, or to hate. In some way, you receive what you give. If you are angry, that is what you are giving, and you get the result.

Anger gets results, but, are they worth the cost? One of my early students, Glen, was a building contractor. He was able to get a lot done with his anger. People jumped when he showed it, giving him a sense of power that he liked. However, after a few years, he disliked anger's other results, such as high blood pressure, a failed marriage, little happiness, temper tantrums from a short fuse, poor sleep and depression. When he started looking for another way to live his life, he finally started to forgive and enjoyed his life more.

The Beatles said it very nicely in the song *The End*:

"The love you take is equal to the love you make."

Forgiveness, love, and peace are choices. They cannot be forced or demanded. We have seen this for the past two thousand years. Priests and clergy counsel forgiveness without teaching effective methods on how to achieve it, and often without modeling it. Or, they tell a person they are forgiven without the person believing or feeling it. Forgiveness will only take place when the desire for love, peace of mind, and joy has become more important than the desire for attack, anger, and getting even. The thing you receive is the result of what you give.

Try this: If you feel you are not getting the positives from life that you deserve, look more deeply at your worthiness, which is in your own eyes only. Self-forgiveness is the key to your inner riches and worth.

Search out your unworthy feelings. Find the guilt associated with the unworthiness. It's there. Take care of it by forgiving.

The Cycle of Victimhood and Guilt

Many people do not know they are caught in a cycle of being a victim that keeps them feeling guiltier and at the effect of others. Here is how it goes:

1. We do something against our moral codes, rules, or values.
2. This leads to guilt, shame, regret.
3. We condemn ourselves and thus, we will accept punishment from our self or others because we feel we deserve it. In addition, there is often fear of attack from a higher being.
4. Our self-protective defenses kick in and then we blame others for what happened, and thus
5. We will attack them, subtly or overtly, thus creating more guilt for ourselves. We will also fear attack from them, which often justifies attacking them more, which keeps the whole cycle going.

This cycle gets worse and worse the more we attack others or ourselves, making us more depressed and unhappy. The attack, whether external or internal, doesn't have to be terrible though sometimes it may be. It can be as simple as talking behind a person's back to try to ruin their standing with others

Forgiveness can enter into this cycle at any point and change it.

If you feel you are giving love and get anger back, you need to sort out deeper issues. Margaret was a loving, religious person whose husband beat her regularly. She always forgave him and went back to him after having left him. It seems that her forgiving caused her to be harmed. This is similar to saying that people who have more than three car accidents should not drive. Rather, it is a matter of finding out what they are doing wrong and correcting it.

If someone loves and gets anger in return, a deeper issue might be the inability to set limits. The ongoing victim usually does not have this ability. We often see this in domestic violence.

Healthy people on the outside ask the victim, "Why do you stay in the relationship?" or "Why don't you get rid of that bum?" These are legitimate questions.

The *victim effect* is a result of the emotional programming of "less than," "not good enough," and "lacking." This usually comes from childhood. In victimhood, there is often complaining and whining; the person sees only the negative, and mainly feels regret, guilt, and resentment. Victims usually attack themselves or are attacked from the outside because in some way they feel they deserves it. This is what needs to be changed. Women fall into this more easily than men because of their long history of abuse and denigration.

On the other side of the same coin is the attacker. The perpetrator also experiences victimhood, but acts it out differently. It was standard in our domestic violence groups to ask the angry man what he feared. If he could answer that honestly, the anger would immediately shift.

When Chuck, a wiry, tough guy, was deliberately cut off on the freeway, he intentionally damaged the car that cut him off while driving down the freeway. When he saw how crazy he was acting, he pulled back in the traffic and exited the freeway. When I asked what was going on, he said no one was ever going to take advantage of him again. In questioning further, he talked about how his father beat him in drunken rage from age five to twelve. At twelve, he fought back, and had been fighting ever since.

Continuing to listen to these victim ideas and thoughts is like letting a child run your life. It is letting an egocentric, weak sense of you run the show. With this happening, you become your worst enemy. Forgiving all abuses and finding self-forgiveness is essential. Forgiveness is the choice to regain peace of mind and love. It brings joy. Some therapists will disagree with me and say the anger is good, but that has never been my experience of ongoing anger.

"There is no spiritual power quite as great as that which comes from forgiving and praying for the enemy. Forgiving our enemies and praying for them generates great spiritual power because it is love."[3]

JOEL GOLDSMITH, SPIRITUAL TEACHER (1892 – 1964)

Meredith, an abused wife, started going to Co-Dependents Anonymous meetings every week, and eventually three times a week until she started feeling better. Co-Dependents Anonymous (CoDA) is a twelve-step program for people who share a common desire to develop functional and healthy relationships. It's adapted from Alcoholics Anonymous but not limited to alcohol. (See Appendix A for The 12-Steps of Co-Dependents Anonymous) In this program, she learned why she kept going back to abuse and even why it kept happening.

She started rehabilitating herself with the 12-steps, which has strong spiritual and forgiveness components. Meredith saw how the pattern of returning to the abuse was an old pattern of her mother's and reflected her mother's lack of self-worth.

In Meredith's case, because her husband would not quit drinking and was becoming more abusive, she escaped and never went back. (Because her husband was alcoholic, she could have gone to Al-Anon[4], but she chose CoDA because she had a friend in it. Al-Anon which includes Alateen for younger members has been offering hope, understanding and support to families and friends of alcoholics. It is also adapted from Alcoholics Anonymous,)

When I talked with her in class, she still loved him but knew she deserved more. Now she was with a man who loved her and treated her well. She was actually in class to work on forgiveness in her family of origin.

Feeling persecuted may come from habitual perceptions of being externally controlled and helpless—a victim of fate. These thoughts may keep people stuck because they don't believe they can actually create positive results in their life, let alone make any difference in the world. Someone or something is responsible for their pain, loss, and failure; "They did it to me!" is their cry. It's hard to find solutions with this attitude in place because "they probably won't work anyway." [6]

The truth about our seeming lack of control is:

1. We are constantly making decisions.

2. Every decision affects our lives.

3. In general, we have a responsibility for what happens to us. [7]

You undo the lie of helplessness by taking more control of your life. You are responsible for what happens in your inner world because you make your own life happen by your choices. Of course, events happen in your outer world over which you have no control, but overall, your choices also affect your outer world. Contentment and joy also come from specific choices you made and continue to make. These facts the victim does not understand, [8] and suffers for it. Compassion helps in forgiving someone, like a parent, who has regularly chosen the role of victim in life.

In your forgiving others, remember that people choose what they think is most valuable to them. They believe it will bring happiness, but it won't necessarily.

Gabrielle thought that being secure was more fundamental than anything else. Thus, she remained married for 30 years to a man who provided her money, but *nothing* else. She paid for her security at the expense of passion and joy. In her forgiving process, she saw that her husband had provided what was crucial to her, security. That changed her whole perspective of him and her.

Looking Deeper

To forgive constant victimization in your own life or that of another, try to find your overriding desires—what was for you most important? There is usually a conflict. The victim gets something from the situation, which keeps him or her in it, but feels lack of control or hopelessness because something else significant is not provided. We all have free will and make choices. If you don't appreciate the choices you or another made, bring in a compassionate perspective and find what was behind the choices. What was most important? In unforgiven situations, for many, being right is often more important than being happy.

"We cannot love unless we have accepted forgiveness,
and the deeper our experience of forgiveness is,
the greater is our love."

PAUL TILLICH

I've counseled several cult members. All admit that even though being in the cult was terrible, it provided something at the time that they felt gave meaning to their life—enough to put up with the abuse. Often, for people to forgive oppressive situations that they chose to remain in, they will have to see that they made choices to be there. Then it becomes a matter of self-forgiving.

"What if you were lied to?" Lorianne, one of my students, asked. "We were all lied to about what the church did and its success. You can't justify that. I would have never stayed in it if I knew it was all lies." I agreed with her and asked, "How do you forgive the church's lying to you so that you can get on with your life?" Each person could work on that question in a different way. That is why I have provided this book.

In her final paper for the forgiveness therapy class, Lorianne dealt with it by seeing that we are lied to all the time, by parents, media, politicians, advertisements, etc. "It seems to be common for people in organizations to do this. Yes, and I lied to my family and friends about how well I was doing and how wonderful the church was when I knew it wasn't true."

Questions: Here are insight-provoking questions concerning a perceived lack of control:
1. What choices did I make that resulted in this situation?
2. What decisions did I make?
3. What decisions can I make now to change it?

Help in Gaining Self-forgiveness

Researchers have shown that our survival mechanisms are fully engaged right after birth.[9] As we get older, we continue to use more of them for our protection and well-being.

Yet, also available to us is something else—an experience that takes us above our daily familiarity. It inspires us toward the best within us as opposed to mere survival. It is the source of our inspiration and love. This experience, in general, is in the domain of religion. There you will find some of the methods to help connect with this religious experience and thought.

As psychology developed in the late 19th century, it labeled this spiritual experience as abnormal. The struggle at the time was between church and science, and between Freud's rising popularity and his dislike of religion. This unfortunate split demonstrates the divide between our spiritual experience and everyday survival modes. Transpersonal Psychology helps people incorporate these seeming separate experiences. In general, though, the schism between religion and psychology remains. This is unfortunate for the field of forgiveness. However, it isn't an accident that religions have used the power of forgiveness for ages—it transforms.

If you are unable to attain forgiveness for yourself, many people can help, including a priest or clergyperson. I certainly have had benefit from church rituals in helping me find forgiveness when I was having difficulty.

Unforgiven situations take tremendous power away. You gain strength when you are able to show compassion for another's situation, as well as your own, and forgive them and yourself.

There is an irony here: This work may be intense and require personal power. But, that power is tied up in the unforgiven. Thus, there is limited energy available in the beginning to do the work of forgiving. This is why forgiveness may be such hard work initially. But, only initially.

"Woe to you, teachers of the law and Pharisees, you hypocrites! You clean the outside of the cup and dish, but inside they are full of greed and self-indulgence. Blind Pharisee! First clean the inside of the cup and dish, and then the outside also will be clean."
JESUS – *MATTHEW 23:25-26*

CHAPTER TWELVE

Dealing with Stress and Trauma

B ecause unforgiven situations create stress for us, we need to
look even further at how to alleviate our reactions to stress so
that we can forgive more easily. This chapter is about dealing with
our own tensions, which might be from family or work burnout,
compassion fatigue, or trauma and its consequences.

In the previous chapters, we went over why we react as we do.
In this one, we'll address some of the serious problems that arise
from these reactions and how to deal with them effectively to keep
them from overwhelming you. Of course, forgiveness is necessary,
but to get there, often you must calm down first.

Stress can be useful. Under stress, we will come up with new
ways to respond when the old ways no longer work. However, too
much stress overloads the system and shuts it down—then your
behavior becomes less rational. Life's pressures often evoke habitual response of fear or anger because flight and fight are activated
pretty easily. Flight comes from fear, which produces anxiety and
panic attacks. At its emotional extreme, we have hopelessness,
apathy and even suicide. Fight in its extreme brings murderous
reactions. We are seeing more of these extreme responses in
schools and workplaces.

It's vital for you to catch the early signs of stress in yourself, and to see those symptoms in the people you are trying to forgive. *Psychology Today* tells us that the experience of stress in the past magnifies your reaction to stress.[1]

We know that traumatic incidents can have devastating effects, but most people get over them in time. However, these painful incidents may have harmful long-term consequences if they are not dealt with appropriately. Because trauma heavily activates the body's stress response, forgiving benefits people suffering from the long-term consequences of traumatic incidents. Often a person's inability to cope with chronic stress comes from earlier trauma in his or her life.

Traumatic or catastrophic events are sudden, overwhelming, and often dangerous, such as a car accident, combat, rape, natural disasters, robbery at gunpoint, living in a war zone, or a near drowning, to name a few. The victim usually feels intense fear, helplessness, or horror at the time or afterwards. While most survivors are able to deal with the memories of the trauma and cope well, a small percentage develops strong anxiety reactions afterwards. When this happens, it's called Post-Traumatic Stress Disorder or PTSD. [2]

Please note: Family, close friends, and professionals who help survivors of these intense incidents can also be affected by the event because of their empathy for the person or people involved.[2a] We'll address this later in the chapter. This is called compassion fatigue.

I've given emphasis to trauma and its effects in the second part of this chapter for two reasons:

1. Trauma often causes seemingly unforgivable situations, especially if there was major loss, death or serious injury.
2. In this time of terrorism, new traumatic events close to us may be quite possible. Thus, we need to be aware of their

effects, especially when those effects might be happening in us, someone close to us, or someone we need to forgive.

You can do something about stress by changing your habitual thought and behavior patterns. Cognitive Therapy helps, as does meditation and prayer. Likewise, Traumatic Incident Reduction (TIR) and Visual Kinesthetic Disassociation (VKD) have been effective in relieving people's trauma experiences. TIR works to decrease the emotional charge of specific traumatic events; VKD is a hypnosis method that does the same.[3] For my own trauma and resulting PTSD, forgiveness worked the best.

In stressful situations, a variety of methods help. A wife who expects a beating might finally decide to protect herself and leave, instead of living in fear. Courage brings new behavior. Finding a different way to respond helps remove the habitual emotion tied to the action. Anything done to change any part of the response will change the whole situation.

We know from psychology and brain studies that shining the light of logic onto emotional distress will help alleviate it. Why? Because the linear thinking, analytical part of the brain is set up to work with our emotional system to calm it down.

The unforgiving person keeps him or herself in a constant state of tension by thinking often about the situation and people involved, or suppressing it so that it is still there but subconsciously. When you add old stress reactions to the normal stress that occurs in our environment, like driving, time schedules, work, or raising a family, you may become overloaded. Therapy can help.

Stress research has shown that when we fail to adapt to what stresses us, the body is affected, causing many symptoms, from tiredness, to a cold or flu, to more serious disease. In earlier times, after a stressful event occurred, for example, a brush with a wild animal, the body could relax and recover. However, today there is no recovery time.

In the stress response, there is a surge of hormones and chemicals in the body, creating changes. If these changes are not allowed to revert to normal through relaxation, trouble will occur.[4] Of course, we can take more vitamins and energy drinks, but remember, if the high power additives and fuel are used all the time in an engine for more speed, it will eventually burn up. It is the same with the body.

If this stress phase continues too long and becomes a normal state, stress exhaustion and burnout take place, causing problems including heart disease, chronic degenerative diseases, and eventually death.

"Chronic stress is like slow poison."

DR. JEAN KING, UNIVERSITY OF MASSACHUSETTS
MEDICAL SCHOOL

The Signs of Stress Overload and Exhaustion

Please take note of the signs and symptoms of chronic stress and burnout to see if they are or were present in the person you are trying to forgive, or in yourself.

Research shows that the chemicals and hormones the body releases during stress have these effects on us:[5]

1. Opens us up to cancer, and chronic infection and disease;
2. Encourages ulcers, swelling, pain, tenderness in the joints, and asthma;
3. May weaken the circulatory system, leading to strokes, heart disease and attack, and high blood pressure;
4. Affects the emotional system causing depression or aggression.

There is even evidence that intense psychological stress can change the brain's makeup, perhaps permanently.[5a]

When stress is chronic, it may easily lead to burnout, which has these physical conditions: [6]

1. Emotional, mental and physical exhaustion
2. Sleep disruptions
3. Headaches, stomachaches, body aches
4. Susceptibility to colds or flu

A person may feel many of the following attitudes and emotions when burnt out: [7a,b]

- Powerless, hopeless, helpless
- Drained, exhausted, sad, bored, cynical
- Frustrated, irritable, anxious, resentful
- Little satisfaction from work, so productivity is low. Sometimes the sufferer doesn't go to work
- Feels trapped in a situation from which one cannot free him or her self
- Unsure about the choice of job or career
- Withdrawn and cut off from coworkers, family and friends
- Insecure about capability, feeling like a failure

All of these are signs that something is drastically wrong. A person with the above feelings needs immediate help. If your unforgiven situation has resulted in these symptoms in you or another, you must understand that you or they were unable to function rationally or compassionately. When I experienced these symptoms, I also felt that life was not worth living. Through the grace of God, the *Power Forgiveness Process* helped me.

In these situations, alcohol and drug abuse often increase. Many times, people use alcohol or drugs to relax and get away from it all. This also includes prescription drugs, nicotine, and coffee. These substances become addictive because they are the only things that relieve the pain or suffering people feel. The problem, however, is not the substance, but the stress reactions that the person is unable to deal with. Around the world, Alcoholics Anonymous, Narcotics Anonymous, and 12-step recovery programs in general, have revealed that addiction is also a spiritual and emotional problem.

Pain

People in chronic pain often exhibit the above symptoms. Those living with unending pain are frequently not in their right mind, often making poor decisions for themselves or others. If you know someone like this, or you are this way, compassion and understanding are needed tools.

Barbara married a disabled veteran after the WWII. He was often in pain. He would alienate people at work with his impatience and then would quit for some reason. He had many jobs—always looking for a better place, and never finding it. His anger and rage scared her. She stayed with him because she knew he was a decent man who had to cope with too much pain. But, she added, his pain didn't justify the pain he inflicted her.

She was never prepared for the next outrage, or dropping of friends, or decision to move. Sometimes they separated. Her religion enabled her to forgive. Sometimes, she forgave only to keep the family together for the kids. His pain took its toll on her too, making her fearful and bitter.

People who have debilitating diseases or chronic pain have a difficult time and are often on painkillers or other drugs. These medicines affect their quality of life and personality. They struggle continually to control the pain and side effects of the medicine. Alcohol and illegal drugs are often used to handle the pain.

People around those in chronic pain also have a difficult time. It's difficult dealing with the emotional setbacks that people in pain cause. Children raised by someone in chronic pain, whether on painkillers or not, may show all the symptoms of those raised by alcoholics.

Max was a great guy; everyone loved him. He was successful at his work. At a party, people would always be around him telling jokes, laughing and drinking. At home, though, he had another face. The pain from an injury years before still tortured him. The kids had to keep quiet, couldn't have friends over, and were often verbally abused. No one outside the household realized what his family endured because "he was a great guy."

You need deep continuing inner work to come to forgiveness with these people. You may be confused because the drugs, alcohol, or medicines can also have their positive effects of relieving the pain so that the person will show a pleasant and even lovable personality. If you are forgiving someone in your past who was like this, the work is worth the effort. I recommend help, though.

Many times, the pain is camouflaged by alcohol or drugs and you miss it; and blame the addiction. This may get even more confusing and difficult when the pain is emotional. The sequence can often happen like this: original injury > pain >drugs or alcohol > their children injured emotionally > their children use drugs or alcohol > their children injured emotionally > on it continues down the generations.

Do everything you can to understand this cycle in your own family and work on it. Forgiving is the best thing you can do for your whole family, people around you, and generations to come.

Dealing with Family Burnout

Here is another fundamental area of stress to look at when you are working on forgiving family members. Dr. Charles Figley, distinguished researcher in trauma and stress, has written about heavy stress reactions that may occur in marriage. When unrewarding experiences replace a couple's dreams and expectations, the marriage will eventually suffer and ultimately end from burnout. *Family burnout,* as he calls it, is the result of efforts to correct or tolerate a bad situation in an intimate relationship. He says that there is a higher probability of family burnout when: [8]

1. One family member has a low level of satisfaction, causing a higher level of distress in the family,

2. The distressed family member disrupts the family routine for a long period of time and

3. The family member's expectation of a quality family life is much different than what he or she perceives is available.

Be aware of past family stress and burnout in doing this work. For example, if you are dealing with upsets with your parents, you need to remember that the level of stress at home affected their behavior. When you look at your family of origin, it is imperative that you step out of your own perspective as a child and view the whole family scene as an outsider, as the adult you are, with the experiences you have. You must do this or you will remain stuck in your own immature reactions. In fact, you are probably older now than your parents were then; consequently, you can be more objective than they were.

Likewise, employ your objective perspective to look at workplace upsets, to see how much workplace burnout is present in the people with whom you are upset. Look at how much you were or are affected by burnout. If your stress exhaustion was or is high, you did or will react with more upset than normal, possibly creating a trauma out of a situation that, for another, might be just an incident.

What You Can Do

In burnout and chronic stress, a person never sees a good way out of the miserable situation. The unrelenting demands and pressures cause him or her to give up searching for solutions.

There are many reasons why a person may react to stress this way, for example, poor belief systems, distorted thinking patterns, or early trauma. Nevertheless, the way out requires active self-examination, often with professional help or with people who can hold a loving and objective perspective for you.

The worst part of chronic stress is that people get used to it and see no way out. When stress is at this unremitting, chronic level, it kills through suicide, violence, heart attack, stroke, and cancer, because it wears people down. Chronic stress is difficult to treat and may require extended medical treatment, psychotherapy and stress management.[9]

If you have seen a friend, family member, or yourself having the above symptoms, please be aware that there are many ways to assist. Although I won't go over all of them here, I will say that doing *Power Forgiveness* allows you to come back more easily from the edge of overwhelm. In years of teaching stress management methods, I can also say that stress reduction methods take much longer to be effective when a person is holding resentments and anger at self or others.

You need to do whatever you can to help yourself manage these continual stresses. A therapist could help. Meditation is effective in reversing this cycle of stress and disease. As mentioned earlier, it is best to calm the mind before forgiving.

Removing upsets that have bothered a person for years, perhaps from childhood, has an obvious positive outcome. My grandmother-in-law did not hold upsets with people. I first met her when she was 96 years old. She was still sharp mentally, and talked wistfully of the newspaper route she had had in her 80s. She still looked attractive and held herself well. Her presence, smile, and loving eyes told me that she had found a secret to life – she had stopped holding onto the upsets of her early years and found peace.

What Do Trauma Survivors Need to Know?

Drs. Eve Carlson and Josef Ruzek have written a careful synopsis for the National Center for PTSD on what survivors of trauma need to know: [10]

- You can't protect yourself or others completely from trauma, it happens to many competent, healthy, strong, good people.
- There may be long-lasting problems following a trauma. Up to 8% of people will have PTSD some time in their life.
- After a trauma, sometime people think they are going crazy or are personally weak. This isn't true. Really are just experiencing the symptoms connect to a trauma reaction.
- Well-adjusted and physically healthy people can develop PTSD. If the trauma were severe enough probably anyone could develop PTSD.

Understanding the symptoms of trauma enables a person to better manage them and possibly decide about getting help. Even if a person does not have long-term effects from the trauma, reactions still occur close to the time of the incident.

Facing your trauma is often too hard to do alone. You might find a trauma therapist to help. There are many agencies that give trauma support and help. Note, however, that psychiatrist, psychologists, psychotherapists, social workers, and family therapists though licensed, are not necessarily trained in trauma work. [11]

Critical Incident Stress Management (CISM)

Around the United States, a powerful crisis recovery procedure is being used which is particularly suited to address the needs of victims of traumatic events. At present, it helps first responders—police, fire and emergency medical service (EMS) personnel—sort out their reactions to particularly difficult trauma scenes. Trained teams do the method, called Critical Incident Stress Management.

The men and women of our police, fire, and EMS departments around the world have my highest regard, because they are the first ones on the site of tragedy and danger. While they are expected to be there and help, that doesn't mean they are immune to what happens. Trauma takes its toll. As a volunteer police chaplain, I saw what they go through, first hand, and trained in CISM to help.

CISM is invaluable because it prevents the long-term consequences of trauma. The CISM team comes together with the first responders within the first hours or first days of the critical incident to help defuse the emotional upsets. The recovery statistics of personnel who have had CISM are impressive compared to those who had no such help.

It gives emphasis to:
1. early intervention,
2. direct action,
3. the gathering of facts,
4. the expression of difficult emotions, and
5. the mobilization of needed resources.

Such CISM interventions can have a deep impact by lessening a serious problem.[12]

This process is not currently used enough, even with first responders, but it needs to be so that we do not lose valuable service people to the traumas they have experienced. Because it helps the needs of victims of traumatic events as well, I hope in the future CISM will be used for all victims of trauma to ease the secondary effects of an immediate trauma. I also hope it will be used with our military service personnel in combat areas who deal with trauma every day. In addition, nurses, doctors and other hospital personnel need it regularly.

Trauma's Long-Term Consequences – PTSD

As noted earlier, a small percentage of people develop and maintain strong reactions to the memory of a trauma, especially when they have not had CISM or some other therapy for defusing the trauma. When a person has intense reactions to a trauma for more than a month, it is called Post Traumatic Stress Disorder or PTSD. In families of American veterans, rates may be high. In countries experiencing current or recent violent conflict, rates of PTSD for the general population may be high, for example: Algeria 37%, Cambodia 28%, and Ethiopia 16%.[13, 13a] In 2007, the PTSD rate for children in the Gaza Strip was 70%.[14]

PTSD is complex and intense. I've studied and worked with it, and had it myself for several years, which eventually forced me into forgiving. I am addressing it here because I've found forgiveness to be essential in dealing with situations that were unbearable. Why? Because there is always someone we judge responsible for the disaster. This can often include the survivor as viewed from his or her own perspective. Research has shown a definite correlation between forgiveness and a decrease in PTSD symptoms.[15]

PTSD was first identified during the Vietnam War. Doctors noticed that returning soldiers were incapacitated by nightmares and persistent flashbacks to the stresses they had experienced. This condition in World War II was called "battle fatigue". In the 1980s, psychologists started using PTSD as a term. Later, they acknowledged it could occur in anyone suffering from prolonged trauma, such as child abuse.[15a]

Dr. Charles Figley, who I mentioned earlier, one of the foremost authorities on the effects of trauma and PTSD, notes the following characteristics in the person with PTSD:[16]

- Re-experiences the most traumatic aspects of the event many times, in flashbacks, memory, or dreams
- Makes efforts to avoid exposure to reminders.
- Is on edge, unable to relax.
- Is unable to think about the event without being obsessed.
- Experiences symptoms for more than a month.

He or she can also exhibits these symptoms:[16a]
- Phobia and general anxiety (especially among former POWs and hostages and natural disaster survivors),
- Substance abuse,
- Depression and/or intense guilt,
- Psychosomatic complaints, increased hospitalization
- An altered sense of time (especially among children),
- Grief reactions and obsessions with death (especially among those who survived a trauma in which someone died or could have died),
- Increased interpersonal conflicts and outbursts of anger,
- Absenteeism, criminal behavior, and truancy.

If there has been family trauma, one or more family members may exhibit these symptoms, which will contribute to family burnout.[16b]

If you are suffering from PTSD, get help, if you are assisting another, get them help and especially get them to help themselves.

Brain imaging studies done by Bessel A. van der Kolk, MD, noted international trauma specialist and author of more than a hundred papers and several books on trauma, tells us that during a traumatic event, the part of the brain that does not have language, shows the most activity. The front part of the brain that is associated with speech and being able to talk about events, literally shuts off during trauma.

When a trauma victim does eventually "speak" it may be with the voice of rage, substance abuse, or even physical violence. This means that people don't necessarily need to talk about trauma to resolve it. Dr.Van der Kolk emphasizes the power of qigong, tai chi, yoga, dancing, and breathing in order to quiet the body down.[18] At his Trauma Center, they teach people self-regulation through biofeedback and use EMDR.[19] See Note A on EMDR and EFT (which has been used successfully for forgiving).

I recommend the National Center for PTSD website if you or someone you know is dealing with PTSD. You can also go to The American Association for Marriage and Family Therapy (AAMFT) webpage for more detailed information on PTSD and also a great deal of information on problems facing today's families.[20]

Forgiving and PTSD

Trauma or its aftermath often occurs because of the action of others. With the continuing lack of acceptance of what happened, resentment builds. Forgiveness can stop the continuing inner dialogue and replaying of abuses or trauma, or both. *The Power Forgiveness Process* works well because it deals with the whole situation in a complete and methodical way. Because of the intensity of the trauma and its long-term effects, I recommend doing the Power Forgiveness work with an experienced counselor.

Here is a letter from a client who had PTSD for 20 years. When I started working with her, she had fear of public places.

"Thank you so much for the time we spent together. The relationship between my husband and me is much better. He now prefaces statements and discussions with me with 'Now that we're communicating' or 'Now that we're friends'. We've already had several heart to hearts (something totally new in our marriage).

In one of them, by way of trying to explain my reactions to things he's said and done in the past, I began to tell him what it was like to be a child growing up in my parents' household. Out of nowhere came this violent discharge of grief that amazed me even while it was happening. Instead of suppressing it, I just let myself go. It lasted about a minute or so and then I was back to normal. It was SO visceral. I have not cried like that in over eight years.

Part of me is obviously very much present with and

connected to all the trauma and drama of childhood, but I keep so much distance between that part of me and my everyday-self and have for so long that I'm still struck with wonder at my reaction. For years I've been hypervigilant not to allow myself to go anywhere near things that are upsetting. Since early on in our marriage my husband pushed many of these childhood buttons; my deliberate compartmentalization of and distancing from the past has also cut me off from any intimacy with him.

Although ignoring the past has its advantages, it doesn't ever really go away. Now, after the relatively brief time you spent with me, I feel ready to tackle anything and everything - in small doses. I no longer care to live so entirely on the surface.

Thanks so much for putting me back on track. It's only the beginning, I know, but thank you for getting me started. And you made it so easy! Thank you!"

Within months of this letter, she and her husband left their apartment of seven years in New York City and moved overseas. Now she travels regularly by herself.

Compassion Fatigue

Another disturbing aspect of trauma is the secondary trauma that may occur from indirect exposure to trauma through hearing a firsthand account of a traumatic event. Repeatedly watching a traumatic event on television can bring this about. The clinician or any person listening to the vivid description of a trauma by the survivor creates thoughts or emotional response to that event which may sometimes result in a set of symptoms and reactions that parallel PTSD, such as re-experiencing, avoidance and being constantly on edge. This secondary result of the trauma is called *compassion fatigue* by Dr. Charles Figley and *vicarious traumatization* by Drs. Laurie Pearlman and Karen Saakvitne.[21]

Clergy, therapists, social workers, and anyone counseling others, need to be aware that dealing with trauma has its impact on them too. Professionals who often listen to people's traumas need to regularly renew a sense of satisfaction, inspiration and support for their work.[22]

Forgiving is effective even in the vicarious trauma of watching it on TV. We can do actions that help the victims and we can do forgiveness work when we find we are upset. If we look, sometimes we'll see that in some way we had a similar situation. The tools are here.

How and Why Self-Forgiveness Helps

We often feel in some way that we are responsible for traumatic events that occur in our lives. You can prevent those incidents from harming you further by finding forgiveness for your mistakes whether they are rational or not. This is vital especially if you have guilt around a trauma and are saying negative things against yourselves. Everything changes by dealing with your *If only* and *I should have* statements through finding forgiveness for yourselves for what happened.

In relationships that have had trauma, forgiveness of self wipes out the guilt and regret so that people can learn from their errors and establish a new way of dealing with future mistakes. Relationships built on love rather than condemnation are more satisfying, and allow us to proceed from our highest self. This is true in all of our relationships.

When people react improperly to a highly stressed situation, they often have regret, shame, guilt, and blame. How badly they acted may seem unforgivable. Forgiveness enters with the understanding that *Reaction happens!* By remembering that the reactive brain is not who the person is, you can step out of blame and away from your own guilt.

Remember also, you are not that reaction. It was only a powerful survival mechanism that inconveniently entered into a situation.

Trauma and Forgiveness

Remember that forgiveness has its timing. If a person is in the middle of a reaction to a terrible event, forcing forgiveness will not work, and will probably upset the person more. Initially, a person who is still reacting might need to use other methods including therapy. For the person willing to look at forgiving, Power Forgiveness therapy may be quite helpful when used along with the other accepted treatments.

I appreciate this comic statement because it hits so close to the craziness of self-condemnation:

From The Management:
The beatings will continue until morale improves!

PART IV

Doing the Work

Up to this time, we have set the stage for for-giving. In this next section, we will focus on what to do so that The Power Forgiveness Process succeeds easily.

"True forgiveness deals with the past—
all of the past, to make the future possible.
We cannot go on nursing grudges even vicariously
for those who cannot speak for themselves any longer. We have to accept that we do what we do
for generations past, present and yet to come.
That is what makes a community a community
or a people a people – for better or for worse."

Desmond Tutu –
From:
No Future Without Forgiveness[1]

CHAPTER THIRTEEN

Successful Preparations for Power Forgiveness

An Overview of Power Forgiveness

As I mentioned in the first part of the book, through the years I noticed different parts, stages and steps in this work of forgiving. You will go through these different levels with each situation you address. Sometimes you will go through them quickly while with other situations, you'll take more time. You will find, though, that the process goes through this natural sequence as you work on forgiving.

It takes time. How long is entirely up to you. Once I made the decision to forgive and committed myself to the process, I worked on it in one long sitting until I felt it was complete. Others find that it works better to take many sessions over a longer period. It really does not matter as long as you follow the *Power Forgiveness Process* outlined here.

Here are the major areas to *The Power Forgiveness Process*:
Part 1 – Identifying all your upsets
Part 2 – Forgiving all your upsets (this has several stages)
 • Stage 1 - opening to the upset.
 • Stage 2 - expanding your understanding and compassion.
 • Stage 3 - realizing you have changed your attitude toward that person.
 • Stage 4 - doing self-forgiveness on what you just forgave in Stage 3.
 • Stage 5 - giving thanks for the healing, then repeating stages 1-4 until all is forgiven.
Part 3 – Feeling the transformation

Forgiveness is a process—a series of actions, each having a set of steps, which brings about viewing a bad situation in a different, more flexible way. Forgiveness is the art form of moving the mind toward being more open, happy, and accepting of others and self. Often forgiving will not be effective until there is understanding and compassion. Once these enter, forgiveness might be automatic or the decision to forgive becomes easier, so that healing can occur.

Making the decision is difficult without digging deeply into the situation and without understanding how the mind is set up to prevent forgiving.

Power Forgiveness

In the book, we follow the different areas of forgiving through many questions exercises and suggestions. Through the years, I have been asked to simplify the process because people may get overwhelmed at its level of involvement. I've found, though, that this isn't necessary because the process itself speeds up as you become familiar with it. Forgiveness for most people is not simple and quick. While it can become faster with practice, initially it takes work. If you have reached this place in the book, you understand this and probably still have more work to do. The initial preparations to help you do this work more effectively follows.

In forgiving, you need to look more deeply at your past with the wisdom of the present and actually change the effects from the past. If you can add humility to the equation through the insight that, in some way, you have done a similar thing, and you forgive yourself, then your forgiving is permanent. This is the basic process and its goal. It brings transformation.

I had a therapists say, "This Power Forgiveness Process can't be effective. This is a lifetime of hurt. You can't let go of it just like that." This perspective comes from schools of thought that do not acknowledge the truth of who we are, and the power of a Divine Source, which assists in all of this. Einstein's statement is relevant here: "No problem can be solved from the same level of consciousness that created it."

If you are in the position of supporting this work for another person, as a facilitator, friend or counselor, you will assist them best by remaining in touch with your own Higher Power and by having a full positive regard for their effort as you witness them releasing resentment. It is far more difficult to do this work alone. The positive regard of the forgiveness facilitator for the person forgiving makes a great deal of difference.

Often, the facilitator/counselor needs to look at the same issues. In my psychotherapy training, we were told that the client would bring the therapist's issues into the room. Perhaps the client cannot or will not forgive, but in the process, the counselor sees something in his own life that is affected. In many ways, the support person or forgiveness facilitator is a participant in the forgiveness process. His or her role is extremely valuable. Your belief in the person affects his or her forgiving.

Review of Secrets & Essentials of Forgiving
The Small Shifts of Heart and Attitude

The most important discovery in doing forgiveness as a process is how quickly it can occur. This is because there are many small transformational shifts of the heart and thoughts that bring about major changes. With each of these shifts, we regain the life energy that was tied up in the mental and emotional upset.

Pay attention to your body during this work:

- Watch for that feeling of "ahhh" and relief.
- Notice shifts inside your body and in your major muscle groups.
- Notice changes in your body temperature and your breathing.
- Pay attention to your energy level and take breaks as you feel you need them.
- Notice shifts in perspective and understanding, which is the Aha! response.

Felt shift questions: Ask these questions to test for the felt shift:

1. Have I felt relief or release while working on this?
2. Is it time to take a break?
3. Have I felt a little love or understanding come into this?
4. Is it done with for now?

Keep the Essentials in Mind

Here are the key points to focus on during the process. Review them and keep them in mind to help your progress.

- **Hold the highest vision** – Focusing on your highest purpose or vision will allow forgiveness to take place. Focus on what inspires you to forgive.
- **Find meaning in forgiving** – Use a core value or principle in your life – like Wild Bill did in the concentration camp

and Amy Biehls' parents in South Africa. Find a deeper meaning in the situation.

- **Commit to the process** – Be willing to forgive. Intend to forgive. Decide to forgive.

- **Feel the feelings** – Keep feelings in view while forgiving. Look for the feelings under the surface. Avoiding difficult feelings is normal but not helpful in this work. You cannot let go of something that is hidden.

- **Find the truth** – Be honest – Truth heals. The truth will set you free! *When the truth is known, healing occurs.* Honesty with our self is of paramount importance to our health and well-being. *Defensiveness will prevent the truth of the situation from being seen and felt.*

- **Ask for Divine help** when you are not sure what to do or how to understand something you are working on. Be silent, and offer it to the Divine Help you have. Turn it over and listen. Have faith in Divine Love.

- **Be Grateful**—Anytime that you can be thankful to a person or about the situation, you change it. At the end of any forgiving, find gratitude. What did you gain from the situation? For what can you be grateful to that person?

The Secrets

The following counseling wisdoms are significant in helping people forgive. I call them secrets because few people use them in counseling.

The Secrets in doing this work:

- **Use your intuition.** Besides basic intuition, most of us have an inner sense of knowing the right thing to do.

- **Get support.** Help from others in forgiving moves you more quickly and easily through it.

- **Break down the situation** – Analyze it piece by piece, person by person. Break down big upsets by listing everything the person has done. Break down an upsets with an organization by listing all of the people who represents that organization. As you think of one, others will come to mind.
- **Look for earlier events** – Search for experiences in the past that are alike or similar to the one you are working on now. *Deal with the earliest people and situations in your life.* Appreciation of life deepens as we mend the upsets with our family, religion & culture of origin.
- **Access humility** – Humility enables us to bring in our compassion to try to understand another's situation. It quiets the snake brain and allows us to step away from the defensive part of us that needs to blame and attack to feel protected.
- **Use your imagination** – To truly understand the worldview of the person you are forgiving, walk in their shoes.
- **Forgive yourself** – *Forgiveness becomes permanent when you forgive yourself for the same thing you have forgiven another.* Then, you will no longer need to project your upset with yourself onto others to protect and feel good about your self

The Principles of Power Forgiveness

I. **The experience of healing is the result of a simple principle of the mind**: *Your thoughts cannot go in opposing directions at the same time and get anywhere.* Resentment, guilt, anger, and fear take the mind in the opposite direction from love, joy, and peace. Until you are willing to let go of these resentments and fears, you won't have the deep change you'd like.

II. **The intention** of Power Forgiveness is to "let it all go". That means all resentments and upsets with anyone and everyone. This is central coming into one's own full potential of life – spiritually, mentally, emotionally and physically.

III. **Willingness is essential** because it provides the beginning of the commitment that leads to forgiving. Sometimes a person needs to manage resistance and objections to forgiving by ensuring that none of the Myths of Forgiveness are standing in the way.

IV. **Put yourself into a comfortable non-threatening environment when you do this work.** The brain does its magic best when we feel safe. Then your higher thinking abilities can start working in harmony to handle your unforgiven stressful situation.

V. **Stop and calm down your stress reactions** anytime that you find you are being run by them. We are a complex mixture of mind, body and spirit not an ancient programmed stress reaction. It's normal for people to misidentify these reactions as themselves. They are not us!

VI. **Forgiveness is a movement of heart that opens us to being more compassionate and loving.** Performing acts of kindness or charity toward our self and others is healing and transformative. This is how forgiveness gets its power for the essence of our being is love.

VII. **Find the metaphor or symbol of the upset** because the mind thinks symbolically. The mind works in metaphors and symbols. For example, words are symbols of complex actions or things. In looking at difficult situations and people, find how they may symbolizes something else in your life that is similar, i.e., a boss might be like dad.

VIII. **Self-forgiveness relieves guilt, shame and the need to blame.** In our own healing, self-forgiveness is as important as forgiving others. Guilt and shame hold us back from living a full and happy life.

IX. **Know your values and beware of judgements.** We condemn others when they do not adhere to our own morals, values, and rules. Guilt and shame arise from not adhering to our own highest morals, value and rules.

X. **Forgiveness is a re-examination of our self and others in a different light.** Re-evaluating the standards by which we judge others and our self is an ongoing practice.

XI. **Our reaction to our outer world is a reflection of our inner one.** As you become familiar with this work, you will recognize that the world you see outside you is a reflection of what is going on inside you. That is why finding the projection is so crucial. Often, people are just showing you things about yourself and your judgements and rules. When you see this, all forgiveness becomes self-forgiveness.

XII. **Love is the key. Love is for giving.**

Preparing for the Process

A. *Have a pen and plenty of paper available.*

B. *Allow yourself adequate uninterrupted time* for this process. Depending on the stage on which you are working, you will need blocks of time of at least thirty minutes to two hours, or more. When I did my process, I worked many hours straight. However, I was quite familiar with inner processing.

C. *Eat, but don't allow food to be a distraction.* Be aware that when you are dealing with a difficult situation you will feel an urge to avoid the tough areas. Pay attention to cravings for food, cigarettes, or caffeine. Sometimes the desire to find distractions can provide a clue to the presence of defense mechanisms that prevent forgiving.

D. *Work with other people* as this can often assist you. Groups of people working together on their own forgiveness process have achieved excellent results.

E. *Have no drugs or alcohol* in your system. I'm not talking of medicines, but recreational drugs. These and alcohol temporarily deaden the consequence of stress. In any kind of inner work, they will often prevent you from going more deeply into a situation.

F. *Meditate, retreat, and relax.* Start with the easy ones first.

Angeles Arrien, PhD, one of my teachers in forgiveness says, "You cannot go further on your spiritual path until you do rectification work on your family of origin, your country of origin and your religion of origin."

Rectify means to make right. My own forgiveness work with my first religion brought back experiences of a deep connection to God that I had as a young person. I would not have regained that experience had I not made things right and moved back into a realigned relationship with my past.

Someone once asked me, "If you know your life is not going well but can't think of any bad stuff done to you, what do you do?" I recommended that he make a list of everything that upset him in the world. Once he wrote down the upsets, he gained a strong inroad into forgotten situations. It is like the smoker who knows he should stop but isn't ready. You have to be ready and willing to deal with what is going on inside yourself to forgive effectively.

A Review of the Basics

- Keep your motivation high through inspiration and your highest vision.

- Write either what is going on with you now or about a specific subject; this might be your most frequently used tool.

Writing down all your upsets and hatreds will provide you with the raw material for your *Power Forgiveness Process.*

- Don't take the most difficult situations first. Look at what you are *willing* to work on and release what you can. That will bring you the energy and the feel for what to work on next.

- Once you progress through some of the major upsets and can let them go, you will find that you have more energy and inner strength, which will move you quickly through the list. In all of this work, *you regain the emotional and spiritual energy* previously tied up in holding the unforgiven offense in place.

- With each act of forgiving, you should feel a change inside— *the felt shift.* When you allow each of the forgiven people to pass through your mind, be aware of your body, your heart, and your muscle tension. With many people on your list, you will know immediately that you have forgiven them because you will feel great; but with others, you will feel there is more to forgive. As you progress, you will forgive more easily, yet still get the same joyful, peaceful, or loving result.

- With true forgiveness, there will be no animosity at all. You will have a neutral or positive experience of the person in your mind. When you feel relief, joy, love or peace with each person you forgive, there should be no upset left. Do the same thing for each person or situation on your list.

- Sometimes a release occurs by simply acknowledging that you have done a similar thing to another.

- Use the Secrets, Essentials and Principles if you are stuck.

- Break down the upset as far as you can.

- As you go along you will find that the process will speed up. You will forgive more easily but still get the same joyful, peaceful, loving result—sometimes even more so. Toward the end, if you are doing the whole *Power Forgiveness Process*, you will just think of the person and be able to forgive because you have regained your personal power and Love.

"One cannot arrive at true nobility of spirit
if one is not prepared to forgive the imperfections
of human nature. For all men, whether worthy or
unworthy, require forgiveness..." [11]

INAYAT KHAN, 1882 – 1927
INDIAN SUFI TEACHER

CHAPTER FOURTEEN

The Power Forgiveness Process

The *Power Forgiveness Process* has three parts or phases.

Part 1 – Facing the unforgiven in our lives
Part 2 – Working on the incidents
Part 3 – Being aware of the transformation

In the first part, you are looking at all of the unforgiven people and situations in your life. You write up lists instead of letting them fester under the surface.

In the second part, you work on one person at a time or one specific thing of many the person did. This part deals with the basics in forgiving which we went over in the first chapters. When you forgive all of the people and no upset is in your life, a transformation happens, which is the third part.

Please Note: Because this is *The Power Forgiveness Process,* we are talking with dealing with ALL of your upsetting people instead of letting them fester under the surface.

If you are just starting out I recommend not writing down all of your upsets all at once unless you are on a retreat, supervised intensive, or close supervision where you are in a contained space and routine so that you are able to focus on the process and not be distracted by all of your upsets.

In doing this work alone, if you get distracted and too upsets you probably won't finish the process without help. If you have read the book completely and have had some success with letting go of your upsets and feel ready, then write down ALL of your upsets. But, you **must** immediately follow through with the forgiving. Don't wait.

If you do not feel comfortable with the process, then just take one upsetting person and work on him or her. Make sure that person is not your most upsetting one. You will get to the most "charged" person but not yet. Get familiar with the process and have some success at doing it first.

Part 1 – Facing the Unforgiven In Your Life

Write down the people, organizations, situations, or places with which you have resentment, hate, anger, fear, or critical judgement. You might find there are many negative acts connected to one person or just one thing. At this stage, you are simply writing down the situations that you **want** to deal with. (Just work with the ones you want to look at. If some are too upsetting, you can address them when you feel more confident with the process. For now do the forgiving that you can, that will bring you the energy to face more the upsetting situations.)

The main questions of this step are:

A. Who or what upsets me?

B. W hat are **all** the things that each person did?

Note: It is necessary to break down their offenses. Make sure you break down each offense into all of its pieces. One situation might have twenty different little situations that need forgiving. Likewise, a person in a big event might have twenty different offenses. Take care of each of those offenses before you work on someone else. It is easier to forgive the 20 separate acts than try to do it all at once.

C. After you have broken the situation down to its smallest parts, work on each piece until you've handled them all.

Here are questions to help look more deeply at A. and B.

1. When I look at my home environment, what do I need to release?
2. Who am I having problems forgiving?
3. Is there something I want to forgive myself for?
4. Are there any situations I just don't have the strength or willingness to let go of and forgive?
5. Are there acts that are completely unforgivable?
6. Are there situations that I am inclined to respond to negatively on a regular basis?
7. Are there situations where I am being ill-treated presently?

Write just enough to jar your memory. One sentence max or a phrase can be enough for the whole thing. This is for you to read, not someone else. You do not need paragraphs. I had 30 pages of one-liners. They weren't funny, but they were all down on paper.

The intention is to write all of your upsets down. Doing it all at once may mean staying agitated and upset in a victim stance, if that is the only emotional state that enables you to include everything. This is often too difficult, though some have done it. I wanted to feel the whole pain so that I could release it all completely. Often it is easier to take sections of your life and contend with those before going on.

After you have written your upset and broken it down, the next step is to choose what to work on first. Because this may be overwhelming, I recommend taking the smaller upsets first and get those out of the way. Some people like to jump into the hard stuff first. We all have our different styles and comfort levels. Few people are able to tackle everything all at once. Most often, it takes one-on-one forgiveness counseling or a forgiveness intensive with another or others to take it all on. Consequently, in one sitting take an area of your life and take care of it. Spend at least an hour on each sitting. When I work with people, I like to do several hours at a time but that depends on you and the person working with you.

Remember to review and use the essentials and secrets.

Part 2 – Working on an Incident
Stage 1 –The Opening Stage –
Unlocking an Upset

This is the preliminary stage for working on an upset. We went over this in Chapters 1 through 8 of the book. A full summary is at the end of Part II in Chapter 9. With the knowledge of the first chapters, this opening stage can go quickly.

Please note that this whole first stage on an upsetting person or single upset with a person can occur in moments. Once you understand each step, it becomes a checklist to make sure each is covered.

Here is a summary of the first stage (See Chapter 9 to go into these more deeply):

1 – Make the choice that feels right.

Break down the upset and select one offense.

2 – Look at your willingness

Make sure you are willing to face that upset.

3 – Focus on what inspires you to forgive.

The stronger the inspiration, the greater the likelihood of success. This inspiration carries your spirit forward to the quest for more understanding and compassion, carrying you through emotional blocks that come up.

4 – Deal with feelings effectively
When you think of each situation, are there other feelings underneath, or mixed up with the main emotion, like hopelessness, humiliation, or guilt? What were you afraid would happen at the time?

5 – Find your needs and the debt owed
Figuring out what the offender owes you is basic, along with the reality of what you want. What do they owe you?
See the needs, wants, and debts summary in Chapter 2.

6 – Look at the real result of holding on to this upset.
What is the payoff for keeping the upset?

- What are the negative consequences of holding on to this upset?

7 – Handle resistance and objections to forgiving
Make sure no Myths of Forgiveness are active. If you need to, look over the Myths of Forgiveness section in Chapter 3 to make sure none are in the way.

8 – See if you can forgive it.

- Can you forgive right now for yourself?
- Even though it is not deserved, can you forgive as an act of compassion toward the other person and yourself?

Taking the First Stage Deeper

The first stage of *The Power Forgiveness Process* deals with the basics in forgiving. Many people are able to get relief with those first steps. 1 through 8 basically follow the first chapters in this book.

The next stages take the process deeper to completion by:
- Delving further into the situation
- Changing our perspective about the person
- Looking at the inner mechanisms that tend to keep the real reason for the upset hidden

- Finding the positive in what happened
- Doing self-forgiving

Continue until all upsets are completed.

Stage 2 – The Understanding Stage – Expanding Understanding and Compassion

Understanding is a basic key in unlocking feelings and a closed heart when dealing with the realm of the heart as you are doing in forgiving,. After the opening stage where you start looking at the upsetting situation, you go into the second stage, where you go over methods and guides to aid in deepening your understanding and compassion for another and yourself. Any one of the following categories can bring the forgiveness you are looking for. Just keep going down the list of methods and their steps until you feel the felt shift of success.

By understanding how the brain works and how we use it, forgiveness students gain compassion for our humanness. Compassion quells the emotional fires of anger and resentment.

In human physiological growth, the emotional (limbic) system develops before the intellectual. Even teenagers' nerve cell developed is not complete in the area of the brain governing intellect. Because of the earlier development of the emotional system, the emotions are quite capable of shutting down our logical thinking side. We know from psychology and brain studies, however, that shining the light of logical analysis onto emotional upsets can help to alleviate the upset. This is because the linear thinking, analytical part of the brain, which is the left frontal lobe of the neocortex, is set up to manage our emotional system.

Ways for Increasing Understanding and Compassion

We can take many avenues to deepen our understanding of one another. This deepening often results in changing our perspective of situations. Change in viewpoint is really the art of counseling, whether it is with a friend, minister, forgiveness counselor, or psychotherapist. The methods that follow will enable you to be your own forgiveness facilitator. However, I recommend you work with someone familiar with this work so that he or she can carry you through the process, instead of your being both client and facilitator.

Here are helpful skills you have been reading about to aid in deepening your understanding of the situation, another person, and yourself:

Skill 1 – Look for Your Rules for Conduct

In our discussion of justice, we saw that it is necessary to be aware of our principles, values, and rules for behavior and conduct.

- Which of your principles did the offender not follow?
- Which of your values were rejected or disregarded?
- What rules were broken?

Now with each rule, principle and value ask:

1. Though others should observe these principles, values, and rules, is my expectation realistic, given the life experience of this person?
2. Have I always been able to follow these principles and rules myself?
3. Have I done the same thing in any way to others or myself?

Skill 2 – Change your Perspective

Shifting the way you see the person or situation is where you can begin to separate the person from his/her actions. As Terry Hargrave, PhD, points out, "When you, as the victim, can begin to understand the limitations of your victimizer, you can also begin to recognize his humanity." [1]

Sometimes, in order to shift our perspective sufficiently, we need a God's-eye-view. In situations that are apparently unforgivable, we must hold to our highest vision for ourselves. In this way, we can accomplish the necessary shift in perspective that will lead us to letting the upset go.

- Ask yourself: "Is it possible there are perspectives other than my own?" Again, initially, just the willingness to look at other perspectives is significant. Our desire to be right often overpowers our desire for the truth of the situation and blinds us from taking other perspectives.

One of my students complained vehemently throughout class about a building contractor who had cheated him and caused his family trouble. He was right from his perspective, and I agreed that what the guy had done was not decent. Nevertheless, I know that when I see a great deal of anger, there is more to look at than being right, if a person truly wants to feel better and heal.

It was not until he wrote his paper for that class that he saw how the contractor had also lost time and money. That shift in perspective, about the situation in general, and specifically about the other person's perspective, helped him to feel better. The change in view does not justify what happened, but it does bring understanding of why the contractor acted as he did.

A. Walking in the Other's Shoes

In your journal, write down the circumstances that surround the event you wish to forgive from the point of view of the person who hurt you. Using what you know of their background and early life, write down their version of this situation. Try to understand what it is like to walk in their shoes. This may be difficult to do, particularly for seriously upsetting situations.

Make use of meditation and possibly prayer to complete these exercises if you notice a great deal of resistance. Note in your journal where you feel stuck.

1. Write down what you believe to be the governing moral code that this person lives by and that should have influenced their behavior in this situation.
2. Write down what you believe were their fears and hopes, likes and dislikes.
3. What was it like growing up in their family?
4. What was it like to come from their culture or time?
5. What are their issues?
6. What is their emotional intelligence?
7. What was their expectation of you, of others?

If you do not have enough information about the person to do this exercise, ask someone who might know. For example, Lucy forgave her father when her aunt told her that, as a child, his father had suffered vicious treatment at the hands of his father, Lucy's grandfather.

As you write their version of the situation, look for the felt shift. Notice any difference in your understanding of the situation. Write any insights about the person that you may have experienced in this exercise. After you get familiar with the process, this can take only moments.

B. *What is the Big Picture?*

1. Write down how this situation might fit into your idea of Karma or a Divine Plan.
2. Was this person in your life to teach you an valuable lesson?

C. *Other Shifting Perspectives Questions*

1. What other ways could I see this situation?
2. Can I listen to others who might have a different viewpoint?

3. Can I get help from others?
4. How would an impartial observer look at this?
5. What have I left out? Have I skipped over anything where I may have contributed to the bad outcome?
6. What have I added that I should not have?
7. Are you holding onto this resentment out of loyalty to someone else?

For Completing this Skill:

- Make sure you have written down all the ways that the offender is correct and justified from his or her perspective.
- Be sure to pay attention to the felt shifts in your perspective and in your feelings during this stage.

Skill 3 – Face Your Defenses

Now that you have looked at the situation from the perspective of what you believe is the offender's point of view, it is time to look deeper.

The mind is set up to defend our goodness and rightness. Thus, as I discussed in Chapter 10, we often push wrongs we have done out of our mind and onto others. Then, we deny we have done that wrong action. One way in which we defend ourselves is by being hurt or indignant. By blaming what happens in our world on others, we seem to maintain our ideal self-image. It takes courage to consider that our reactions may have their source in the specific defense mechanism of projection – blaming another to avoid the pain of feeling at fault oneself.

If you can see that you have done a similar thing to that which upsets you about another, forgiveness becomes easier because humility has entered your perspective, enabling understanding and compassion to occur. For the moment, our defense about that wrong is undone. It will come back again if self-forgiveness for that action is not complete, which is why there is a self-forgiveness stage in this work.

Here are other questions to help you look for signs of projecting:
1. How would an impartial observer view this?
2. What have I added that I should not have?

Facing Defenses Summary Questions
A. Detach from it all by asking, "How would an impartial observer view this?"
B. See if you have done something similar yourself – perhaps not in magnitude, but in context – maybe not to others, but to yourself.
C. If you have, ask yourself:
    a. Can I forgive this person for doing the same thing I've done? Or for breaking an unrealistic value, moral code, or rule that I have?
    b. Can I forgive myself for doing the same thing?

So far, in this situation, you have:
- Examined your own responsibility in maintaining your hurt and resentment,
- Shifted your perspective sufficiently that you are able to see the offender's humanity,
- Looked at your own unrealistic expectations,
- Found unenforceable values and unrealistic rules,
- Gained more compassion and understanding for another's viewpoints.

Skill 4 – Work with Ways to Feel More Positive

A. Find a Deeper Meaning in the Event

Forgiveness will increase your capacity to love because it requires a shift in your vision of the world. With this new perspective, it's possible to look for a deeper meaning in the situations that you have released through forgiveness.

Questions to ask yourself:
1. What has this hurtful experience taught me about myself, the world, or other people?
2. How have I matured from this experience?
3. What have I learned about love and compassion, as a result of this experience?
4. How have my values changed?

B. *Appreciate What You Gained – Be grateful*

Gratitude is a powerful method for change that works at anytime. In forgiveness work, look for and acknowledge ways that the person has helped you. There are different possibilities and perspectives on this. Even a negative role model could have taught you something positive. For example, Ron was in a particularly unkind and vicious cult whose leader opposed the concept of love. Seeing how terribly people treated each other in this unkind cult, he decided to live his life as much as he could with loving kindness as his goal.

When you extend thanks to those who have taught you a major life lesson, you send love, the greatest healer. That love, oddly enough, heals you as you give to another.

Being thankful makes it easier. A powerful contemplation is to ask yourself, "What am I thankful for from this situation?" You ask this over and over until you are feeling grateful. I've seen people start this inquiry seemingly having nothing to be thankful for. They had to search their mind for anything to be thankful for. In the end, they realized that they were appreciative of many things as a result of this situation.

C. Give love

Can you imagine holding the person you are trying to forgive and just love them no matter what? Hold them as a mother or father would their child, perhaps not agreeing, but still loving. You might still disagree, but not with anger, or resentment.

Remember:

- At any time as you work on this, you might feel a <u>shift</u> inside yourself. This could be all you need to change it for good. You can always come back to it at a later time if need be. You will be quite surprised at what a small shift in perspective can do!! .

▶ **If** you forgave, go to the next piece in the situation you have already broken down.

▶ **If** you could not forgive the piece you were working on:

▷ See if it will break down further. Then do the opening steps on the newly broken down upset.

OR

▷ Look back further. Ask these questions:
1. What in my past reminds me of this?
2. Is there an earlier situation in my life that might be similar to this one?
3. What do I need to let go about my past, including my family of origin, to help me in this?

Then go back and do the above Understanding steps on these new items.

▶ **If** no change – take another incident from Stage 1 and work on it, and come back to this later.

Remember:

- If you find that it has not lifted, ask:
  1. "What other ways could I see this situation?"
  2. Are there others I might talk with who have a different perspective?
  3. Can I get help from others?
- Be silent, and give it to the Divine Help you have. Turn it over and listen. Have faith in Divine Love. You have done all you can do. Remember to ask for Divine help in seeing this a different way!

Stage 3 – Realization Stage

During your work on this person, you will feel a shift in your perspective and attitude. When this happens, take time to feel the change within and think of the person again to see if there is any resentment or hurt left. If there is, go back to where you left off in the Understanding Stage.

When you forgive the person or a specific action they did, the first level of forgiving on this is complete. Sometimes your work in forgiving will go fast. You might go through each stage in minutes. As long as you feel a definite emotional shift on each person's unpleasant action, you are doing fine. Eventually you will be able to forgive the person completely as long as you keep doing the steps on all their offending deeds.

When you feel forgiveness has occurred with this specific thing move onto the Self-Forgiveness Stage around this specific action.

End Result of the Realization stage

Somewhere along the way by using these skills for expanding understanding and compassion, you will:

- shift positively in your perspective about the situation or the person, and

• realize forgiveness for the person

When that occurs, go to the Self-Forgiveness Stage to carry the forgiveness work to completion on that specific offense.

Stage 4 – Gaining Self-Forgiveness

Because the world we see reflects our own mind and thinking, it is always useful to see that what you are dealing with pertains to yourself. Thus, for forgiving to be permanent, you need to address a second level of forgiveness, which is dealing with your own similar deeds.

The first part of this stage is personal responsibility. Here, you look at what the person did in the situation you have just forgiven to see if it has something to do with you. Here are questions that might help:

1. Is this unforgiven situation mirroring something about me?
2. Have I done anything similar to others? Or perhaps only to myself? (The magnitude might not be the same but is there a similarity?)

Note: Without self-forgiveness, there is the possibility that the upset will continue in other ways with other people.

The second part is to forgive yourself for the similar action you might have done to others or to yourself.

I don't know what it will take for you to gain self-forgiveness. Many people finally just decide to let go of the burden they have been carrying. Peter said to me after he did the process, "I saw that I have been in pain for enough years. That pain was my amends. I just decided enough is enough and was able to let go of the upset I had with myself on each thing that came up. As I did I felt more compassion for myself and could see how much I had been torturing myself. Each act of forgiveness was a relief for my heart."

Self-forgiveness questions: Use the following questions on the person you are dealing with in this situation.(Even though you might have been working on self-forgiveness earlier, this stage focuses on ensuring that your forgiveness work is completed.)

1. Am I prepared to forgive myself for the same transgressions I am willing to forgive in another?
2. Can I forgive myself for the same offense I have forgiven in others?
3. Do I feel any guilt around my own transgression for which I need to forgive myself?
4. What will it take me to forgive myself for this? Do I need to make amends to anyone?
5. For those with a Christian orientation, this question might help: Can I accept God's forgiveness of me on this?

When you feel you have forgiven yourself, you naturally go to the next stage to finish off this situation.

Stage 5 – The Healing Stage – Thanksgiving

With the completion of that incident, you have forgiven the other and then yourself. You experience a break in the intensity and a natural movement toward thanksgiving occurs. Here are questions to aid in the conclusion of the offense from that person. In this stage, you look at what you have learned and how it helped you.

Is there is something you gained from having this person in your life? Here you appreciate how far you have come in your life, and change your perspective of what happened with that person. Other questions from the gratitude section to assist are:

1. What can you be grateful for in this situation? What did it teach you?
2. Did its influence in your life make you stronger, more capable, or successful?
3. What did you learn?

4. How did the person or people help you?
5. How have they helped others?
6. How did they affect a positive change in your life?

When you have forgiven the situation and yourself, feel the successful completion of that situation. You should not feel animosity, and normally, there will be a sense of loving kindness toward the person involved.

In non-threatening situations, you might even want to extend appreciation to the person. For example, when Mary Lou dealt with an upset with a mentor, she sent her a letter of appreciation for the help the mentor had given her through the years.

Any of these ways might be appropriate to give appreciation:

• Thank you letter
• Flowers
• A letter of acknowledgement
• Acknowledging them in person

There may even be a desire for reconciliation. For now, just keep doing the process and go to the next part of this step, which is clearing up the next upset.

The Second Section of this Healing Stage is to take another situation that is bothering you. Go through the same process to success in forgiving that person and you by returning to the Healing stage until eventually there is nothing left to forgive. Repeat the stages until *all is forgiven.*

When all of your upsets are let go of, a peace, love, and joy will be there for you that you haven't felt for a long time. This takes you into the next part.

Part 3 – Transformation

Initially you might not notice all the changes that will happen in your life. Some will be subtle, some will be big. They will not only affect you but will spread to others around you. This is similar to the Christian concept of Grace. Of course, this experience is not restricted to Christianity but is experienced in every religion, because it is a letting go of our conscious upsets and moving into our heart. What actually happens is that the mind is able to move to another level of functioning. How long this stage lasts is up to the individual.

It doesn't mean that one is permanently enlightened, only that the person reaching this transformation views situations differently than before and functions in a more capable way. She or he will carry some of their not-so-normal behavior forward, especially those qualities not addressed with the forgiveness process. Power Forgiveness is not the ultimate life process, but it does enable a person to function at a higher level, giving a person effective tools to let upsets go more easily, allowing faster recovery and renewal.

Thank you for persisting. Bless you for doing this work.

Note: In Appendix F you will find the Summary of the *Power Forgiveness Process*. If you use it, just make sure you follow what I've said in this chapter and the preparations one, because that summary required the knowledge of Chapters 13 and 14.

The Shortened Power Forgiveness Process

When you find things are moving quickly for yourself, and you 1) understand projection and 2) can see it in your life, you might try this shortened form of the *Power Forgiveness Process*.

My own transformation came from the following steps. You have to remember though that I had had years of training in what is in this book concerning processes and defense mechanisms. And I had inner spiritual help. All of this enabled me to look inside myself and come up with answers.

If you have that inner skill and experience, you can try these steps. If you find you can't see how you have done the same acts in a metaphorical way, this shortened process won't work. That perspective is crucial in this specific process. If you don't feel the joy and increased energy from doing the following steps, then go back to the more complete process in this chapter and use it.

The Original Process

These steps begin after you have:

A. Found all the upsetting situations and people in your life and written them down, and

B. Chosen one person you are willing to work on.

With one of the offenses the person has done, ask:

1. What am I feeling about what they did?
2. What was I afraid of?
3. What value, law, rule or moral code of mine did they break?
4. Do I have an unreal expectation for them or myself to hold that law, value or rule?
5. Have I done the same thing in any way to others or myself?
6. Can I forgive them for doing the same thing I've done? Or for breaking an unreal value, moral code or rule that I have?
7. Can I forgive myself for doing the same thing? (An essential step.)
8. What are all the things I can be grateful to them for?

Then chose something else the person has done that you are willing to work on and do steps 1 – 8.

The next section of the book addresses how to keep an open door to transforming and forgiving.

Part V

After the Process

To maintain these benefits and to strengthen
them, there are several key actions to remember:
- Keeping a regular practice
- Staying inspired
- Finding inner and outer support
- Using in-depth tools for further forgiveness

"The ineffable joy of forgiving and being forgiven
forms an ecstasy that might well arouse
the envy of the gods."

ELBERT G. HUBBARD (1856 – 1915)
AMERICAN WRITER, ARTIST, AND PHILOSOPHER.

CHAPTER FIFTEEN

Continued Healing

After Deep Change

T he transformation I have been speaking of is a spiritual re-
birth. The potential of life opens up to us. The sense of
much deeper spirituality is often apparent. Dr. Herbert Benson
has an excellent book on the effects of this peak experience called
The Break-out Principle.

After you have done your forgiveness work, you'll find your life
has improved in many ways. These include:

- Release from emotional prison
- Living from the heart
- Finding a deeper meaning for your life
- Reconciliation possibilities

Without a way to channel this joy, love and deepening of life, a
crisis of meaning may occur in one's life. If we look at the Christian *born-again* experience, people become active in their churches,
and/or help and do activities to make a difference in their community. I believe it is natural to want to help others. Having a
positive effect in the world satisfies us. As social beings, we need
to feel we are moving in a direction that is noteworthy–not only to
us, but also to the greater whole–socially, spiritually or even na-
tionally.

Release from Emotional Prison

At this point in your inner work, you have let go of old hurts that have been holding you hostage. Once you release them, you free yourself from the destructive cycle of reliving the injury every time you think about it. Letting go of those wounds brings back plenty of positive emotional energy.

Forgiveness removes emotional blocks so that you'll see a more clear vision for your future. When you release yourself from the emotional prison of resentment, joy is the natural by-product. Joy is your best guidepost in aligning with the truth of who you really are, your authenticity. You can be fully in touch with the peace or love that gives your life meaning.

> "Love is the victor in every case.
> Love breaks down the iron bars of thought,
> shatters the walls of material belief, severs the chain
> of bondage which thought has imposed,
> and sets the captive free." [1]
>
> – ERNEST HOLMES,
> THEOLOGIAN, AUTHOR AND SPIRITUAL TEACHER

Living from the Heart

Any action motivated by resentment will lead you away from expansion, love, and joy. This includes servitude, which may sometimes masquerade as service to others; the difference is that the underlying motivation is resentment at feeling trapped. True service to others carries a surge of positive energy and love. This is living from the heart.

Forgiveness, particularly when done as a regular practice, allows you to live from the heart in joy and peace. Whether it is in your work or your close relationships, be mindful of the movement of the heart. To live from love requires a way to release these negative emotions once we have heard what they have to tell us. Holding onto them and re-feeling these emotions is what causes the damage to our capacity to love.

From my own experience, find help to correct your unloving thoughts if you aren't able to undo them yourself.

Deeper Meaning

Not only will your capacity to love increase but your vision of the world, yourself, and other people will shift. With this new perspective, you will discover a deeper meaning in your life because of what has happened to you. You might even have a God's-eye-view of your life instead of the restricted self-centered view you had before.

An example of this perspective is from a local police officer's dream that had this kind of effect on me. Jack has 20 years in law enforcement and has led an intense life. One night in a dream, he was surfing, which was his favorite sport. As he was going down an enormous wave, an angel flew next to him and said, "This is it!" He understood in the dream that it meant that this was the end of his life, and he said, "Well, this has been a great life, thank you very much. I have lived this life to its fullest. Thank you."

When I have relayed this story to others, they all have had the same reaction as he did. They felt much better about their life, and about what they went through and who they had become.

Forgiveness Affecting Us after Death?

Noted MD and near-death-experience researcher, Dr. Raymond Moody, wrote a book, *Saved by the Light,* with Dannion Brinkley about Brinkley's near-death-experiences (NDE). Whether NDE's are true or not we may never really know, I am going by what this well-known psychiatrist, Dr. Moody, reported.

While clinically dead, Brinkley reviewed his life from all angles, facing with horror all the damage he had done to others, and how those foul deeds rippled out creating even worse events. He was revived and vowed to reform his behavior and help other people. Because of the damage to his body from the first death and his heavy workload, sometime later he died again. This time *the review* included all the good he had done in his later life. He saw how those he had helped went on to help others. Then he heard a clear powerful, loving voice that said, "You can't get to the next level without forgiveness." He decided at that moment to let all his upsets go and forgive. Suddenly, he was part of the light of heaven. He had learned that forgiveness is an essential part of being in the Light. He was then told to go back and give this message to people.[2]

Reconciliation Possibilities

Reconciling if it occurs in a relationship, can feel like a blessing, but forgiveness does not always lead there. The person with whom you have the upset may be deceased, no longer in your life, or simply not open to a relationship with you. In such cases, reconciliation will not be possible, but forgiveness does not depend on it. You let your upset go whether you reconcile with that person or not.

After doing your forgiveness work, if you desire reconciliation, I recommend the following books:

- *Forgive for Love: The Missing Ingredient for a Healthy and Lasting Relationship,* by Fredric Luskin, Ph.D.;
- For Christians, Part Three of *Forgiving and Reconciling: Bridges to Wholeness and Hope,* by Dr. Worthington.

Besides helping you feel better, sometimes reconciliation is possible for the benefit of the person you have forgiven. After Kirk and Nate had entered into a financial arrangement, Kirk did not keep the agreement and Nate came out the loser. Nate, however, had forgiven Kirk and let the matter go but had nothing more to do with him. Later, a friend told Nate that Kirk was devastated by the situation and regretted losing their friendship. Nate called Kirk and apologized for not remaining in touch. Then, Kirk said, "I've been stuck for six months. I just cannot move in my life and I can't change anything about that situation. I'm sorry." For Nate, the matter was over when he forgave Kirk. For Kirk it was important for them to be reconciled. Nate said later, "If I had not wanted to reconcile, Kirk would not have come back into my life and enriched it, and he would have remained stuck with the loss of our friendship, and I would have too."

This ability to let go and reconcile is not solely human. In the book, *Natural Conflict Resolution*, Filippo Aureli from John Moores University, UK, and Frans de Waal from the Yerkes Primate Center at Emory University, document reconciliation in no less than 27 species of primates, including bottlenose dolphins and goats [3]

The ideal of the spiritual movement, Seicho-NO-IE, is to be reconciled with everyone. As the founder said:

"True reconciliation cannot be achieved by patience or forbearance with one another. To be patient or forbearing is not to be reconciled from the bottom of your heart. When you are grateful to one another, true reconciliation is achieved." [4]

I have found this idea and process to be quite helpful, not only in reconciliation, but also in self-forgiveness. Even further, we are really talking about reconciliation with life itself – to be grateful for everything and everyone in our life. This idea has been valuable to me through the years, especially when I get upset about events that are happening around me. When I can see the situation or person with gratitude, I feel reconciled. I can then more easily come up with an efficient solution to the problem that I perceive.

Giving a Meaningful Apology

When we see the importance of forgiving there is a desire to help people forgive especially when we have been hurtful to another. An apology is an especially effective way to help clean up the situation. Beverly Engels book, *The Power of Apology: Healing Steps to Transform All Your Relationships*, is a useful resource.

Maintaining Regular Practice

Keeping up a regular practice of forgiveness is the most effective way to maintain your success in this work *and* to quickly release upsets that arise. Although you might get surprisingly upset about something, you will be able to regain your balance and peace of mind more readily, and handle upsets with greater ease.

The best way I've found to maintain a regular practice is through an *evening review*. At the end of each day, make it a practice to forgive the upsets that occurred that day. For me, the best time to review the day is in the evening when I can find some quiet and uninterrupted time.

1. Mentally go over your day and clean up any upsets that have accumulated – those that you did not let go of at the time.
2. Release them.

If you find that you are having a repeated upset, you can be sure that forgiveness is necessary.

Re-Forgiving?

Just because you've rid yourself of all the upsets you can think of doesn't mean that more will not come up to deal with. Through the years, more upsetting events and memories might emerge. You have the tools now to sort them out. If you maintain a regular forgiveness practice, you won't be overwhelmed with what might come up.

If a major situation arises that you thought you forgave, know that there is just more work to do. When you look closely, you will see that what has come up now is a different aspect of that situation. Likewise, people you thought you forgave might again come up. This different aspect of them was not forgiven originally.

Arnie finished the *Power Forgiveness Process* feeling great for months. One night an old girlfriend contacted him and they proceeded to get into an argument. He was daunted because he thought he was finished with his upsets with her.

Please note: Your processing does not guarantee upsets will not occur again. They will! This is because our defense mechanisms are still there, as is the reptilian brain. Sometimes we forget our commitment to our highest potential and sometimes we go on automatic and get surprised. These will probably all happen. You will find, however, that you will sort out what happened faster and forgive more easily, feeling back on top more quickly than ever before.

Humor

You might even find that you will laugh more at your reactions as opposed to condemning yourself. With that laughter all aspects of forgiveness will come.

"Laughter is the shortest distance between two people."

VICTOR BORGE

A new phenomenon called Laughter Clubs, was started by Indian physician, Dr. M. Kataria. Today, the laughter movement has become a global phenomenon with over 6000 clubs in 60 countries. Because Laughter Clubs realize the great power of laughter and its efficacy as the best prescription for wellness, they have brought laughter to the lives of many people suffering from upsets that are physical, mental and emotional. They even have a forgiveness laughter![5]

Beware of Old Habits of the Mind

Even though you have transformed your mind, old neural brain patterns may still show their face. You are still human. Reactions will occur but will dissipate more quickly.

The day after my own transformation, I woke up with the same early morning reaction to the day that I had had for months, "Oh no, not another day!" Then I came to my senses, remembering that the day before had been incredible. I understood that my reaction was just an old habit. It went away immediately. I heard that *Oh no!* reaction upon waking up for another couple of weeks with its strength diminishing each morning. At the end, I laughed at it. The laughter and joy remained for years upon awakening.

Feed Yourself the Good and Positive

In religion, as in traditional psychology, there is the question of how to deal with upsets. In psychology, we analyze what is happening and has happened in the past. We might try to change present behaviors or get an understanding of past events that might have caused the upset. We have done a great deal of that in this book. Handling a problem at its own level can take quite a long time to resolve, but it works.

It is more efficient to take care of the problem from a higher level of magnitude—the spiritual state of mind. From this level, changes occur more easily. To get to this level of mind, the question becomes, "Where are you putting your attention, your conscious mind?" The approach is to move toward the positive aspects of life and towards the Divine. The only problem with this placement of mind is that a mind in turmoil has difficulty finding the positive. Unforgiven situations will always continue to create turmoil until you work with them.

Even after forgiveness, or without it, there is often the question of how we find the positive. This is a question of desire. To feel better more often, *feed* your mind more of what it needs.

What is the best food for your mind? If you want peace, then feel peace, be more peaceful. It is not always what is in your mind that is the problem, but what you keep feeding your mind.

Gene, a client and cult survivor, spent years in recovery from the atrocities of being mind-controlled by a particularly abusive cult. Every day he replayed the upsets, hurts, and betrayals. "Eventually, I became so depressed that I saw no reason to keep on," he confided. Through the help of friends, he started letting go and forgiving. However, that was not the only thing he did. He started going to a church that was loving. He meditated. He read inspirational books regularly. He stopped watching the news and commentators on TV. He started hanging out with people who provided a more positive influence for him. He started feeding himself better mind, soul, and heart food. His depression went away, and he was able to maintain feeling good by keeping inspired and positive as opposed to bringing himself down with the daily onslaughts of negative news and views.

Mary, a psychotherapist, said her whole therapy practice changed by seeing that it is not enough to stop negative thought patterns. "We must put in the positive. Just like in a good diet, we need to increase the good food, not only stop the bad."

Values and Strengths

By putting attention on our highest values and strengths, we function better. Dr. Seligman, the father of Positive Psychology, has the Values in Action (VIA) non-profit organization.[6]

This research organization is advancing the science of positive psychology by undertaking the systematic classification and measurement of widely valued positive traits, which they call character strengths; examples are authenticity, persistence, kindness, gratitude, hope, humor, forgiveness and so on—each of which exists in degrees in us. Forgiveness is only one of the strengths.

The idea is to find your key strengths to take advantage of them and to strengthen ones you want to be stronger.[6a] For more information on these strengths and developing them, I recommend Dr. Seligman's book, *Authentic Happiness: Using the New Positive Psychology to Realize Your Potential for Lasting Fulfillment.*[7]

The forgiving mindset lets us engage our tragedies and trauma at a higher level so that healing can occur. To me, the ultimate work is the one that lets us know The Divine and Sacred of Life. While Power Forgiveness definitely opens the door for this, there are many other qualities besides forgiveness that need developing after opening the door to forgiving.

In-Depth Tools for Forgiving

CPR –Three concepts, Communication, Perspective, and Responsibility, are at the heart of successful forgiveness.
- Communicating about what is going on
- Shifting your perspective or viewpoint on it, and
- Taking Responsibility

These function as ongoing individual practices in the overall forgiveness process. Think of these three activities as three categories of tools in your toolbox.

You will use them continuously during your forgiveness work. You will recognize most of them from the previous chapters. I have brought them together here so that you can go down them quickly to use what might work for you in the moment instead of going through the whole *Power Forgiveness Process.*

The following is a summary. (For more in-depth work on these, see Appendix B.)

Communication

- Talk to yourself and others about the situation. Use journal writing and dialoguing plus conversations with others to communicate the hurt and your desire to forgive.
- Pray as a method of communication.
- In your imagination, communicate thoughts of love flowing from your heart to the offender's, until you feel a shift in attitude and energy.

Perspective

- Walk in the other person's shoes. Empathy for the one who hurt you can be the key to free you.
- Take a broader perspective: look at the big picture, the God's-eye-view.
- Observe the negative consequence of holding on to this upset.

Responsibility

- Recognize your responsibility in keeping the upset alive. See how you have participated.
- Be aware of defense mechanisms that are keeping you from letting go. Be honest with yourself. Have you done the same thing to others or yourself?
- Search for the rules that you feel have been broken. Are they valid? Whose rules are they? Do you always follow these rules?
- Look at how you may be benefiting from not forgiving; what are *the payoffs?*

Stay Inspired

Make it part of your practice daily to read inspirational materials that keep you aligned with your highest vision for yourself. Associate with like-minded people.

With the forgiving mind active in your life, spiritual understanding deepens. In contrast, those who cannot forgive condemn themselves to constricted lives of fear and anger requiring them to develop protection and defenses.

So look now and see if there are inspirational writings, a church, or organization that can help you to continue with forgiveness.

Give Support—Help People Forgive

The most powerful way to maintain your forgiving attitude is to teach it. Some people have also formed Power Forgiveness groups to help others forgive. This is the original vision that I had of the earth becoming more harmonious and peaceful – people helping others forgive. It went on like that spreading around the world. We have the tools to do it. The Forgiveness Foundation is here to help.

Give forgiveness workshops at your church, community center, or local college. Use this book as a guide.

"As a goal commonly advocated by all the world's religions,
forgiveness can be a truly transforming experience
that allows us to move beyond our
often selfish desires and needs."

HUSTON SMITH
THE WORLD'S RELIGIONS, 1989 ED.

CHAPTER SIXTEEN

The Ultimate Result

F orgiveness is an act of inclusion—that is what love is. It includes. That is what The Divine is. Our joy at the deepest level of ourselves is to go beyond our small stimulus-response self. At the highest level, we want an alignment with integrity—God in Its many aspects.

I have seen people who are enthusiastic about forgiveness go out to teach it at their church or in other places. Some, like me, have had inner visions of what they might do to help. This is why I created *The Forgiveness Foundation*, I spoke of in Chapter 1. It came out of a vision of the possibility of a forgiving world, and out of a prayer for guidance about what I was to do with my life. My mind opened up and I saw people all over the world helping others to forgive. I kept hearing The Forgiveness Foundation. A year later, it was a legal, approved non-profit.

What You Can Do

Whatever movement there is inside you that gives more meaning to your life is essential. Start where you are, not where you think you should be. Meditation is a great tool to align with the Divine Inspiration that is always there to assist. We have inner help to realign our mind and heart, which will assist us through the infinite possibilities in our life. The primary step is lining up our mind with the Divine Mind. While mistakes and disappointment will always occur, the tool of forgiveness and aligning with our Higher Power will bring joy, as well as love. With forgiveness, it's easier to align with the Sacred Tabernacle within – the Source of life and love. Peace and understanding will then come naturally.

"Go confidently in the direction of your dreams. Live the life you have imagined."

HENRY DAVID THOREAU

Increasing Trust

To connect to the highest potential of life takes trust.

Trust takes time. We are not used to it. Our reptilian brain is still there and wants to protect us. It warns us of the pitfalls and shows us the negatives. This is natural. Fears will still come up, but now we deal with them more easily. Building trust in life, as well as in love, takes an inner practice of continually going back to peace and love. Then inner help will be more available for us than we ever thought possible to manifest what we want in our lives.

The secret to trust is gaining self-forgiveness. You cannot trust in life if you feel you are unworthy of life's gifts. I remember a story from a workshop by Doris Donnelly called *Seventy Times Seven*, where a man lost all of his brother's and sister's money that he had invested. Of course, he felt terrible. It was a bad mistake. Each family member forgave him. Nevertheless, he would not accept their forgiveness and removed himself from the family altogether. This was a terrible loss for him and them.

I believe that the greatest source of long-term unhappiness is being away from our connection with our highest nature, the

Divine Aspect of life, whatever you may call it. The greatest reason for our separating from this true Source of life is resentment and grudges. Cleaning these up is a primary step to a fulfilling life. Forgiveness is, of course, a vital step, like digging a foundation and pouring the concrete. The development of our Spiritual nature, however, is beyond the scope of this book.

Ongoing Forgiving

Through new life experiences, you are continually made aware of past incidents that might bring up resentments. If you don't take care of them, they will accumulate again, causing disaffection with life. The forgiveness done in the past was valid for those things that you forgave. Now you need to forgive the issues presenting themselves today. For many, the second level of forgiving is much easier than the first. For others, those new areas of forgiving might be the deeper ones that were repressed and hidden from view. These might be more difficult.

Jeremy felt great about his forgiveness work on his parents and had a pleasant relationship with them when he was on one side of the state and they were on the other. When he moved into the same city and saw them more often, old issues he had forgotten re-emerged. These caused a rift with his parents until he finally sat down and did a "mini" forgiveness intensive specifically around the old issues he'd forgotten.

As we forgive more and more, we become a "forgiving person" instead of a person who just uses forgiveness.

Final Statement

Neither the field of psychology nor religion understands mental and emotional health. A continuing use of forgiveness can change the face of mental health because it puts our mind's well-being into our own hands, opening us up to a potential which is far greater than that provided by our survival mechanisms alone.

The field of mental health must change. Though, there are good methods in psychology that help a person let go of upsets and heal relationships. I believe that psychology is not effective enough in bringing mental and emotional health to our society because of the rejection of the concept of forgiveness and the importance of letting go of all upsets. Thus, forgiveness continues to be misunderstood because it is associated with condoning, reconciliation, and being hurt again.

For the health of our society and communities around the world, we can no longer allow this maligning of forgiveness to occur. We cannot afford declining mental health and increasing acts of violence. The legal and prison systems in the United States and around the world are operating mainly on retribution, revenge and punishment with little mediation and rehabilitation involved. This can change. We can start using forgiveness in our lives for taking care of our own mental health and setting limits on harm to others and ourselves.

As I've shown throughout this book, there is a reason for the unacceptability of forgiving even beyond the rift between psychology and religion, which is the rift in our own minds as well. It is the split between our highest and true-self versus our basic survival-self. Both are part of us. One gives us our highest vision and goal of community, peace, and kindness. The other protects us by seeing limitations and problems but can also keep us small, fearful, and seeking revenge.

Forgiveness raises our ability to remain in control of our thinking, pointing it toward the highest within us to bring a joy, peace, and love far greater than we have had before.

Forgiving is critical to our mental health, emotional well-being and spiritual fulfillment.

The Ultimate Result

I've met people through the years who don't understand the emphasis on forgiveness that many people have. It is not that they are unforgiving, just the opposite. They don't hold upsets with people. They have the humility within them not to take offense at people or God when bad things happen. They retain a love of life and Spirit. This requires a state of mind that has great compassion and understanding for neighbor and self. I believe this capacity is in each of us because The Divine is available to each of us.

The ultimate result of this work is the deepening of our connection to others, to life, and to the Divine Presence and sacredness in our lives. With the tools of forgiveness:

- We can have love, peace and kindness among us;
- We can be our genuine selves, living the joy we deserve; and
- We can have a knowing bond to the Source of life and love.

A Vision for Forgiveness

Because we already have sufficient forgiveness methods right now to transform our lives to ones of love, peace and joy:

- We will promote forgiveness sufficiently so that people will not doubt the power of forgiving.
- We will choose to be happy instead of being right.
- We will chose to be loving in relationships for we know that is more rewarding than being resentful.
- We will recognize that we are the first to be healed by forgiving. We never know how it will affect another.
- We will understand that without forgiveness first, there is no true reconciliation.
- We will teach our children how to forgive and to grow up willing to forgive so that they will have happier lives with much less conflict.

- Our hearts will allow differences with other people without blame for those differences.
- Friends will counsel friends to forgive instead of just agreeing with how bad things are.
- Individual and couples counseling will use the many methods of forgiving to help people let go of the upsets with themselves and others.
- Schools will expect social proficiency through teaching communication skills, forgiveness, and conflict and anger management so that students' minds will be open to creative win-win solutions to a conflict.
- Clergy will not only preach that forgiving as important, but will teach people how to do it. They will put on forgiveness intensives and workshops to enable their congregants to clear their minds and hearts in order to live deeper spiritual lives – experiencing God.
- Conflict Resolution programs throughout the world will use forgiveness regularly. There is no true conflict resolution without the movement of heart that forgiveness gives. Forgiving brings the capacity to hear what the other person is really saying or wanting.
- Anger control groups will use forgiveness as an important tool for healing.
- Conferences on healing will address forgiving as a powerful agent for health instead of barely mentioning it.
- PTSD will no longer be so incapacitating because forgiveness of self and others will be part of the healing process.
- Psychology will hold the torch of forgiveness as a precursor to mental health.
- Law students and medical students will be taught the power of forgiving as a regular course of study in their schools.

- Judges will require defendants to go to counselors or groups on forgiveness when appropriate.
- Nations will ensure that their representatives and most valued negotiators are also accomplished in forgiving.
- Nations will establish and promote their own Truth and Reconciliation programs to bring about healing among races, ethnic groups and religions.
- The Forgiveness Foundation will no longer be necessary because churches, schools, universities, governments, and households will have taken up the cause of forgiveness.
- The healing among religions and nations will bring us to a new era of non-violent, compassionate communication and interaction.

Thank you for developing the skills to forgive.

APPENDIX

A. The 12-Steps of Co-Dependents Anonymous
B. 24 Forgiveness Methods – CPR For Forgiving
C. Prayer of Reconciliation

D. 1. How We Are Likely To Feel When Our
      Needs Are NOT Being Met
   2. Feelings Likely To Be Present When
      Your Needs Are Being Satisfied.
E. The Principles of Attitudinal Healing
F. Power Forgiveness Process Summary

"Forgiveness is the answer to the child's dream of a miracle by which what is broken is made whole again, what is soiled is again made clean." [9]

DAG HAMMARSKJOLD
FORMER SECRETARY GENERAL OF THE UN

The 12-Steps of Co-Dependents Anonymous

1. We admitted we were powerless over others, that our lives had become unmanageable.
2. We came to believe that a power greater than ourselves could restore us to sanity.
3. We made a decision to turn our will and our lives over to the care of God, as we understood God.
4. We made a searching and fearless moral inventory of ourselves.
5. We admitted to God, to ourselves, and to another human being the exact nature of our wrongs.
6. We were entirely ready to have God remove all these defects of character.
7. We humbly asked God to remove our shortcomings.
8. We made a list of all persons we had harmed and became willing to make amends to them all.
9. We made direct amends to such people wherever possible except when to do so would injure them or others.
10. We continued to take personal inventory and, when we were wrong, promptly admitted it.
11. We sought through prayer and meditation to improve our conscious contact with God, as we understood God, praying only for knowledge of God's will for us and the power to carry that out.
12. Having had a spiritual awakening as the result of these steps, we tried to carry this message to other codependents and to practice these principles in all our affairs.

Working In-depth with the Forgiving Ways

24 Forgiveness Methods – CPR For Forgiving
~ Ways to Breathe Healing into Your Life ~

Communication

Communication often enables us to step out of an upset and achieve a better understanding of a situation. Communicating with people who agree with our grievances and resentments keeps our upsets in place. Relief occurs by communicating with others, our self and beyond our self, with the intention of gaining insight. Here are some communication methods you can use.

Letters of Hurt, Response And Gratitude
See The Letters Exercise in Chapter 6 & 7 for this.
Do not send the first two letters, but consider sending the gratitude one.

Dialogue Process
Writing a dialogue process in your journal about the situation is powerful. Engage your full honesty and mind. You do this by writing about your upset and then asking yourself questions that come to mind about the situation. When you write start with one of the questions. You might then ask, "How could they have done this?" Then search your mind for a possible answer. Once answered, ask the next question that comes to mind. We often do this with friends when we try to understand something, which can allow intuition to come forward. Then ask the next *burning* question that comes up for you.

Another version of this process is to answer the question as if the other person is actually answering it.

To start, ask yourself what you would like to know the most about the situation you are dealing with. Any of these questions will help start the process.

- Down deep, what is causing this upset?
- How can I take control of my anger, revenge, and attack thoughts?
- How can I see a different viewpoint in this situation?

Sending Love

Flow love from your heart to the person you are upset with until you feel a shift in attitude. In your mind, actually picture him or her in front of you and hug them, sending love to them from your heart. Do this until you feel a heartfelt connection with them. Can you love them no matter what? Can you hold them as a mother or father would hold their child, perhaps not agreeing, but still loving?. That would be enough for the upset to be gone. You might still disagree, but not hatefully, angrily or resentfully. Forgiveness is a movement of heart. Hold the person and feel the love dissolving the upset until it is gone.

Communicating with Others for Information

- Is there anyone who would give another viewpoint and not just side with you?
- Is there someone from whom you can get more information about the person you are trying to forgive?

Perhaps you could talk with a brother or sister of the person, a friend, or others who might be able to give you a better perspective of the person. A client gained compassion and forgave his father when he learned from his aunt how vicious his father's father had been to him.

Prayer

Prayer is a very powerful vehicle for help in forgiveness. All of the following types of sincere prayers are effective methods for relief.

- Pray: For help to see it differently, like repeating over and over, "Please help me to see this in a different way."
- Pray: To be relieved of the upset altogether.
- Pray: For reconciliation if that is what you want.
- Say it over and over until a change is noticed. "I forgive you, you forgive me, we forgive each other." The key is to feel it happening each time.

Be prayed for by people. There are prayer groups in most churches that will pray for people. I have been prayed for and got significant results, even though I did not know at the time that I was being prayed for.

Research findings in the past few years are showing that prayer effects healing. This has been known in the religious community for a long time, but now actual research in hospitals is proving it. People being prayed for recover sooner from serious problems—even when they do not know they are being prayed for. (Dossey 1993)

You repeatedly say "I forgive" with full intention thinking of all of the aspects of the situation. See the Angel of Forgiveness Prayer in Chapter 4 at *The Simplest Forgiveness Practice.*

Feelings

Communicating your feeling about a situation is important. Without looking at feelings, a situation often will not release. You have to be aware of what is there to be able to release it.

Write about or talk with another person about any of the feelings that are affecting you in a situation. They may be sadness, anger, hurt, depression, apathy, guilt, embarrassment, humiliation, regret, blame or shame, to name a few. All the different feelings need looking at. You can ask:

- "What am I feeling about what they did?"
- "What was I afraid of?"

Journaling

Keep a log in your journal of:

- How often the upset comes into your mind during the day.
- The situations that trigger it.
- Earlier times this has occurred.
- Write on how forgiveness can change these recurrences.

Thankfulness

In forgiveness work, looking for and acknowledging ways that the person has helped you is powerful. There are different possibilities and perspectives on this. Even as a negative role model, a person could have taught you something positive. When you extend thanks to them, you are sending love, the greatest healer.

- What did you learn from them?
- How did they help you?
- How have they helped others?
- How did they effect a positive change in your life?

Having thankfulness in general in a person's life makes it easier. A great meditation/contemplation is to ask yourself, "What am I thankful for?" You ask this repeatedly until you are feeling great. I have seen people start this having to search their mind for something they are thankful for. In the end, they are appreciative of many things in their lives.

Appreciation

Any of these ways might be appropriate to give appreciation:

- Thank you letter or Flowers
- A letter of acknowledgement
- Acknowledging the person when with them.

Talking with the person directly

- Is there any way to talk with the person to come to a better understanding of what happened?
- Can you do this without it becoming abusive or harmful to either of you?
- If you can, it helps to let go of trying to get your point across. Just try to understand what their mindset was. You might be surprised.

Perspective: Different Ways of Seeing the Situation

The fixed, unmoving perspective or viewpoint holds resentments and grudges in place and does not allow forgiveness to occur. Thus,

any way that can be used to loosen that unmoving perspective will help in letting go of its negative effects. Here are different ways to work on seeing the situation in a different way.

Projection

Turn around the situation you are looking at and ask:

- Have I done the same thing to another? Or to myself?
- Is this similar in any way to something I have done to another or myself?
- Is this similar to a family pattern or the actions of someone else in my family?

Walking in the other's shoes

- How do they see the world? What do they fear? Love?
- What are their likes and dislikes?

- What was it like growing up in their family?
- What was it like being in their culture or time?
- What is their emotional intelligence?
- What was their expectation of you, of others?

If you cannot answer these questions, then you have no idea about this person.

Finding who

Often behind the broad issue situations in the world that you do not like, for example, racism, there is a person or several people who represent that situation in your mind.

- Who are the people you think of when you see this upsetting situation?
- What is it about their behavior that upsets me?
- What does their face look like, what did they specifically do?
- Was every person like them doing the same thing?
- In your experience, have all of them been the same way?

Challenge

- Can you see it as a challenge to overcome rather than a punishment or attack? What would be the challenging solution?
- How would an impartial observer view this?
- Is there anything else going on here that you have a hunch about?

The Big Picture

- Are you sure they are not in your life to show you something about it?
- Could this be part of a Divine Plan or Karma? Or, to show you a better, more effective or happier way of being?

Turn it around

- Write down all the ways that they are correct and justified from their perspective.

Highest perspective – *See* the love

- What would the highest part of yourself do? Why?
- How would you see them with the eyes of love? (For Christians it could also be, what would Jesus do?)

Responsibility

Regardless of what a person says or does to you, your response is your responsibility, not anyone else's. Here are methods to help:

Validity and reality of rules broken

- List all of your values, laws, rules, or moral codes that they broke.
- Looking at each, ask: 1. Where did this rule come from? 2. Is it a valid rule, code, etc. or one that needs re-evaluation?
- Then ask: 1. Do I have an unrealistic expectation of them to hold that law, value or rule, especially if I have done the same thing in any way to others or myself? 2. Do I have an unrealistic expectation for myself to observe that law, value, or rule?

Amends & asking for forgiveness from another

- Do you need to make amends for the harm you have caused?
- What do you need to do to make it right?

Payoff

- What do I get by keeping the upset going? Write down any benefits. Who benefits and how?
- Is being right more important than being happy?

Being a Victim

- How long has your victimization by them been going on? How long is it okay to let them be in control of your happiness?
- Can you perceive yourself as a possible contributor to the problem and not just the victim?

Negative consequence of holding on to this upset

Sometimes people do not realize the negative effect that holding onto their unforgiven situation is causing in their lives. Here are some questions to look at around this:

- What are you really getting out of this upset? List the negatives.
- What is happening to your family by holding onto it?

- How strong are love, peace, and joy in your life? Could being finished with this situation increase love, peace, and joy in your life?

Personal Responsibility

- Do I want to keep this situation alive?
- Even if "they" seem to be the sole cause of the problem, how might be I keeping it going?
- Is my logic getting in the way of the right thing to do in this situation?
- Are my emotions getting in the way of the right thing to do in this situation?
- Am I turning people to side with me to justify my position?
- What was my part in all of this? Did I make it worse?
- How can I take care of myself better?

Gratitude

Gratitude is a powerful method for change that works at anytime.

- What can I be grateful for in this? What did it teach me?
- Did their influence in my life make me stronger, more capable, or successful?
- What did I learn from them in the end for which I am grateful?

Prayer of Reconciliation by Dr. Masaharu Taniguchi
(Some sentences removed for simplicity by Dr. Dincalci.)

What is the Prayer of Reconciliation? As the name implies, it is a prayer in which one becomes reconciled with any and all persons with whom there has been discord or disharmony of any kind. Why must we become reconciled? So that we may live in peace with all persons and things around us. ...

"...True reconciliation cannot be achieved by patience or forbearance with one another. To be patient or forbearing is not to be reconciled from the bottom of your heart. ..."

In performing the prayer of reconciliation, chose a quiet place, assume a humble attitude, and call the names of the persons with whom you wish to be reconciled. The persons so called will come to you though they may be unaware of it. Believe this. Visualize their faces in your mind's eye, and recite the following prayer aloud if possible. Repeat each passage over and over again. There is no limit to the number of times you should repeat them. Do the prayer to your heart's content. Repeat the prayer the next day and as many days as is required to effect thorough reconciliation. When you are able to see the faces in front of you break into a beautiful smile, you have accomplished reconciliation.

The Prayer of Reconciliation

"I have forgiven you. You have forgiven me.
I have forgiven you. You have forgiven me.
You and I are one under God.
I love you. You love me.
I love you. You love me.
You and I are one under God.
I am grateful to you. You are grateful to me.
I am grateful to you. You are grateful to me.
You and I are one under God.
There is no longer the slightest ill feeling between you and me.
I pray for your happiness from the bottom of my heart.
May you be blessed with increasing happiness.
Thank you very much! Thank you very much!

How We Are Likely To Feel When Our Needs Are Not Being Met

afraid	dislike	horrible	passive
aggravated	displeased	hostile	perplexed
agitated	distressed	hot	puzzled
angry	disturbed	hurt	reluctant
anxious	downhearted	impatient	resentful
apathetic	dread	indifferent	restless
bad	embarrassed	infuriated	sad
bitter	embittered	insecure	scared
blue	exhausted	irate	shaky
bored	fatigued	irritated	shocked
brokenhearted	fear	jealous	skeptical
cold	frightened	let-down	sorry
confused	frustrated	lethargy	spiritless
dejected	furious	listless	surprised
depressed	grief	lonely	suspicion
despair	guilty	mad	terrified
disappointed	hate	mean	troubled
discouraged	heavy	miserable	unhappy
disgusted	helpless	nervous	upset
disheartened	horrified	overwhelmed	worried

Feelings Likely To Be Present When Your Needs Are Being Satisfied

affection	elated	glorious	quiet
amazed	electrified	glowing	radiant
appreciation	encouraged	grateful	satisfied
astonished	energetic	happy	secure
blissful	enjoyment	helpful	sensitive
calm	enthusiastic	hopeful	splendid
carefree	exhilarated	inspired	surprised
cheerful	expansive	joyful	tenderness
confident	exuberant	loving	thankful
contented	free	optimism	thrilled
delighted	friendly	peaceful	tranquil
eager	fulfilled	pleasant	trust
ecstatic	glad	proud	wonderful

From *Nonviolent Communication: A Language of Life* by Dr. Marshall Rosenberg, www.NonviolentCommunication.com

The Principles of Attitudinal Healing

Dr. Jerry Jampolsky outlined a core framework or set of Attitudinal Healing principles to help people to let go of fear, discard negative and hurtful thoughts from the past, and remove inner obstacles to peace. These include the following:

1. The essence of being is love.
2. Health is inner peace.
3. Giving and receiving are the same.
4. We can let go of the past and the future.
5. Now is the only time there is.
6. We learn to love ourselves and others by forgiving rather than judging.
7. We can become love-finders rather than fault-finders.
8. We can be peaceful inside regardless of what is happening outside.
9. We are students and teachers to each other.
10. We can focus on the whole of our lives rather than on the fragments.
11. Because love is eternal, death need not be viewed as fearful.
12. We can always see ourselves and others as extending love or giving a call for help.

Power Forgiveness Process Summary

There are three major parts to the *Power Forgiveness Process*:
1. Finding your upsets
2. Forgiving all your upsets (contains five stages each with several actions.)
3. Feeling the transformation

First Part – Finding all your upsets
A. Who upsets me?
B. What are all the things that they did? Make sure you break down the event into bite size pieces.

Second Part – Forgiving – Dealing with your upsets
In this part, you are taking each of your upsets and completely dealing with it. This part is split into five stages, each with several actions to do.

Stage 1 is opening to the person, the upset, or part of it.
Stage 2 is expanding your understanding and compassion.
Stage 3 is realizing forgiveness.
Stage 4 is self-forgiving on what you forgave in Stage 2.
Stage 5 is giving thanks for the healing.

Stage 1 – The Opening Stage – Unlocking an Upset
Follow these steps or actions. Once you have the pattern down it can go quite quickly.
1. Take a specific person in the incident to work on.
2. Ask, "Am I **willing** to work on this upset and person?"
3. Look at what **inspires** you to work on this.
4. Feel the **feelings**:
   a. What do I feel when I think of the person involved in this situation? For example, sad, depressed, angry, hurt, anxious.
   b. Apart from the main emotion you feel when you think of the person, are there other feelings underneath or mixed up with that main one, like hopeless, guilt, humiliation, or shame?
   c. What were you afraid would happen at the time?
5. Find your **needs** and the debt owed.
   a. What do they owe you for having to feel what you have felt?
   b. What do you need out of the situation?

    c. What would satisfy you?

    d. Is it realistic that you would ever get that?

6. Look at the **consequence** of holding on to this upset.

    a. What benefits do you get by keeping the upset going?

    b. Are you holding onto this resentment out of loyalty to someone else?

    c. Is being right more important than being happy?

    d. What are you really getting from this upset? List the negatives.

    e. What is happening to the people closest to you by holding onto the upset?

    f. Could being done with this situation increase love, peace, and joy in your life?

    g. How long has your victimization by them been going on?

    h. How long is it okay to let them be in control of your happiness?

7. Can you perceive yourself as a possible contributor to the problem and not just the victim?

8. Ensure no **resistance** to forgiving. See The Myths.

Remember

- Take time to relax, meditate, or contemplate on the highest in yourself while doing this inner work.
- Listen to that highest aspect.
- Look at the highest goal you have for yourself that this situation might be stopping, either in its existence or in your own attitude?
- Question you always needs to ask yourself are:

    a. Can I decide to forgive right now for myself?

    b. Can I decide to forgive as an act of compassion toward the other person?

Now keep on going.

Stage 2 – The Understanding Stage – Expanding Understanding and Compassion

    Skill 1 – Look for violated principles, values, and rules.

        a. What principles of yours did the offender reject?

        b. Which of your values were disregarded?

        c. What rules were broken?

Now take each rule, principle, and value and ask:

d. Though others should observe these principles, values, and rules, is my expectation realistic, given the life experience of this person?

e. Have I always been able to follow these principles and rules myself?

f. Have I done the same thing in some way to others or myself?

Skill 2 – Find Other Viewpoints Than Your Own
A. Walk in the other's shoes

1) Write down what you believe to be the governing moral code that this person lives by and that could have influenced their behavior in this situation.

2) What was their fear?

3) What was their expectation of you, of others?

4) Write down all the ways that they are correct and justified from their perspective.

General questions

5) What it was like growing up in their family.

6) What was it like coming from their culture or time?

7) What are their issues?

8) What is their emotional intelligence?

B. What is the Big Picture?

1) Was this person in your life to teach you some important lesson?

2) How might this situation or person fit into your idea of Karma or a Divine Plan?

C. What other ways could you see this situation?

1) Can you get help from others?

2) Can you listen to others who might have a different perspective?

Skill 3 – Face Defenses That Prevent Forgiving –

A. Detach from it all by asking, "How would an impartial observer view this?"

B. See if you have done something similar yourself – perhaps not in magnitude, but in context – maybe not to others, but to yourself.

If you have, ask yourself:
1) Can I forgive him or her for doing the same thing I have done? Or for breaking an unrealistic value, moral code, or rule that I have?
2) Can I forgive myself for doing the same thing?

Skill 4 – Develop a Positive Attitude
A. Find meaning in the event
1) What has this hurtful experience taught me about myself, the world, or other people?
2) How have I matured because of this experience?
3) What have I learned about love and compassion as a result?
4) How have my values changed?
B. Be grateful
1) What am I thankful for?
C. Give love
1) Can you imagine holding the person you are trying to forgive and just love them no matter what? Hold them as a mother or father would their child, perhaps not agreeing, but still loving. You might still disagree, but not with anger, or resentment.

▶ **If** you forgave, go to the next person on your list for this situation.
▶ **If** you could not forgive the piece you were working on:
   ▷ See if it will break down further. Then do the opening steps on the newly broken down upset.
OR
   ▷ Look back further. Ask these questions:
     4. What in my past reminds me of this?
     5. Is there an earlier situation in my life that might be similar to this one?
     6. What do I need to let go about my past, including my family of origin, to help me in this?
Then go back and do the above Understanding steps on these new items.

▶ **If** no change – take another incident from Stage 1 and work on it, and come back to this later.

Stage 3 – Realization Stage

When you feel a shift in your perspective and attitude, take time to feel the change within you. Think of the person again to see if there is any resentment or hurt left. If there is, go back to where you left off in the Understanding stage.

When you feel forgiveness with the specific thing that this person did, move to self-forgiveness around this specific action.

Stage 4 – Self-Forgiveness Stage – personal responsibility.

Since the world we see reflects our own mind and thinking, ask:
1) Is this unforgiven situation mirroring something about me?
2) Have I done something similar myself to others? Or perhaps only to myself? (The magnitude might not be the same but there is some similarity.)
3) Do I feel any guilt for my own transgression for which I need to gain forgiveness?
4) Can I forgive myself for the same thing for which I've forgiven them?
5) What will it take to forgive me for this? Do I need to make amends to anyone?
6) For those with a Christian orientation, this question might help: Can I accept God's forgiveness of me on this?

Stage 5 – The Healing Stage – Thanksgiving

Here are some questions to aid in the conclusion of the offense.
1) What can I be grateful for in this situation? What did it teach me? Perhaps it made you stronger, more capable, or successful?
2) What did I learn in the long run for which I can be grateful?
3) How did the person help me or help others?
4) How did they effect a positive change in my life?

Continue with Part Two of the Power Forgiveness Process

Repeat the actions of this part until all is forgiven.

Third Part – Transformation

Initially you might not notice all the changes that will happen in your life when you finish all your forgiveness, for your mind will actually be moving to another level of functioning.

NOTES

Introduction
1. See Coelho 1996   2. See Guyton   3. Ibid

Chapter 1
A. *NIH* is one of the world's foremost medical research centers
1. See Legaree 2007
2. See Sevrens
2a. McCullough, et al (2000)
3. Legaree2007
4. See CBS News
4a. Willson 1999
5. See MacLean
6. See Dubruc 2002
7. See MacLean
9. See Pert 1997
10. Healy 2007
11. Bio-medicine 2003
12. Potenza 1996
13. Abagayle 2009

Chapter 2
Note A -Type A individuals can be described as impatient, excessively time-conscious, insecure about their status, highly competitive, hostile and aggressive, and incapable of relaxation. They are often high achieving workaholics who multi-task, drive themselves with deadlines, and are unhappy about the smallest of delays. Because of these characteristics, Type A individuals are often described as "stress junkies." – From Wikipedia.
1. See Legaree 2007
2. McGinnis 2006
3. See Wohl 2008   4. ibid
5. See Science Daily 2007
6. See Brehm
7. See Smalley p 91
8. Research by Dr. Redford Williams, See Goodier
10. Gendlin, 1981
11. See Reid, 2000
12. See Wikipedia-TRC, 2006

Chapter 3
A. Jerry's book on Attitudinal Healing is *Teach only Love.*
1a. See Gordon, et al 2000
1b See Warren 2006
2. See Luskin 2007
2b. See Clottey 1999
3. See Tutu 1999 p271
4. See Warren 2006
5. Siegel 1999
6. This comes from the title of a little inspirational book, popular in the 70s & 80s written by Dr. Jerry Jampolsky
7. See Arbinger 2006

8. See McInnis, N. 2006
9. Coelho 1996

9a. Engel 2001
10. See Rosenberg 1999

Chapter 4
2. See Toussaint, et al, 2008
3. See Luskin, 2000
3a. Ibid   3b. Ibid
4. See Enright, et al, 2000
5. Luskin 2007
6a. personal communication
6b. personal communication
7a. Kiecolt-Glaser, et al, 2005
7b. See Real Age, 2006
8a. See Loukas 1995
8b. *Univ. Of Michigan 2000*

9. See Allen 2009 *Judy Allen wrote a book about her experience with cancer, entitled, The Five Stages of Getting Well.*
10. See Smedes 1988
11. slightly changed by me - the word heart was changed to reactions
12a. Personal communication
12b. Some people use Catholic rosary beads to do this.

PART II   1. Berg 87

Chapter 5
1. Begley 2007
2. Healy 2007
3. See Amen, D. G. 2006a
4. See Do Amaral 2003
5. See Frantz_2005
6. See Wikipedia- Frontal Lobe, (2006)
7. See Miller 2002
8. See Amen, D.G. (2006)a.
9. See Do Amaral 2003
10. See Le Doux 2000
11. See Lewis P37
12. See Christison 2002
13. See Wikipedia - amygdala
14. See Do amaral (2000) limbic system
15. See Amen, D.G. (2006)a.
16. See Amen, D.G. (2006)b

17. See Lewis et al
18. See Amen, D.G. (2006)a.
19. See Sagan
20. See Steiner C
21. Van der Dennen, 2005
22. Ibid
23. See Do Amaral
24. See Prettyman 1997
25. Maclean 1990
26. Ledoux 2000
27. See Amen, D.G. (2006)a.
28. Do Amaral
29. See De Beauport 1996
30. Ibid
31. Maclean 1990
32. Ledoux 2000
33. See Khan

Chapter 6
1. See Hall 2005 2. Ibid
3. See Caine
4. See Begley 2007   5. Ibid

6. Lewis, et al 2000
7. Ibid   8. Ibid
8a. Rosemergy 2009
9. Ibid p.118

10. Bob received his version of the letters from Dr. John Gray of *Men are from Mars, Women are from Venus* fame.

Chapter 7
1. See Reid 2000
2. See Ritchie 1978
3. See Arrien 1991
4a. See McKay, et al, 1981
4b. Ibid
5. Rosenberg See p. 88
7. For an excellent series of

11. See ho'o pono pono
12. Quoted in Forgiveness We articles on intuition, see Dr. Daniel Benor's website at www.healthy.net.
8. See Clark 1971
9. Benor 2002 10. Ibid
11. See Benson 1976
12. See Blakeslee 2005
13. See Figley 2000

Chapter 8
1a. See Einstein (2) from a letter in 1936 to a child who asked if scientists pray.
1c. See Jantsch 1980
2. See Young 2004, chap 10
3. Quoted in Williamson
4 . See Einstein5. Wikipedia-12

Steps 2006
6. See AA 1976
7. See Seligman 2004
8. See Arrien 1991

Chapter 10
1. See Einstein 1972
2. Quoted in Heartquotes
3. See Amen, D.G. (2006)a.

3a. About.com 2009
4. Katie 2003
5. See McKay, et al, 1981
6. Ibid

Chapter 11
1. See Lynch 2007, p101
2. See Merton
3. Goldsmith
4. See: http://www.al-anon.alateen.org/ for more information on al-anon. and see the appendix for the al-anon steps.

5. Berg 1987
6. Mckay
7. Ibid
8. Ibid
9. See Lewis, et al, 2000

Chapter 12
Note A -EMDR is a powerful method to help people resolve of fear and problems through the use of eye movement. It is only done by licensed therapist. A similar approach done by everyday folks is called EFT. It is easy to use and learn, has no negative side effects and is empowering. For more info, go to the EFT website at emofree.com

1. Capri 1996
2. Figley 2002 2a. Ibid
3. Figley 2000
4. Capri 1996
5. Ibid 5a. Ibid
6. Young 2004
7a. Helpguide.org is an excellent website providing expert, non-commercial information on mental health and lifelong wellness.
7b. Helpguide.com 2006
8. Peeples, 2000
9. APA 2004
10. Carlson, 2005
11. You might contact the Association of Traumatic Stress Specialists (ATSS) website to find information and their links to organizations to find a trauma therapist in your area.

12. Flannery 1999
13. I don't have figures for Iraq and Afghanistan.
13a. Friedman (2006)
14. ROTA (2008)
15. Witvliet, et al (2004)
15a Friedman (2006)
16. Figley 2000, 2002
16a. Figley, 2002
16b. Figley 2000, 2002
17. Carpi, 1996
18. Starnes 2005
19. Van der Kolk 2009
20.http://aamft.org/families/inde x_nm.asp
21. Zimering, et al, 2003
22. Peeples 2000

Chapter 13 1. See Tutu 1999

Chapter 14 1. Foltz-Gray, 2002

Chapter 15
A. You can answer a free questionnaire at www.authentichappiness.com to find your main character strengths.
1. Ernest Holmes 1984 p331
2. Brinkley 1994
3. Dugatkin 2005
4. SNI

5. Kataria, M. 2009
6. VIA, 2005
6a. Seligman 2002

BIBLIOGRAPHY

♦ AA (1976) *The Big Book*, Alcoholics Anonymous World Services, Inc.

♦ APA (2004). *The Different Kinds of Stress*, Retrieved 6/2006 from the American Psychological Association Help Center webpage: www.apahelpcenter.org/articles/article.php?id=21

♦ Aba Gayle, (1995) Personal correspondence.

♦ Aba Gayle, (2009) retrieved 2/4/09 from http://www.catherineblountfdn.org/rsof.htm

♦ About.com (2009) retrieved 2/7/09 from http://grammar.about.com/od/mo/g/metaphorterm.htm

♦ Allen, J. *Judy tells her moving story of using the Course to find healing for cancer,* Retrieved 2-16-09 from the Circle of Atonement http://www.circleofa.org/articles/HealingJudyAllen.php

♦ Amen, D.G. (2006)a. Retrieved 6-4-06 from http://amenclinics.com/bp/systems/limbic

♦ Amen, D.G. (2006)b. Retrieved 6-4-06 from http://amenclinics.com/bp/articles.php?articleID=10

♦ Arbinger Institute, (2006). *The Anatomy of Peace: Resolving the Heart of Conflict,* San Francisco: Berrett-Kohler.

♦ Arrien, A. (1991). Personal notes from lectures in 1991

♦ Begley, S. (2007) "In Our Messy Reptilian Brains," *Newsweek Web Exclusive* April 09, 2007, Retrieved 1/16/09 http://www.newsweek.com/id/35728

♦ Berg, C. (1987). "The Art of Return," *Parabola* - Volume XII, Number 3, Aug.1987 Society for the Study of Myth and Tradition

♦ Benor, D.J. (2002). Intuition, *The International Journal of Healing and Caring,* Volume 2, No. 2, Retrieved 11 Aug06 www.healthy.net/scr/column.asp?ColumnId=34&ID=728

♦ Benson, H. (1976). *The Relaxation Response,* NY: HarperTorch.

♦ Bio-Medicine (2003) "New scientific study finds women more forgiving than men" retrieved 1/17/09 from http://news.bio-medicine.org/biology-news-2/New-scientific-study-finds-women-more-forgiving-than-men-3496-1/

♦ Blakeslee, Sandra (2005). Hypnosis can profoundly change brain, *New York Times,* Published on 11/22/05, Retrieved 12/15/05 from http://www.ajc.com/news/content/health/1105/22hypnosis.html

♦ Borysenko, J., (1993) *Fire in the Soul: A New Psychology of Spiritual Optimism,* NY: Warner Books, Inc.

♦ Brehm, B.A. (1994). Type A revisited: Is Type A behavior OK?, *Fitness Management Magazine,* September 1994, Vol. 10, No. 10, p. 24, Los Angeles, Calif. Retrieved 8/19/06 from www.fitnessmanagement.com/FM/tmpl/genPage.asp?p=/information/articles/library/labnotes/labnotes0994.html

♦ Brinkley, D., Perry, P., Moody, R. A. (1994). *Saved by the Light,* NY: Villard Books.

♦ Caine, R & Caine, G. (2006) "The Brain/Mind Learning Principles", Retrieved 7/6/2006 www.cainelearning.com/pwheel/expand/

♦ Cambridge Advanced Learner's Dictionary, http://dictionary.cambridge.org

♦ Carlson, E.B., & Ruzek, J. (2005). *Effects of Traumatic Experiences,* A Fact Sheet for the National Center for PTSD of the Department of Veteran Affairs, Retrieved 4/26/2006 from http://www.ncptsd.va.gov/facts/general/fs_effects.html

♦ Carpi, J. (1996). Stress: It's Worse Than You Think, *Psychology Today,* Jan/Feb 96 Retrieved 4/23/2006 from http://www. psychology-today.com/articles/pto-19960101-000027.html

♦ CBS News (2007) "Suicide Epidemic Among Veterans," November. 13, 2007 Retrieved 1-21-08 http://www.cbsnews.com/stories/2007/11/13/cbsnews_investigates/main3496471.shtml

♦ Christison, MaryAnn (2002). *Brain-Based Research and Language Teaching,* English Teaching Forum Online, Volume 40, Number 2, Bureau of Educational and Cultural Affairs, Retrieved-http://exchanges.state.gov/forum/vols/vol40/no2/p02.htm

♦ Clark, Ronald W. (1971). *Einstein: The Life and Times, p 622,* World Pub. Co., New York, Retrieved 8-10-06 from "Einstein's Last Thoughts" www.einsteinandreligion.com/lastthoughts.html

♦ Clottey, K., Abadio-Clottey, A. (1999). *Beyond Fear – Twelve Spiritual Keys to Racial Healing,* H.J. Kramer, Tiburon, CA

♦ Coelho, P. (1996) *By The River Piedra I Sat Down and Wept: A Novel Of Forgiveness,* From the "About the book" section, Harper Perennial; Translation edition

◆ De Beauport, E. (1996) "Crossing the Threshold of the Unconscious: Into The Basic Brain," Retrieved 7-13-06 from www.motley-focus.com/crossing.html Taken from her book: *The Three Faces of the Mind: Developing Your Mental, Emotional, and Behavioral Intelligences*. Elaine de Beauport with Aura Sofia Diaz. Quest Books. (1996) Wheaton: The Theosophical Publishing House.

◆ Do Amaral, J.& de Oliveira, J. (2003). *Limbic System: The Center of Emotions*, Retrieved 7-12-2006 from http://www.healing-arts.org/n-r-limbic.htm

◆ Donnelly, D. (1993). *Seventy Times Seven – Forgiveness and Peacemaking*, Pax Christi, Benet Press, Erie PA

◆ Dossey, L. (1993). *Healing Words- The Power of Prayer and the Practice of Medicine*, Harper Collins, NY

◆ Dubuc, B. (2002). "The Brain from Top to Bottom," *The Evolutionary Layers Of The Human Brain*, Retrieved http://www.thebrain.mcgill.ca

◆ Dugatkin, L.(2005. "Why don't we just kiss and make up?," *New Scientist*, 5/7/05

◆ Einstein, Albert (1972). *New York Post, November 28, 1972*. Retrieved 8-9-06 from www.ivu.org/history/northam20a/einstein.html

◆ Einstein (1)Retrieved 2-7-08 from http://thinkexist.com/quotation/a-person-experiences-life-as-something-separated/411055.html

◆ Einstein (2) Retrieved 08- 11-06 from "Quotes by Albert Einstein," http://quotes.zaadz.com/Albert_Einstein

◆ Engel, B. (2001) The Power of Apology: Healing steps to Transform All Your Relationships, NY: John Wiley & Sons, Inc.

◆ Enright, R.D., Fitzgibbons, R.P. (2000). *Helping Clients Forgive: An Empirical Guide For Resolving Anger And Restoring Hope*, Washington DC: American Psychological Association.

◆ Figley, C. R. (2000). *Post-Traumatic Stress Disorder*, American Association for Marriage and Family Therapy -AAMFT -Clinical Update Volume 2, Issue 5, Sept. 2000, Retrieved 12/29/05 from http://www.aamft.org/families/Consumer_Updates/PTSD_AAMFT_Clinical_Update.htm

◆ Figley, C. R. (2002). *AAMFT Consumer Update on Post-Traumatic Stress Disorder*, American Association for Marriage and Family Therapy, Retrieved 5/15/06 www.aamft.org/families/Consumer_Updates/PTSD.asp

♦ Flannery, R.B. Jr. (1999). Psychological Trauma and Posttraumatic Stress Disorder: A Review, *International Journal of Emergency Mental Health*, 1999, 2, 135-140. Retrieved from www.icisf.org/Acrobat%20 Documents/TerrorismIncident /PsyTrauPTSD.pdf

♦ Foltz-Gray, D. (2002). "Start Forgiving," *Arthritis Today*, 9-10/2002. Retrieved from http://www.drrandijones.com/newsltr4.htm

♦ Foundation for Inner Peace (1975) *A Course In Miracles*, Sausalito, CA

♦ Frantz, R. (2005). "Introduction To Intuition," *Two Minds: Intuition and Analysis in the History of Economic Thought*, Berlin: Springer. Retrieved 5-03-07 from http://www-rohan.sdsu.edu/~frantz/docs/Chapter1.pdf

♦ Friedman, M. J. (2005). *Posttraumatic Stress Disorder: An Overview*, A National Center for PTSD Fact Sheet, *Dept. of Veteran Affairs*. Retrieved from http://www.ncptsd.va.gov/facts/general /fs_overview.html

♦ Guyton, R.(1995) *The Forgiving Place*, Waco: WRS Publishing.

♦ Gendlin, E. (1981). *Focusing*, NY: Bantam.

♦ Goldsmith, J. (1984). *Living by Grace*, NY: HarperCollins.

♦ Goodier, S. "A Life That Make A Difference", retrieved 11/2/02 from http://lifesupportsystem.com/

♦ Gordon, K. C., Baucom, D. H., & Snyder, D.K. (2000). "The Use Of Forgiveness In Marital Therapy." In M. C. McCullough, K. I. Pargament, & C. E. Thoresen (Eds.), *Forgiveness: Theory, Research, and Practice*, pp. 203–227, NY: Guilford Press.

♦ Hall. D. (2005). "Social Support," Health Plus – Vanderbuilt Faculty and Staff Wellness Program, Wellsource, Inc. Retrieved 1/10/06 http://vanderbiltowc.wellsource.com/dh/content. asp?ID=563

♦ Healy, M (2007) "Humans may be hard-wired to have a soft spot: The predisposition to forgive appears genetic and may have been selected through evolution" *Los Angeles Times*, Dec. 31, 2007 Retrieved 1/17/09from www.psy.miami.edu/faculty/mmccullough/Media% 20Coverage/Humans%20may%20be%20hard%20wired_la_times.pdf

♦ Heartquotes, retrieved 5-18-07 http://www.heartquotes.net/ Anger.html

♦ Helpguide.org (2006) "Emotional and Psychological Trauma: Causes, Symptoms, Effects, and Treatment", retrieved 5/11/2006 from www.helpguide.org/mental/emotionalpsychological_trauma.htm

♦ Holmes, E. 1984. *Living the Science of Mind*, Marina del Rey: DeVorss and Co.

♦ Ho'oponopono, From classes with: Keoki Sousa, Sept-Oct 1999, Maui Community College, Maui, HI and Kapi'ioho Lyons Naone, June - July 1999, Bailey House, Maui, HI

♦ Jampolsky, G. (1990). *Out of the Darkness into the Light: A Journey of Inner Healing*, NY: Bantam.

♦ Jampolsky. G. (2000) *Teach Only Love: The Twelve Principles of Attitudinal Healing*, Beyond Words Publishing, Inc, Hillsborough, Oregon

♦ Jantsch, E. (1980). *The Self-Organizing Universe: Scientific and Human Implication of the Emerging Paradigm of Evolution*, Pergamon, NY, NY

♦ Kataria, M. (2009) "Laughter Clubs" retrieved 2/6/2009 from http://www.laughteryoga.org

♦ Katie, Byron, (2003) *Loving What Is: Four Questions That Can Change Your Life*, NY: Three Rivers Press.

♦ Khan, H.I., *The Sufi Message of Hazrat Inayat Khan* - Volume VII – IX, Retrieved 6/2005 http://wahiduddin.net/mv2/IX/IX_9.htm

♦ Kiecolt-Glaser, J. K., Loving, T. J., Stowell, J. R., Malarkey, W. B., Lemeshow, S., Dickinson, S. L., Glaser, R. (2005). Hostile marital interactions, proinflammatory cytokine production, and wound healing. *Archives of General Psychiatry* 62(12):1377-1384. Retrieved on 4/19/06 from http://archpsyc.amaassn.org/cgi/content/abstract/62/12/1377

♦ Le Doux, J. (1996) *The Emotional Brain: The Mysterious Underpinnings of Emotional Life*, New York: Simon& Schuster

♦ LeDoux, J. (2000) Emotion Circuits in the Brain, *Annual Reviews Neuroscience* 23:155–184 retrieved 1-30-09 www.csmn. uio.no/events/2008/machamer_docs/ledoux.pdf

♦ Legaree, T., Turner, J., Lollis, S. (2007) "Forgiveness and Therapy: A Critical Review of Conceptualizations, Practices, and Values Found In the Literature." *Journal of Marital and Family Therapy*. The American Association for Marriage & Family Therapy. Retrieved 2/02/09 from: www.highbeam.com/doc/1P3-1270855471.html

♦ Lewis, T., Amini, F., & Landon, R. (2000). *A General Theory of Love*, NY: Random House.

♦ Loukas, Chris (1995). Faith, forgiveness help crash victim heal, *The Press Democrat*, December 25, 1995, Santa Rosa, CA.

♦ Luskin, F. (2000). *Forgive For Good : A Proven Prescription for Health and Happiness*, pp 77-93, San Francisco: Harper.

♦ Luskin, F. (2007) *Forgive for Love: The Missing Ingredient for a Healthy and Lasting Relationship*, NY: HarperOne.

♦ Lynch, M.J. (2007) *Big Prisons, Big Dreams: Crime and the Failure of America's Penal System* NJ: Rutgers University Press.

♦ MacLean, P. D. (1990). *The Triune Brain in Evolution: Role in Paleocerebral Functions,* NY: Plenum

♦ McCullough, M. C., Pargament, K. I. , & Thoresen, C. , (Eds), (2000) *Forgiveness: Theory, Research, and Practice,* NY: Guilford Press, p.3,

♦ McInnis, N. (2006). Retrieved June 5, 2006 http://www.mediamessage.com/OURCHIVE/forgivenesspractice. htm#Staying%20in%20the%20Grace

♦ McKay, M., Davis, M., & Fanning, P. (1981). *Thoughts & Feelings: The Art Of Cognitive Stress Intervention,* Oakland: New Harbinger.

♦ Merton, T. (1955) *No Man is an Island,* Retrieved 6-6-07 from http://www.octanecreative.com/merton/quotes.html

♦ Miller, J. (2002). Science searches the brain for mystical experience: Newberg, Delio and the mystery of the brain, *Science & Theology News,* July 1, 2002, Retrieved July, 19, 2006 http://www.stnews.org/print.php?article_id=1696

♦ Myss, C., (1996) *Anatomy of the Spirit: The Seven Stages of Power and Healing,* NY: Three Rivers Press

♦ Potenza, (1996) a talk on forgiveness given July 1996

♦ Peeples, K.A. (2000). Interview with Charles R. Figley: Burnout In Families and Implications for the Profession, *The Family Journal,* 8: 203-206. Retrieved 11/17/2004 from http://mailer.fsu.edu/~cfigley/burnout.htm

♦ Pert, C.B. (1997). *Molecules of Emotion: Why You Feel the Way You Do.* New York: Scribner.

♦ Prettyman, J.W. (1997). *Deep And Deeper: Deep Blue vs. The Triune Brain,* Retrieved 7-12-06 www.americanreview.us/deepblue.htm

♦ Real Age, Inc., (2006). April 21-Tip of the Day-A Case for Peace, Retrieved 4/19/2006 http://www.realage.com/news_ features/tip.aspx?v=1&cid=16586

♦ Reid, F., Hoffmann, D. (2000). *Long Night's Journey Into Day: South Africa's Search for Truth & Reconciliation,* Iris Films, Retrieved 2/25/2008 from http://www.irisfilms.org/longnight/

♦ Ritchie, George G., M.D. (1978). *Return From Tomorrow,* Fleming H. Revell, of Baker Book House Company, Old Tappan, NJ

♦ Rosemergy, J. (2009) Email of 2 March 09

♦ Rosenberg, M. (1999). *Nonviolent Communication- A Language of Compassion,* PuddleDancer Press, Del Mar, Ca.

◆ ROTA (2008). "ROTA (Reach Out To Asia) and Save the Children Collaborate to Support Children in Gaza Strip." Retrieved 4-15-09 from http://www.reachouttoasia.org/output/page275.asp

◆ ScienceDaily (2007). Outwardly Expressed Anger Affects Some Women's Heart Arteries, Source: Cedars-Sinai Medical Center, 1/15/07 Retrieved 6-8-07 from www.sciencedaily. com/releases/2007/01/070114185909.htm

◆ Siegel, B. (1999). *Prescriptions for Living: Inspirational Lessons for a Joyful, Loving Life,* NY: Harper Paperbacks.

◆ Seligman, M. E. P. (2002). *Authentic Happiness: Using the New Positive Psychology to Realize Your Potential for Lasting Fulfillment,* NY: Free Press.

◆ Seligman, M. E. (2004). Happiness Interventions That Work: The First Results, *Authentic Happiness Coaching News,* Vol 2, Number 10 5/3/2004, Retrieved 7/13/2004 from http://www.AuthenticHappinessCoaching.com

◆ Sevrens, J. (1999) *Learning to Forgive,* San Jose Mercury News, 9/6/99

◆ Smalley, G. (2001). *Food and Love: The Amazing Connection,* Tyndale House Publishers, Wheaton, IL, p. 91

◆ Smedes , L. (1988). *Forgive and Forget: Healing the Hurts We Don't Deserve,* NY: Pocket Books.

◆ Snopes.com (2006) Grandma's Cooking Secret, Retrieved 7-1-06 from the Urban Legends Reference Page: http://www.snopes.com/weddings/newlywed/secret.asp

◆ Starnes, G. (2005) "The Psychophysiology of Trauma" Returning Warriors Blog, 5/16/05 Retrieved 1-17-09 www.returningwarriors.org/2005_05_01_archive.html

◆ Steiner, C. *Transactional Analysis and the Triune Brain,* Retrieved 7-9-06 from http://www.emotional-literacy.com/triune.htm

◆ Taniguchi, M. (1931). *Holy Sutra,* Special Maui Edition 1987 Hawaii: Seicho-No-IE.

◆ Toussaint, L., Williams, D., Musick, & Everson-Rose, (2008). "Why forgiveness may protect against depression: Hopelessness as an explanatory mechanism," *Personality and Mental Health,* 2, 89-103.

◆ Tutu, D.M. (1999). *No Future without Forgiveness,* NY: Doubleday.

◆ University Of Michigan, (2000) "New Study Shows Link Between Hopelessness And Hypertension," *ScienceDaily,* 2/18/00 Retrieved January 31, 2009, from www.sciencedaily.com/releases/2000 /02/000217100606.htm

◆ Van der Dennen, J.M.G. (2005). "Ritualized 'Primitive' Warfare And Rituals In War: Phenocopy, Homology, Or...?" Retrieved 6-12-06 from http://irs.ub.rug.nl/ppn/280499396

◆ Van der Kolk, B., (2009) "Specialized Treatment Approaches" *The Trauma Center at Justice Resource Institute* Website, retrieved 1/21/09 http://www.traumacenter.org/clients/spec_svcs_treatment.php

◆ VIA – Values in Action (2006). Retrieved 4/25/2006 http://www.viastrengths.org

◆ Warren, R. (2006) Some exerpts from a Rick Warren article on forgiveness from the Spring 2006 issue of "The Worshipper" Magazine. Retrieved 6/05/09 http://exubfjc.wordpress.com /2006/12/18/rick-warren-on-forgiveness/

◆ Wikipedia- Amygdala (2006) The Amygdala, Retrieved 7/09/06 from http://en.wikipedia.org/wiki/Amygdala 7-9-06 Wikipedia-12Steps, (2006*). The Twelve Steps,* Retrieved 7/06, http: //en.wikipedia.org/wiki/12step_program#The_Twelve_Steps

◆ Wikipedia –TRC (2006). *List of truth and reconciliation commissions,* from Wikipedia, Retrieved 7/2006, http://en.wikipedia.org/ wiki/List_of_truth_and_reconciliation_commissions

◆ Wikipedia-Frontal Lobe, (2006*).* Retrieved 7/9/06 from http://en.wikipedia.org/wiki/Frontal_lobe 7-9-06

◆ Williamson, M., (1995) *Illuminata: A Return to Prayer,* NY: Riverhead Books.

◆ Willson (1999) "Memorandum: Accelerated Mortality Rates of Vietnam Veterans," retrieved 3/8/09 http://www.brianwillson.com/awolvetmemo.html

◆ Witvliet, C.V.O., Phipps, K.A., Feldman, M.E., & Beckham, J.C. (2004). Posttraumatic Mental and Physical Health Correlates of Forgiveness and Religious Coping in Military Veterans. *Journal of Traumatic Stress,* 17, 269-273.Wohl, M. J A; DeShea, Wahkinney,. (2008) "Looking Within: Measuring State Self-Forgiveness and Its Relationship to Psychological Well-Being." *Canadian Journal of Behavioural Science.* Canadian Psychological Association, Retrieved 2/02/09 from www.highbeam.com/doc/1P3-1485110721.html

◆ Worthington, E. (2001) *Five Steps to Forgiveness,* NY: Crown Publishers.

◆ Worthington, E. (2003). *Forgiving and Reconciling: Bridges to Wholeness and Hope,* Downers Grove, IL: InterVarsity Press; Revised Edition

✦ Young, M. A. (2004). *The Community Crisis Response Team Training Manual-Second edition*, National Organization for Victim Assistance, and The Office for Victims of Crime - U.S. Department of Justice, Washington, DC. Retrieved 3/5/03 from www.ojp.usdoj.gov/ovc/publications/infores/crt/

✦ Zimering, R., Munroe, J., Gulliver, S.B. (2003). "Secondary Traumatization in Mental Health Care Providers," *Psychiatric Times*, April 2003, Vol. XX, Issue 4, Retrieved 4/27/2006 from http://www.psychiatrictimes.com/p030443.html

PERMISSIONS

I GRATEFULLY ACKNOWLEDGE permission to quote from the following copyrighted works:

✦ To Dr. Fredric Luskin for permission to quote from *Forgive For Good* : *A Proven Prescription for Health and Happiness*

✦ To Dr. Jerry Jampolsky for permission to quote from *Out of the Darkness into the Light: A Journey of Inner Healing,*and from *Teach Only Love: The Twelve Principles of Attitudinal Healing,*

✦ To Paulo Coelho for permission to quote from *By The River Piedra I Sat Down and Wept: A Novel Of Forgiveness,*

✦ To PuddleDancer Press for permission to quote from *Nonviolent Communication- A Language of Compassion* by Dr. Marshall Rosenberg.

✦ To Cindy Funfsinn and David Smith for permission to quote from *Anatomy of the Spirit* by Caroline Myss – www.myss.com

✦ To Luzie Mason for permission to quote from *Fire in the Soul: A New Psychology of Spiritual Optimism,* by Dr. Joan Borysenko

✦ To Julie Noordhoek of Baker Publishing Group for permissions to quote from *Return From Tomorrow* by George Ritchie.

INDEX

ABOUT THE AUTHOR

For the past 18 years, Dr. Jim Dincalci has been working on methods to help people forgive. The sources of these forgiving ways are not only the modern ones of psychology but also the traditional spiritual methods and cross-cultural healing practices. He has spent over 40 years learning and professionally using emotional, spiritual, mental, and physical ways to help people feel better and heal their lives.

His master's is in Counseling Psychology, and his doctorates are in Religious Studies and Divinity. He started training in psychology in graduate school at New York Medical College in 1968. Since then, he has learned and used scores of effective methods for healing the mind, spirit, and body. These methods helped him in his own forgiveness transformation in 1993.

In addition to his years of private practice, his counseling experience includes facilitating domestic violence groups and working for the Hawaii Departments of Health and of Education as a clinical therapist in the state's school system.

For over 45 years, he has studied world religions and their practices, including cross-cultural indigenous healing ways. Thus, he integrates into this book not only the effective thought and emotional processes of psychology but also the time-proven spiritual methods and perspectives, such as specific prayers, meditations, and inspirational viewpoints that aid in forgiving.

In addition to thirty years of private practice and public seminars, he has presented at the professional conferences of the Association of Transpersonal Psychology and the Campaign for Forgiveness Research. He has also taught his forgiveness work in universities, hospitals, schools, and churches.